LONDON, TILBURY & SOUTHEND RAILWAY
and its locomotives

LONDON, TILBURY & SOUTHEND RAILWAY
and its locomotives

R. J. Essery

OPC
Oxford Publishing Co

Cover:
The late George Heiron's well-known painting depicting the LT&SR at Plaistow c1911 with 'No 37' class No 47 *Stratford* on a Fenchurch Street to Southend train along the direct line via Upminster. Compare with the original photo on page 53.

Back cover top:
No 59 *Holloway* at Southend with a train of Midland Railway stock for St Pancras. *Collection R. J. Essery*

Back cover, bottom:
A pair of 0-6-2T engines, Nos 41985 and 41986, haul a train of tank wagons in connection with the oil traffic that was the mainstay of the Thames Haven branch. *Collection R. J. Essery*

Half title page:
The third and final LT&SR armorial transfer was of 11½in diameter and was applied to locomotives and coaches. The central feature is the gateway to Tilbury Fort flanked by the shields representing London to the left, Essex to the right and Kent below. *BR W2096/2*

Frontispiece:
Rebuilt 'No 37' class No 47 *Stratford* heads an ordinary passenger train, probably from Southend to Fenchurch Street. The square panel lettered LTSR carried on the lamp bracket at the top of the smokebox and the white circular disc with a red cross denoted that the train was running via Upminster. *F. Moore*

Title page:
'No 37' class engine No 44 *Prittlewell* in its original condition, heading a train of LT&SR stock at Southend for Fenchurch Street. *Collection R. J. Essery*

East Ham on 16 August 1958 with LMS Class 3F 0-6-0T No 47484. The engine appears to be fitted with ATC gear and carries a front steam heating hose. *H. C. Casserley 94141*

First published 2001

ISBN 0 86093 561 2

© R. J. Essery 2001

Published by Oxford Publishing Co

an imprint of Ian Allan Publishing Ltd, Hersham, Surrey KT12 4RG
Printed by Ian Allan Printing Ltd, Hersham, Surrey KT12 4RG

Code:0111/0201/A3

Bibliography and Sources Consulted

The late Kenneth H. Leech
National Railway Museum, York
Public Record Office, Kew

The Blackwall and Millwall Extension Railways, Geoffrey Body, Avon Anglia, ISBN 0 905466 51 9
Stepney's Own Railway, J. E. Connor, Connor & Butler, 1984, ISBN 0 947699 08 2
London Tilbury & Southend Album, George Dow, Ian Allan, ISBN 0 7110 1085 4
Midland Style, George Dow, HMRS, 1975, ISBN 0 902835 02 5
An Illustrated History of LMS Locomotives Vol, 4 Bob Essery & David Jenkinson, Silver Link Publications, 1987, ISBN 0 947971 16 5
An Illustrated Review of Midland Locomotives Vol 1, R. J. Essery & D. Jenkinson, Wild Swan Publications, 1984, ISBN 0 906867 27 4
Midland Wagons Vol 2, Bob Essery, OPC, 1980, ISBN 0 86093 041 6
The Romford-Upminster Branch, K. A. Frost, 1964
The Midland Railway, A Chronology, John Gough, Railway & Canal Historical Society, 1989, ISBN 0 901461 12 1
LMS Engine Sheds Vol 4, Chris Hawkins & George Reeve, Wild Swan Publications, 1984, ISBN 0 906867 20 7
The Illustrated History of LMS Standard Coaching Stock, David Jenkinson & Bob Essery, OPC, 1991 Vol I ISBN 0 86093 450 0; 1994 Vol II ISBN 0 86093 451 9; 2000 Vol III ISBN 0 86093 452 7
Locomotive Liveries of the LMS, D. Jenkinson & R. J. Essery, Roundhouse Books, 1967
The London Tilbury & Southend Railway, Peter Kay, 1996, Vol 1 ISBN 1 899890 10 6; 1997 Vol 2 ISBN 1 899890 19 X
The Thames Haven Railway, Peter Kay, 1999, ISBN 1 899890 27 0
Midland Carriages, Vol 1, R. E. Lacy & George Dow, Wild Swan Publications, ISBN 0 906867 19 3
Midland Carriages, Vol 2, R. E. Lacy & George Dow, Wild Swan Publications, ISBN 0 906867 36 3
The Railways of Tottenham, G. H. Lake, Greenlake Publications, 1945
Locomotives and Rolling Stock of the London, Tilbury and Southend Railway, R. W. Rush, The Oakwood Press, 1994, ISBN 0 85361 466 0

The Engineer
Engineering
Loco Profiles No 27: Tilbury Tanks, K. H. Leech, Profile Publications, 1972
Locomotives Illustrated No 101: LT&SR Locomotives, RAS Publishing, 1995
The London Railway Record
The Railway Magazine
Railways South East
SLS Journal

Various London, Tilbury & Southend Railway, Midland Railway and LMS Railway public and working timetables. Original Midland Railway distance diagrams.

Contents

During the Great War, the Baltics were employed on hauling coal trains and some authors have suggested they were used on the Toton to Brent trains. I think it is unlikely they ran that far north and suspect they were employed on the section between Wellingborough and Brent. Many of the trains from the Nottinghamshire coalfields were remarshalled at Wellingborough before working forward. This picture, taken near Elstree, shows an up mineral train hauled by No 2102 with 2-4-0 No 130 as the pilot engine. This engine has the tender weatherboard that was fitted to a number of engines at this time and the arrangement would have ensured a draughty footplate for the engine crew. *Locomotive Publishing Co courtesy Richard Taylor*

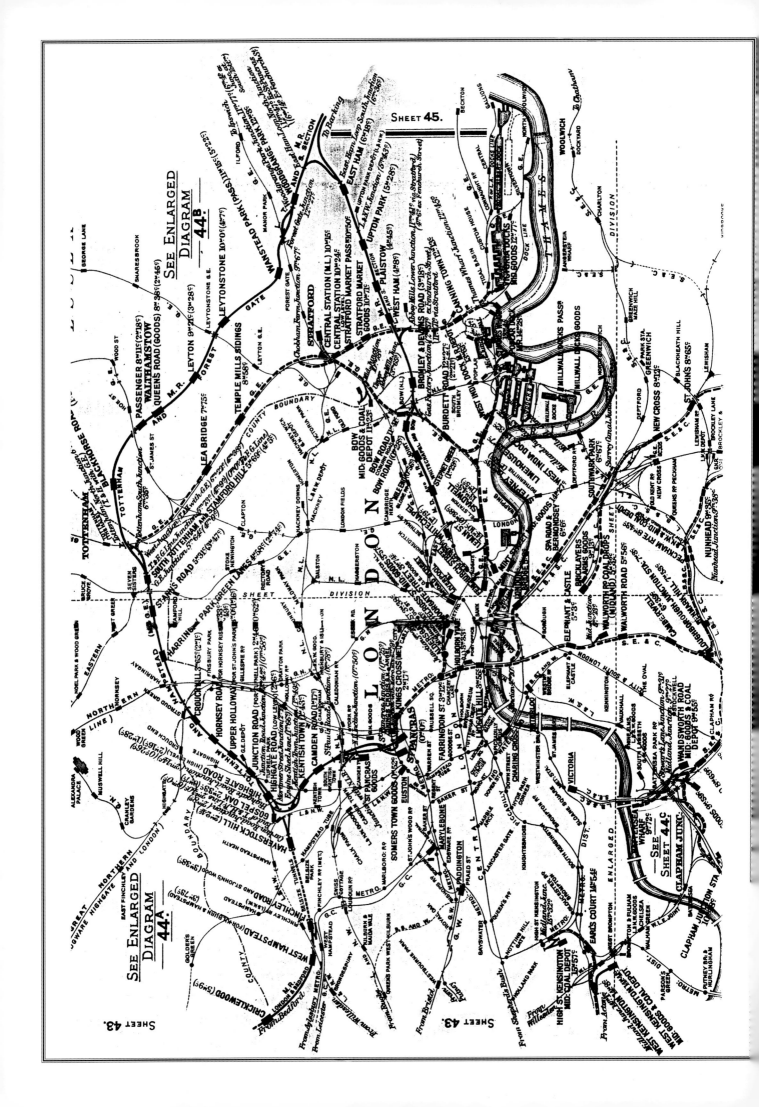

Introduction

It would probably be a good idea to begin by explaining how and why this book came to be written. Readers with an interest in matters related to the Midland Railway may be aware that some years ago Wild Swan Publications published the first of a series of books describing the locomotives of that company. It would have been possible to continue by describing the locomotives of the LT&SR and to leave it at that, but gradually the idea of describing the railway and its traffic, together with the locomotives that handled it, began to emerge and it is in this manner that this work is presented.

This book is not a detailed history of the line; Peter Kay's clinical examination of the minute books and similar archival material has left few stones unturned. However, his work has left the opportunity of writing a history from an alternative viewpoint. Therefore I have begun with an historical survey of the LT&SR in order that readers will be aware of the railway's development, and continue by describing the railway in general terms. I have made use of the various Board of Trade inspection reports; I place great importance upon these records. Although often written in a style of English that at times may be seen as stilted or rather old-fashioned, they provide an accurate and factual account of what existed at that point in time. I have ensured this material can be clearly identified from my own findings by reproducing it in italics.

During the past few years, Fred James and I have been engaged in sorting and cataloguing the Derby Collection of Midland and LMS Railway standard locomotive drawings held at the NRM, that also includes the surviving LT&SR locomotive drawings. The drawings used in this book have largely come from that source. This NRM material has been augmented by information gleaned from a detailed study of the Derby Locomotive Works order books, held at the PRO office, Kew, and I believe that much of this information has never been published before.

The principal emphasis of the line history has been largely directed towards the years when the LT&SR owned its own locomotives and then became part of the Midland Railway. However, I have continued the traffic story into the British Railways period when steam operation was still in being, and the story of the LT&SR locomotives until the last was withdrawn from service.

I undertook a considerable amount of research during the early 1990s but for various reasons this was set aside and I felt that the material would never see the light of day. Therefore I express my thanks to Peter Waller and the team at Ian Allan for accepting this book and including it within the prestigious OPC imprint.

I never saw the LT&SR, the Tilbury section of the LMS or British Railways in the days of steam; it would have presented a fascinating picture, very different to the steam railways in the Midlands that I knew in my youth. Recording the story of our Victorian railways is a satisfying and rewarding task when using both primary and secondary material. The name

Left:
This copy of part of Sheet 44 from the 6th edition of the Midland Railway distance diagrams has been included to show the LT&SR lines in the London area. The original Bishopsgate terminus is now shown as GE Goods and the routes from both Bishopsgate and Fenchurch Street can be seen. The map also shows the joint lines, the Tottenham & Hampstead and the Tottenham & Forest Gate Railways.

Right:
This impressive head-on picture of No 80 *Thundersley* was taken at Stratford on 11 March 1956. The locomotive was withdrawn in June 1956 for preservation as part of the National Collection and it was photographed in conjunction with RCTS London, Tilbury & Southend celebrations.
Collection R. J. Essery

Kenneth Leech is one that is closely associated with the LT&SR, both as an employee and author of many articles about the company. A few years before his death, when I explained what I was trying to write, he was kind enough to permit me to quote freely from his work and these writings have provided both a source of information and inspiration to me when recording the story of this remarkable railway. Therefore it is to the memory of Kenneth Leech that this volume is dedicated.

I would also like to acknowledge the help that I have received from the staff at the Public Record Office at Kew and to my friends at the National Railway Museum, Dieter Hopkin, Richard Taylor and Phil Atkins. Others, whose contribution must be acknowledged and who have helped me in various ways, are Roy Anderson, Andy Brown, Jack Braithwaite, Audrey Field, F. C. Garwood, Tony Overton, Allan Sibley and Stephen Summerson. Finally, I must acknowledge the immense debt that I owe to John Edgington who went through the manuscript and made numerous helpful suggestions before the work went to the publisher.

Bob Essery,
Rolleston on Dove,
Staffs, 2001

Abbreviations

From time to time I have used initials rather than write the name of a railway in full. These are:

ECR — Eastern Counties Railway
GER — Great Eastern Railway
L&BR — London & Blackwall Railway
LMS — London, Midland & Scottish Railway
LNWR — London & North Western Railway
LT&SR — London, Tilbury & Southend Railway*
MR — Midland Railway
NLR — North London Railway
T&FG — Tottenham & Forest Gate Joint Railway
T&HJR — Tottenham & Hampstead Junction Railway
THR&DC — Thames Haven Railway & Dock Company

*During the independent lifetime of the LT&SR two name styles were used. In the early days the style was 'London, Tilbury & Southend Railway' and this appeared on all material, ranging from share documents, letterheads, handbills, timetables, printed forms, etc. By 1900 the style had changed and the use of the comma generally ceased, the company name being shown as 'London Tilbury & Southend Railway'. For consistency, 'London, Tilbury & Southend Railway' has been used throughout this book.

Taken at Plaistow in the final years of the company, this evocative picture shows dual-fitted 'No 51' class engine No 59 *Holloway* and the larger 'No 79' class locomotive No 81 *Aveley*. *Collection R. J. Essery*

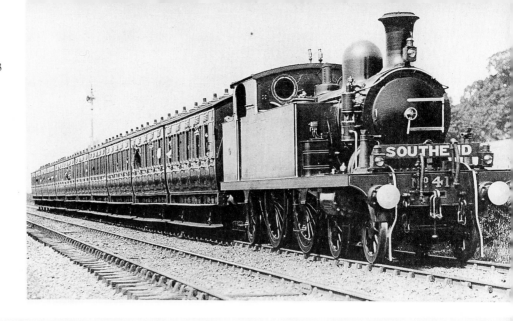

This picture of 'No 37' class engine No 41 *Leytonstone* was taken in 1903 and shows an LT&SR engine at the head of a St Pancras to Southend 11-coach train of Midland Railway four-wheel stock. *Collection R. J. Essery*

Above:
This pre-1903 photograph was taken at St Pancras and would have made a very colourful scene. To the left there is No 5 *Plaistow* and to the extreme right, GER 2-4-0 No 497. The three Midland Railway locomotives are, left to right, a Kirtley 2-4-0 and two Bogie Singles. This was the servicing point for locomotives that were to work trains away from St Pancras. Note the pit, used for oiling and inspection purposes, beneath the Kirtley 2-4-0 and the clinker and ash following fire cleaning and similar preparation work. *Collection Jack Braithwaite*

Right:
LMS No 2152, old No 43, at St Pancras in 1946/7 painting style: unlined black with yellow lettering, no shading. *C. R. L. Coles Ian Allan Library*

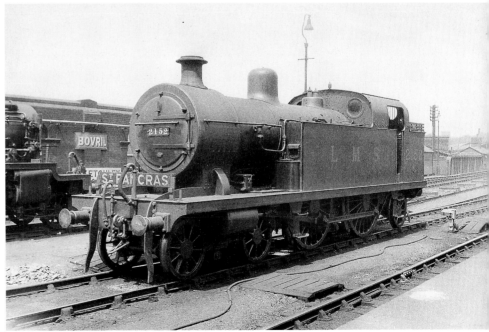

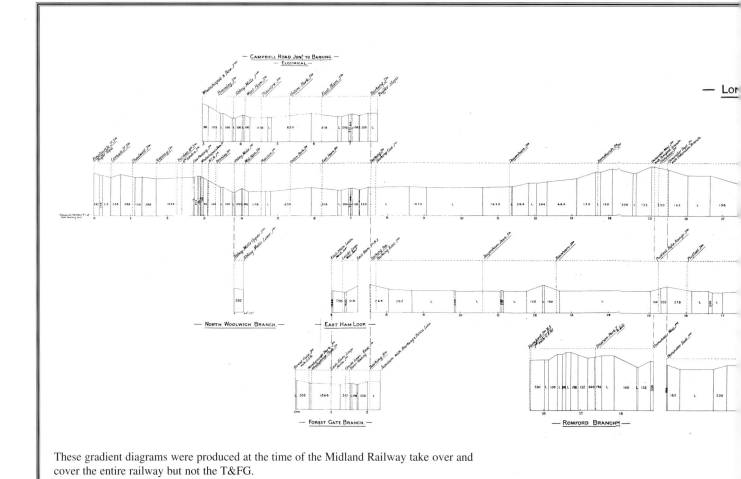

These gradient diagrams were produced at the time of the Midland Railway take over and cover the entire railway but not the T&FG.

LT&SR Diagram

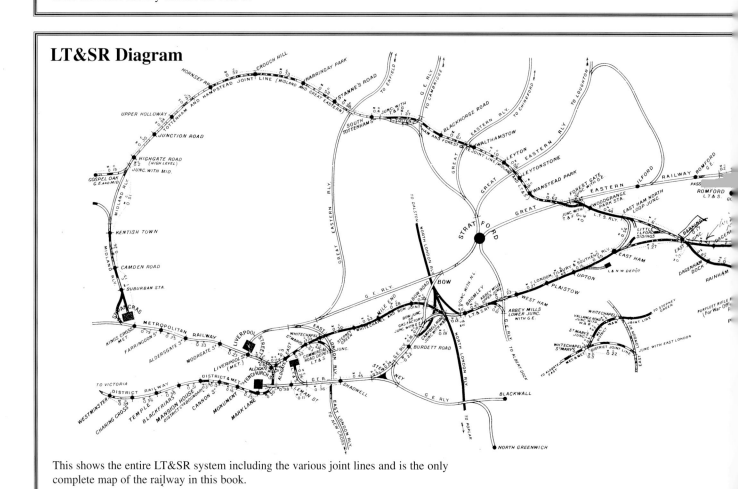

This shows the entire LT&SR system including the various joint lines and is the only complete map of the railway in this book.

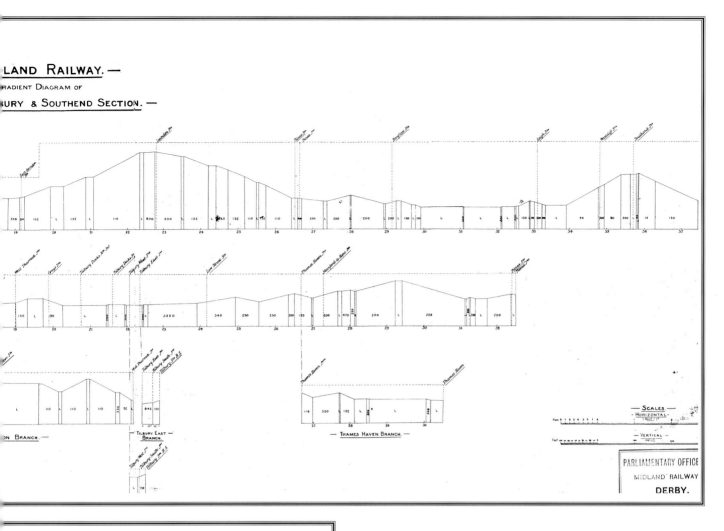

LAND RAILWAY. —

GRADIENT DIAGRAM OF

BURY & SOUTHEND SECTION. —

TILBURY EAST BRANCH. —

THAMES HAVEN BRANCH. —

SCALES.
HORIZONTAL
VERTICAL

PARLIAMENTARY OFFICE
MIDLAND RAILWAY
DERBY.

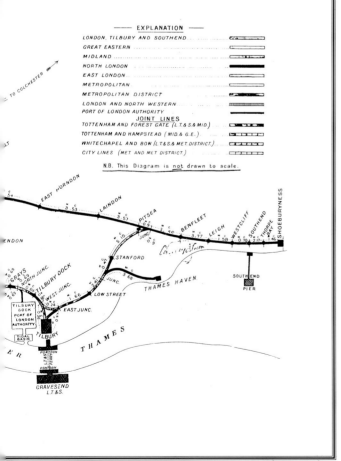

EXPLANATION

LONDON, TILBURY AND SOUTHEND	
GREAT EASTERN	
MIDLAND	
NORTH LONDON	
EAST LONDON	
METROPOLITAN	
METROPOLITAN DISTRICT	
LONDON AND NORTH WESTERN	
PORT OF LONDON AUTHORITY	

JOINT LINES

TOTTENHAM AND FOREST GATE (L.T.&S.& MID.)	
TOTTENHAM AND HAMPSTEAD (MID.& G.E.)	
WHITECHAPEL AND BOW (L.T.&S.& MET.DISTRICT.)	
CITY LINES (MET AND MET DISTRICT)	

N.B. This Diagram is not drawn to scale.

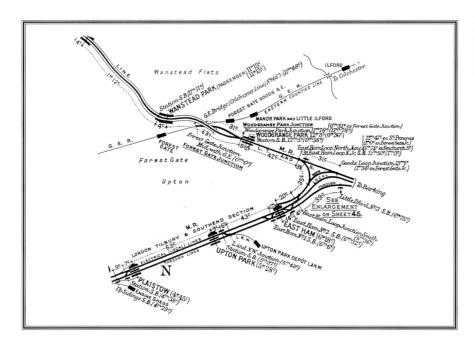

Fig 1 This is an extract from the Midland Railway distance diagrams and has been included to show the stations and junctions in the East Ham area.

This 16 August 1902 picture illustrates an up Metropolitan District Railway train for Hammersmith at East Ham, hauled by Metropolitan District Railway 4-4-0T No 23. *Collection R. J. Essery*

Almost 53 years later this photograph, taken at East Ham, shows British Railways Standard 2-6-4T No 80102 on an up parcels train made up of a single bogie passenger brake van. *T. J. Edgington*

Part One:
The Railway System

I. Historical Background

At the beginning of this historical review of the LT&SR I am tempted to suggest to readers that this was a somewhat unusual railway. Its early years were such that it was leased to the contractors who originally built the line for a period of 21 years. This arrangement meant that the company did not own any locomotives or rolling stock until after the period of the lease came to an end. Moreover, the London, Tilbury & Southend's very beginning was as a company which two other companies promoted, namely the Eastern Counties Railway and the London & Blackwall Railway. It was not until 1862 that the concern was finally incorporated as a separate company.

Another unusual feature was that, although it was a railway set in the south east of England, with its main line described in the company title, throughout its entire existence it was never to own a London terminus. The company was only able to gain access to its headquarters at Fenchurch Street, at the western end of the railway, by the use of running powers. In due course, we will look at the services to and from Bishopsgate and tell the story of the L&BR's Fenchurch Street station, the principal London end of the railway, although the company also used other stations. Another interesting feature was that when the company began to own locomotives it was (with the exception of two engines that came to the company by chance) to remain faithful to the tank engine configuration.

Comparison of the statistics given in Chapter 3 clearly reveals that the LT&SR was, above all, a passenger railway and as such fitted well into the Midland Railway's scheme of things. It seems likely that but for World War 1, and later the 1923 Grouping, the line would have been electrified but this was not to be and steam operation was still in place at the time of Nationalisation in 1948. Truly, the person who described the LT&SR as 'the jewel in the Midland Railway's crown' chose his words wisely; they were an accurate description of a railway whose story begins in 1836.

On 4 July 1836 the Eastern Counties Railway bill received Royal Assent and on the same date the Thames Haven Railway & Dock Company's ambition to build a line from a junction with the ECR's projected line at Romford via Mucking to Shell Haven was confirmed by an Act of Parliament. The ECR's line to Romford was opened in 1839 and continued to Colchester, which was reached in 1843, but by that date the Thames Haven Railway & Dock Company had made no progress whatsoever. Such was the sorry state of affairs that a further Act was required to renew their powers and this was confirmed on 3 July 1846 but, even so, progress was not possible due to the lack of funds.

At this time, Gravesend was a favoured resort for Londoners, in part due to the popularity of the Rosherville Gardens. In addition, Southend, whose pier was to become the

longest in Europe, was developing into a resort that was, by a fair margin, the closest sea bathing centre to London. Although not part of our story, the events to be described did have a bearing upon the development of the LT&SR and we begin by noting the volume of passenger traffic carried by various steamship companies from London, mostly from Blackwall pier, to Gravesend. This potentially lucrative two-way traffic attracted the attention of certain railway promoters, leading to a special meeting of the L&BR shareholders held on 24 November 1851. At this meeting a resolution was passed with the objective of combining with the ECR, and apply for powers to build a railway from a junction at Ilford, on the ECR on to Tilbury & Southend.

The London, Tilbury & Southend Extension Railway received Royal Assent on 17 June 1852. The authorised railway was to begin from a junction on the ECR close to Forest Gate station and was to proceed to Tilbury via Barking, Rainham, Purfleet and Grays. From Tilbury the line of railway would continue through Stanford-le-Hope (originally known as Horndon), Benfleet and Leigh before reaching Southend. In addition, two short branches to Tilbury Fort would form a triangle that would enable passenger trains to reach the terminus.

Just beyond the station there was a ferry where passengers for Gravesend and Rosherville could be conveyed in steam-driven ferry ships owned by the railway company. The passing of this Act enabled the LT&SR to enter into an agreement with the THR&DC whereby a single-track line was to be built from a junction at Mucking to Shell Haven. By the time this agreement was made the contractors, Peto, Brassey & Betts, had commenced to build the line from Forest Gate to Tilbury.

This part of the LT&SR was not difficult to construct, the countryside traversed did not require any engineering works of note and there are no tunnels at all on any part of the railway, or deep cuttings or viaducts on this section. The easy terrain enabled the first section of railway, which was double track, to be opened from Forest Gate, described as Ilford in the Board of Trade inspection report, through to Tilbury Fort on 13 April 1854. From the outset, the motive power and rolling stock to work the railway was supplied by the ECR. Shortly after the line was opened the contractors leased the railway for a period of 21 years at 6% per annum on the share capital, together with the additional payment of Debenture interest. On 13 April 1854 Captain Wynne of the Royal Engineers, on behalf of the Board of Trade, inspected the new railway. His report was brief and to the point. *'The London, Tilbury & Southend Railway commences from a junction with the Eastern Counties Railway and terminates at Tilbury, a distance of about 20 miles. The line commences at Ilford on the ECR about seven miles from the Bishopsgate Street station. I found the*

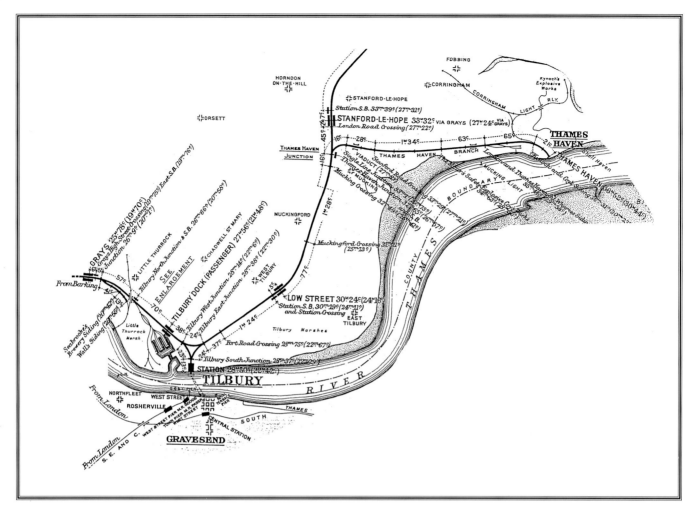

Fig 2 An extract of the Midland Railway distance diagrams showing the junctions around Tilbury and the Thames Haven branch.

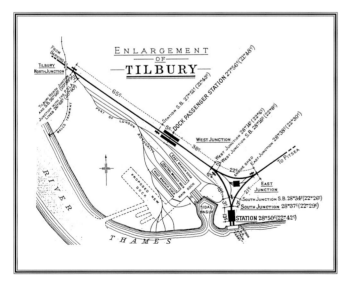

Fig 3 An enlargement of the 1913 Midland Railway distance diagrams that shows the Tilbury area with the various junctions, stations etc.

permanent way, which is laid double, well ballasted and to be good, and the platforms, signals of the line complete, and I am of the opinion that this portion of the LT&SR between Ilford and Tilbury may be opened without danger to the public using it.'

In order to maintain continuity with the various Board of Trade reports, I have included here the reports for the remainder of the line to Southend. The next report, dated 5 May 1855, was in respect of the section between Tilbury and Leigh, which was equally brief and appears to have been signed by a Lt-Col Wynne, who I assume was the same officer now promoted to a higher rank. *'That I have inspected a second line of rails on the London, Tilbury & Southend Railway, between Tilbury and Leigh, and I have to report what I found. This second line of rails, which completes the last link required for a double line of railway communication between London and Southend, well laid and in good order. And it is my opinion in a fit state to be opened for the safe conveyance of the public.'* A further report that I have found was dated 19 June 1855, Col Wynne also signed it but this report was not complete and covered only the section from Leigh to Stanford-le-Hope, a distance of 11 miles 74 chains. He reported that, *'the permanent way, which is laid in a single line is in good order and the few bridges which run over the line of sufficient strength and the platforms signals'*. (At this point the report ended but I expect he was about to write 'satisfactory', or something similar.

Col Wynne also wrote the report for the final section of the line, dated February 1856. I have to say that his handwriting was awful but in essence this is what he said. *'I have inspected the extension, 2 miles 44 chains in length of the London, Tilbury & Southend Railway from the temporary terminus at Leigh to the parliamentary terminus at Southend. I found the permanent well laid and the bridges, platforms completed and satisfactorily constructed. Part of the railway is carried on an embankment'* and at this point it becomes impossible to understand the exact words that he used. However, the meaning was clear. He was concerned about the section of line that ran close to the high water mark and the need for the ballast to become established. The Board of Trade Minute Paper dated 29 February confirms this was passed on to the Secretary of the London, Tilbury & Southend Extension Railway. The words used were in keeping with the period and they are quoted in full: '*My Lords do not object to the portion of line being opened for public traffic provided Colonel Wynne's recommendations as to a reduced state of speed, until the ballast of the line is fully established, be adhered to.*'

From an early date, arrangements had been made for the LT&SR trains to use the L&BR's terminus at Fenchurch Street where an enlargement of the existing station was required; this was opened on 19 November 1853. The station at Fenchurch Street was one of two London terminal stations that intending passengers could use. Understandably, the ECR also required access to the line so that trains from the ECR could depart for Tilbury from Bishopsgate, with the sections of outward trains from both Fenchurch Street and Bishopsgate being combined at Stratford. At this point inward trains were also divided, prior to being worked forward as two separate trains. These combined trains ran from Stratford to Forest Gate Junction

over the ECR, where they joined the LT&SR line for their journey on to Tilbury.

As I have mentioned, the extension to Horndon was opened on 14 August 1854, but just prior to this an amendment to the original line of railway had been agreed. The London, Tilbury & Southend Railway Amendment Act of 3 July 1854 enabled the company to overcome some of the restrictions included within the original act by moving the line of railway inland from the original coastal route. This deviation required both an embankment, a cutting and more importantly some steep gradients at Laindon. In addition to the inland deviation, the act authorised the construction of the Thames Haven branch. On 1 July 1855 the line was opened to Leigh, and then on 1 March 1856 to Southend, which, at that time, was a small town with a population of less than 3,000 people.

At first the LT&SR provided but a single line of railway from Tilbury to Southend even though the land purchased was sufficient to carry both an up and a down line. The Board of Trade refused to sanction passing loops over this section and this restricted the train service which could be operated. These operating problems led to the need to create fresh capital, which would allow the railway to be doubled. With the completion of a double line of railway an improved service commenced in May 1856. This enabled the company to begin

An early view of Rainham station, looking towards Barking, with the rather austere design of signalbox.
Collection T. J. Edgington

This undated but early 1950s view is also looking towards Barking. The overbridge and platform building are the same as in the previous view. Note the LMS hawkseye station nameboard with the additional 'Rainham' on the top panel.
Collection T. J. Edgington

Purfleet station on 28 November 1930, looking towards Barking. *F. Moore, courtesy V. R. Anderson*

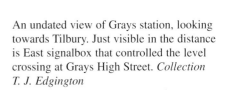

An undated view of Grays station, looking towards Tilbury. Just visible in the distance is East signalbox that controlled the level crossing at Grays High Street. *Collection T. J. Edgington*

A delightful c1900 picture of Grays High Street which also shows part of the East signalbox that controlled the level crossing. There is not a motor vehicle in sight. *Collection V. R. Anderson*

Above:
The junction for Seabrooks Brewery was five chains east of the signalbox shown on page 16 above and the Brewery siding can be seen in Fig 2. The locomotive is one of the pair of tender engines of the No '49' class shunting traffic at the brewery. Unfortunately it is not possible to identify individual wagons with certainty, although most appear to be LT&SR vehicles. The Midland diagram on page 18 does not show all the private lines in the sidings, so it is impossible to determine where the brake van has been set aside while shunting takes place. *Collection R. J. Essery*

Centre right:
The original platform arrangement at Stanford-le-Hope was staggered as shown here. London Road level crossing is in the foreground with the up platform in view. The photographer was looking towards Tilbury. *Collection V. R. Anderson*

This picture of Stanford-le-Hope station was taken from the new up platform, looking towards Pitsea. *Collection R. J. Essery*

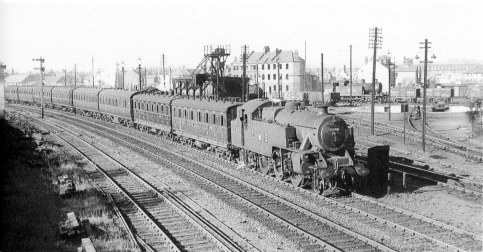

Left:
Tilbury Dock station is shown in the centre of Fig 3; here we can see the station with the station signalbox just to the left of the locomotive hauling the passenger train. The photographer was facing Barking in this undated picture. *Collection R. J. Essery*

Centre left:
This 1948 view of Tilbury shows one of the new Fairburn 2-6-4T engines, No 2248, at the head of a Fenchurch Street to Tilbury train. The leading two and rear two coaches are ex-LT&SR vehicles, the centre four are LMS standard vehicles. The first coach is No 17317, which began life as LT&SR No 45 to Diagram 10, built in 1911. It became MR No 3842, carrying this number until 1933 when it was renumbered again by the LMS. It was withdrawn in April 1956. Beyond the turntable is LMS-built 4-4-2T No 2130. *Collection R. J. Essery*

Below:
Taken about 1934 this panoramic view of Tilbury shows the new Riverside station. The road access is to the right and the ferry is the SS *Edith*. Built by A. W. Robertson & Co of London in 1911, the ferry remained in service until 1961. *Derby Collection NRM DY18085 & DY18084*

A view of Gravesend taken from the bridge of a ferry crossing the River Thames in 1932. The goods and vehicle pier at West Street is in the centre and the London, Chatham & Dover Railway pier and station are to the right. *Derby Collection NRM DY17724*

the tradition of fast business trains from Southend to the City of London. The operating problem, due to the need to reverse trains at Tilbury, was overcome when track improvements were made and a triangular junction was opened.

Almost a year previously, the Thames Haven branch had opened on 7 June 1855. At first, the company provided a service of two non-stop expresses which ran between Thames Haven and Fenchurch Street. Later the importance of this line was to decline with the opening of the Tilbury Docks complex and soon, other than workmen's trains, the branch was to carry goods traffic only. The build-up of passenger traffic along the line from Liverpool Street created problems of congestion at

Stratford. An attempt to solve this led to an Act of Parliament on 7 July 1856 authorising a direct route from Barking through East Ham, Plaistow and Bromley to the L&BR at Gas Factory Junction. In addition, a loop at Abbey Mills linked the LT&SR with the North Woolwich branch of the ECR.

The Board of Trade inspection report written by Captain Tyler, Royal Engineers was rather comprehensive. I have extracted some parts of it in order to provide a contemporary view of a new railway that had just been constructed. The report began: *'The permanent way was laid with double-headed rail that weighed 65lb to the yard. The joint and intermediate chairs weighed 28 and 21lb respectively. The*

Thames Haven Junction with the line to Southend to the left and the branch to Thames Haven to the right, as photographed on 4 November 1950. The signalbox, to a Midland design, was built in 1927. The junction signal, made by the Railway Signal Company, was erected on 2 July 1900; it is a curious arrangement of a part-lattice and part-solid post, with replacement Midland arms and fittings. *Collection R. J. Essery*

Another view of Thames Haven Junction signalbox. The strange white building was probably in connection with the electrification work that was being undertaken on the main line. The branch to Thames Haven is just visible behind the signalbox. *Collection R. J. Essery*

I believe this two-coach plus a passenger brake van train, hauled by 0-6-2T No 41985, is for workmen in connection with the Thames Haven branch. *Collection R. J. Essery*

Taken on 3 April 1954, these two pictures show the old passenger station at Thames Haven. The line was closed to passenger traffic in August 1880, but there were occasional trains to meet steamers until 1909. Workmen's trains used the station from January 1923 until about 1955. *T. J. Edgington*

sleepers were laid transversely, and were 3ft apart on the average.' The ballast was described as being *'remarkably good'*. He continued: *'None of the modern improvements have been employed for receiving the joints of the rails, the ordinary cast-iron chair and wooden key having been used for that purpose. The works are very heavy for so short a line, comprising a brick viaduct containing 42 arches, and numerous bridges, of wrought iron, cast iron, timber and brickwork, with spans of from 12ft to 137ft. The bridge with a span of 137ft is composed of a centre and two outside bow and string girders, resting upon brick abutments. Cast iron is employed in conjunction with wrought iron.'* His report continues with a detailed technical description of the bridge and the tests that he made in order to ensure that it was strong enough. The first test was made by using six engines and tenders, three on each line of rails. This resulted in some rivets on the diagonal braces shearing off.

A second test saw the use of four trucks loaded with rails and chairs added to the weight of the engines and placed on the bridge. He calculated that the weight was 270 tons or about two tons per lineal foot for the two lines. One train was left on

the bridge while the other was run past and then both trains were left on the bridge for 15 minutes. Eventually he was satisfied and reported: *'No permanent set resulted when the load was removed and the deflections ultimately obtained were 2¹⁄₁₆ inches from the middle girders.'* He concluded: *'Under these circumstances I am of the opinion that this bridge may at once be safely used for traffic; but I consider that to render it a satisfactory structure diagonal braces of a more suitable description should be added to it to increase the stiffness.'* He also wanted arched connections to be added to the main girders and wrote that the company's engineer had given him a certificate confirming that this work would be completed by 1 May. He then wished to re-examine the bridge.

In the report he also referred to a wrought-iron viaduct 362ft in length and noted that the other works appeared to have been substantially and carefully constructed and that they stood the tests that he applied to them with the engines used on the larger bridge. The report is concluded by giving the distance between two rails and any obstructions at the side of the line as 3ft 6in, the amount that was usually required. Therefore, *'Subject to the above remarks, I beg to report my opinion that*

These three pictures, taken on 21 May 1927, show the old station as seen from the pier, the old station river frontage, and the derelict cattle pens. At one time a considerable amount of cattle came through Thames Haven. *All Collection R. J. Essery*

Below:
Southend-on-Sea on 21 August 1936 with an ordinary passenger train for Fenchurch Street departing, hauled by No 2134 of the 1927 batch of Class 3 passenger engines. The train is made up of ex-LT&S coaches. *Real Photographs 24072*

Right:
Westcliff-on-Sea was less than a mile to the west of Southend and this undated picture was taken facing there. *Collection R. J. Essery*

Below left:
A west-facing view of Westcliff-on-Sea illustrates a train for Southend made up of four-wheel coaches hauled by the appropriately named 'No 37' class engine, No 38 *Westcliff. Collection R. J. Essery*

Below right:
The delights of pre-Great War Westcliff are advertised by this Midland Railway poster. *Derby Collection NRM DY9616*

the Bow and Barking branch of the LT&S Railway may be opened for traffic without danger to the public using the same.'

Running powers in perpetuity were granted to the LT&SR over the two miles of railway between Gas Factory Junction and Fenchurch Street station. With the opening of this line on 31 March 1858, all LT&SR trains ceased to run over the section from Bishopsgate to Stratford in order to join LT&SR lines at Forest Gate.

Nevertheless, the ECR introduced a passenger service between its station at Bishopsgate and the LT&SR at Barking, made easier by the granting of running powers to the ECR by the LT&SR from Forest Gate Junction to Barking. Additional running powers were granted to the ECR, which enabled the company to work its trains from Gas Factory Junction to the North Woolwich branch via Bromley and Abbey Mills Junction. Fortunately at the time these lines were constructed this part of London was sparsely populated; the explosive growth of London in an eastward direction was yet to come.

As already noted, the LT&SR did not become a separate entity in its own right until 1862 and we now come to the point where we must record what happened. A special meeting of the shareholders of the company was called on 17 December 1861 with the objective of promoting a bill to constitute what I have called the LT&SR Undertaking as a separate company. This bill received Royal Assent on 16 May 1862 and under its terms the company was to have nine directors, three each from the

two original owning companies, namely the L&BR and ECR, with the other three being nominated by the shareholders of the LT&SR. In addition, the bill completely divorced the capital of the LT&SR from the two promoting companies. This legal change in respect of the LT&SR just pre-dated the creation of the Great Eastern Railway — the ECR amalgamating with four other East Anglian companies on 7 August 1862 to form the new railway. Although it was to remain independent until the Grouping of 1923, the London & Blackwall Railway was leased to the Great Eastern Company by an Act of Parliament dated 19 June 1865 and in effect became part of the GER from 1 January 1866.

A further junction with the LT&SR, by what could be described as a 'northern' railway company, came in 1869 when, on 18 May, the North London Railway branch from Bow (NLR) to Bromley (LT&SR) was opened. This new connection enabled trains from the NLR to run through to Southend by exercising their running powers. Furthermore, the 20 March 1867 agreement between the London & North Western Railway, the NLR and the LT&SR, gave the two northern companies running powers over the entire LT&SR system. Exactly how much use of these powers was made is not entirely clear but the first known use of them was to establish a service of trains between Bow and Plaistow, a service that ran until 1916. Other than the possibility of special trains, in particular during the Great War period, I do not

Upton Park on 14 March 1959, showing an up District Line electric train at the platform. *Collection V. R. Anderson*

believe the LNWR exercised its running powers over the LT&SR, the NLR working the LNWR traffic. There is a picture in *1850-1925 Vintage Album* by John Kite of an excursion at Westcliff-on-Sea hauled by two LNWR 18in goods engines c1920. Although he lived at Westcliff between 1908 and 1922, he told me that he did not recall seeing an excursion train hauled by an LNWR locomotive.

The LNWR had a depot at Upton Park between Plaistow and East Ham. This began as a ballast siding, and a letter from the LT&SR to the Board of Trade on 20 November 1874 read: *'I have just completed for the London & North Western railway company a siding into a ballast field communicating with the LT&SR at a point 77 chains east of the Plaistow station. Protected by signals, locked points etc and I shall be obliged by you informing me whether this will be inspected by the Board of Trade and if so when such an inspection will take place.'* The Board of Trade replied the following day advising that Captain Tyler be appointed to make the inspection and also requesting a sketch showing the position of signals etc. Unfortunately, the sketch has not survived but we do have a copy of Captain Tyler's report dated 24 November 1874. He described the location thus: *'A ballast siding, and two crossover roads have been connected with the passenger lines. The points and signals are to be worked from a signal cabin, which has been constructed and supplied, with the necessary locking apparatus; but rods and wires are disconnected pending the sanction of the Board of Trade, which may now, in my opinion, be granted.'* The Midland Railway distance diagram shows the junction to the short branch to the LNWR Upton Park depot which was 78 chains east of Plaistow station. At some later date the ballast siding was closed and the LNWR opened its goods and coal depot on the same site in 1895.

Before leaving Upton Park I must record the opening of the station. The LT&SR wrote to the Board of Trade on 5 September 1877 requesting an inspection before Friday next, but according to an internal Board of Trade note the LT&SR did not include a plan of the new station. Maj-Gen Hutchinson was appointed to inspect the new station and his report was dated 12 September 1877. He said: *'There has been a signal cabin in connection with a ballast siding for some time past at Upton Park, and the new station is protected mainly by the previously existing signals. The station has been constructed in compliance with the requirements of the Board of Trade except*

in the following particulars. 1. The up starting, up distant and ballast siding signals should be either repeated or made visible from the cabin. 2. A handrail is required for the staircase leading from the platform to the booking office. 3. A clock visible to the platform is required. Subject to the speedy completion of these requirements the Board of Trade need not, I submit, object to the opening of Upton Park station. A footbridge between the two platforms has been ordered and is to be shortly erected.'

According to the Midland Railway distance diagram, Upton Park station was 63 chains east of Plaistow station and 15 chains to the west of the junction of the LNWR goods station branch. The original signalbox remained in service until 1903 when Upton Park was enlarged to have four platforms.

To the best of my knowledge, there were to be no further developments of note on the LT&SR and in due course the lease to Peto, Brassey & Betts expired on 3 July 1875. In 1866, Peto and Betts were bankrupted and Brassey died in 1870 so the line just ticked over for the next five years under the management of Brassey's executors. Understandably, they did not wish to become involved in any unnecessary investment, although they were required to bring the line up to the agreed standard prior to the expiry of the lease. In advance of this, talks were held by the LT&SR directors with a number of companies, namely the Great Eastern, London & North Western and North London railways, but it came to naught. Peter Kay covers this period very well in his first volume and those who are interested in these developments are recommended to read his findings.

The LT&SR Period of Operation

After the directors of the LT&SR had failed to persuade the directors of the Great Eastern to lease the line various negations took place that ultimately led to an agreement being made with the Great Eastern railway company to work the line. The GER was prepared to continue to provide locomotives for a period of five years, until 30 June 1880, and rolling stock for two years, and the various details about tolls, costs, etc were agreed before the lease expired. Faced with the need to rebuild the system the directors of the LT&SR began by appointing Arthur Lewis Stride, at the time a district engineer with the London, Chatham & Dover Railway, as Resident Engineer and General Manager. Stride, who was appointed to the board as Managing Director in 1889, Deputy Chairman and Managing Director in 1905 and finally Chairman and Managing Director in 1906, became the father figure who piloted the company forward. From the time that he arrived, when it was somewhat run down, he was to develop it until it became one of the best run and most profitable railway companies in the kingdom. It is also worth recording that the act of 13 May 1875 legally empowered the LT&SR to either lease the line or arrange for it to be worked by another company; however, as I have said, the directors declined both options. In addition, this act also empowered the company to raise fresh capital which was certainly required to finance the re-equipment programme due to be implemented.

The first major improvements centred on the signalling which, at that time, was virtually non-existent. The railway was largely worked on the time interval system and other than Bromley Junction signalbox there was no interlocking on the railway. However, under Stride's direction, by 1881, points and signals were interlocked and the block telegraph established. Considerable improvements were made to the permanent way

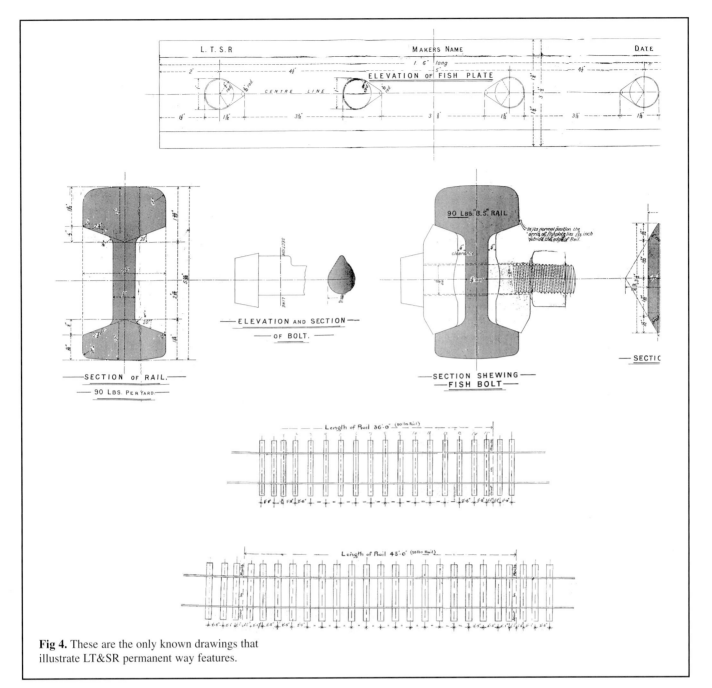

Fig 4. These are the only known drawings that illustrate LT&SR permanent way features.

using 72lb/yd steel rail to replace the 65lb/yd iron rail previously employed. Very little information has come to light about the LT&SR permanent way other than the drawings reproduced here. The need to service and repair the company's locomotives and rolling stock called for the establishment of repair shops, and Plaistow was selected as the site for this work after the contract with the GER had expired. Thomas Whitelegg was to take charge of the locomotive department and we record these developments later. New coaching stock was placed in service, running on four wheels with a tare weight of less than 10 tons, which was in line with the general practice then found elsewhere in Great Britain. At first the coaches were fitted with the Clarke & Webb chain brake but in 1885 the company was to opt for the Westinghouse brake, which was fitted to all passenger stock. At first, oil lamps were used to illuminate the coaching stock but before the turn of the century coaches began to be equipped with electric lights. The LT&SR was one of the first companies to adopt this form of illumination for its passenger vehicles, moving from oil to electricity and, as far as I am aware, never used gas.

The final major legal change to affect the company, prior to the Midland Railway takeover, came in 1882. This was a further Act of Parliament, passed on 24 July in that year, covering a number of separate issues. It is probably convenient at this point to deal with the section which established the LT&SR as a fully independent concern controlled by its own shareholders who appointed five directors. This effectively removed the control of the company from the GER who hitherto, via the original agreement, appointed six of the nine directors allowed. Notwithstanding this change it seems reasonable to presume that the GER and the L&BR still retained a considerable financial interest in the company, but I have been unable to establish to what degree.

In addition to these legal niceties, further additions to the railway network were authorised with a five-year period to complete the work in question. Authority was given to raise £600,000 in capital together with borrowing powers for an additional £200,000 in order to finance it. These new works were as a direct result of the rivalry between the various

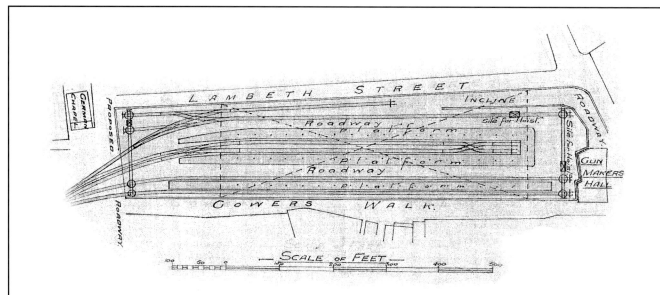

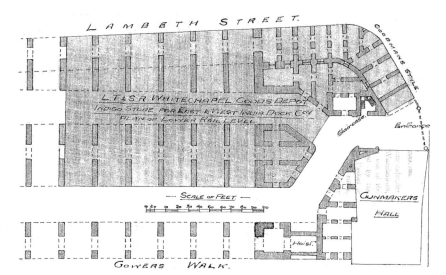

Fig 5 This three-part drawing of Commercial Road goods depot is described on the plan as Whitechapel and shows the original arrangement of the new warehouse that was built by the LT&SR. *Collection R. J. Essery*

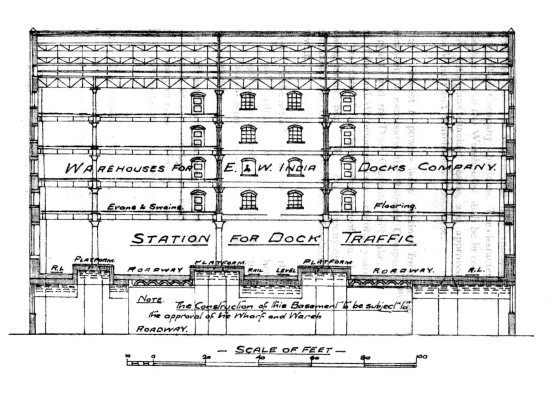

independent dock companies within the port of London, which led to the decision of the East & West India Dock Company to build a deep water dock downstream at Tilbury in an attempt to take the lion's share of the developing traffic on offer and to restore the company's fortunes. At this period in time the growth of industry in the Great Britain was considerable and there was a need to find additional dock capacity to move manufactured products overseas. In the circumstances it was not surprising that the East & West India Dock Company should seek to build this new enterprise, their existing docks being unable to cope with the larger steamships that were entering service. Once it was decided to undertake the project it meant that it would require the LT&SR to move the traffic both inward, for loading on to ships, and outward, from the dock area, for all imports. The responsibility for this work now lay with the LT&SR to ensure that facilities would be built and the traffic handled. In order to accomplish this the LT&SR resolved to build a number of additional lines, which were included within the 1882 act. The new work can be summarised thus:

1. To handle the increasing volume of goods traffic a new goods station would be built at Commercial Road, Whitechapel, at the end of a 27-chain branch that left the L&BR near Leman Street at Christian Street Junction.
2. To build a direct line between Barking and Pitsea over a length of 18 miles 78 chains. This line was seen as not only diverting London-Southend traffic away from Tilbury but also being able to generate valuable commuter traffic.
3. To extend the line on from Southend a further 3 miles 32 chains to Shoeburyness. It is worth noting that previous attempts to build a line to Shoeburyness had not been successful. However, the act authorising the line required, quite understandably, that it be kept away from the 'powder magazine' at South Shoebury. One source quotes that the required distance was to be 132yd, but the author does not know exactly how this precise figure was established.

The work, undertaken by Kirk & Parry, contractors from Sleaford, Lincolnshire, speedily got under way and the first section between Barking and Upminster was opened for traffic on 1 May 1885, while the shorter extension to Shoeburyness had opened in the previous year on 1 February. The final sections of the 'direct' line were opened on 1 May 1886 to East Horndon (later renamed West Horndon in 1949), with the more difficult section to Pitsea on 1 June 1888. Maj-Gen Hutchinson's report, dated 27 April 1885, has survived and the

salient points that he made are reproduced as follows.

'I have inspected the Barking and Upminster section of the Barking and Pitsea Extension Railway of the London, Tilbury & Southend Railway. This line, which extends from Barking to a temporary terminus at Upminster, is 7 miles 71 chains, and is double throughout, with sidings or additional lines at the few stations, Dagenham, Hornchurch and Upminster. The steepest gradient has an inclination of 1 in 132 and the sharpest curve a radius of 40 chains. The permanent way consists of bullhead rail steel rails in 24ft lengths, 72lb to the yard, fished at the joints, and cast-iron chairs 42¾ lb each, secured to the sleepers by three wrought-iron spikes in each; of rectangular sleepers, 9ft by 10in by 5in, laid 2¼ft from centre to centre at joints and 2ft 5in elsewhere. Of gravel ballast 1ft deep below the under surface of the sleepers. The rails are secured to the chairs by outside oak keys and the width at the formation level is 30ft.' Although it is not entirely clear, I suspect that there were two alternative methods of fixing the chairs to the sleepers depending upon whether they were at the rail joints or not.

The report continues by describing the bridges: *'Few over bridges all constructed with concrete abutments faced with blue bricks, widest span 25ft, formed with brick arches.'* It also refers to the use of cast and wrought iron for the girder tops. The construction of the underbridges was similar and the longest span was 70ft. It referred to eight culverts, the widest being 20ft, all having arched tops resting on brick, and concrete and brick walls. It concluded: *'These works appear to have been substantially constructed and to be standing well, except the 20ft culvert at 4 miles 47 chains, where there is a bulge on one of the wing walls which should be carefully watched.'* Maj-Gen Hutchinson was satisfied with the strength of the girders under test.

He continued by confirming that *'there are no tunnels on the line and no level crossings and that the line is fenced with post and rail fencing. The stations are well arranged and contain all the necessary accommodation; footbridges, pathways have been provided. The signal and block telegraph arrangements have been provided for in the new signal cabins at:*

	Working Levers	Spare Levers
1. Barking East	14	11
2. Dagenham	14	6
3. Hornchurch	14	6
4. Upminster	13	11

Interlocking in these cabins has been correctly carried out.

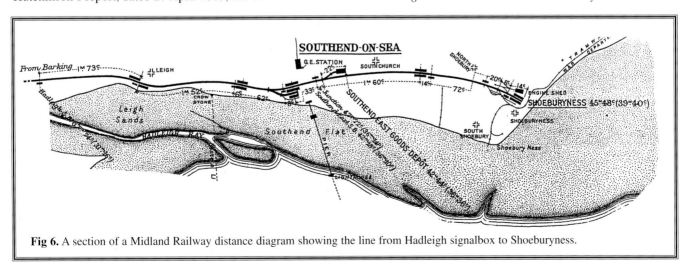

Fig 6. A section of a Midland Railway distance diagram showing the line from Hadleigh signalbox to Shoeburyness.

Photographed on 20 October 1892, this shows 'No 1' class engine No 32 *Leyton* at Pitsea, with Driver W. Haydon. The locomotive displays a Fenchurch Street destination board and the coalbunker is full, which suggests that there were coaling facilities at Pitsea. The safety valves are simmering, indicating the locomotive will shortly be working a train to London. This picture is most useful as it clearly shows the jack on the top of the wing tank as well as some fire irons. I suspect that there are other fire irons on the top of the right-hand side tank as well. The lubricators can be seen on the engine platform and there are no rainstrips on the cab roof. Both enginemen appear to be in a uniform, cap and jacket without a collar. *Collection Jack Braithwaite*

'An engine turntable has been provided at Upminster, (which will become a permanent station) and the traffic is, I am informed to be worked for the present as between Fenchurch Street and Upminster.

'The ballasting of the line was not quite complete when I inspected it but this will be finished by the end of the month and I have no requirements to record. Arrangements have been made at Upminster to prevent the contractor's train, which are [sic] working on the extension being constructed, from running on the lines without the signalman's permission. I am therefore able to report that the new line between Barking and Upminster is fit for passenger traffic.'

The work also entailed new stations at Barking and at Pitsea. Maj-Gen Hutchinson's report dated 22 April 1886 read: 'I have inspected a further portion of the Barking to Pitsea extension line of the London, Tilbury & Southend Railway. This portion is a double line, 3 miles 59 chains long, commencing at Upminster station and extending to East Horndon station, a temporary terminus. The permanent way is similar in all respects to that of the previously inspected portion of the line. It is in good order, except that the ballasting and boxing up are not in all cases yet completed. The steepest gradient has an inclination of 132 [1 in 132 is the modern way of expressing gradients] and the sharpest curve a radius of 120 chains.' He went on to describe the bridges and to confirm the use of post and rail for the fencing. He added: 'The works appear to have been substantially constructed and are standing well. The cast-iron girders have sufficient theoretical strength. There are no tunnels and no level crossings of public roads.

'The only new station is at East Horndon, where good accommodation has been provided and a footbridge for communication between the platforms. The following are the only requirements, which came under my notice.

'1. At Upminster substitute for the semaphore signal leading from the sidings to the main line a disc signal. 2. At East Horndon the points to the down end of No 5 crossing should be worked by a separate lever; these points should in their normal position stand open for the siding (so as to act as safety points with regard to the line in progress beyond East Horndon) and should be locked in this position by lowering of 17 down home signal. The down line should·be only used for contractor purposes.'

His report concluded by recommending that the new line between Upminster and East Horndon be opened for passenger traffic.

A further inspection of the line between East Horndon and Pitsea took place on 24 May 1888; once again Maj-Gen Hutchinson was the inspecting officer. He confirmed that the steepest gradient was 1 in 110 and the sharpest curve had a radius of 40 chains. He continued by referring to the new stations that had been built at Laindon and Pitsea Junction, the latter to take the place of the original Pitsea station, and confirmed that he was satisfied with the arrangements. The final section of the line was opened on 1 June 1888.

There was one further matter to require the Board of Trade's attention and this was at Laindon. On 17 November the Board of Trade was advised that when the line through the site of Laindon station was being built it was found to be advisable to raise the track to avoid the probability of flooding. The Board of Trade was also told that a nearby road had been raised by about five or six feet higher than originally proposed. The LT&SR engineers confirmed that the road authorities had sanctioned this change. Needless to say, the Board of Trade did not raise any objections.

The 'Tilbury cut off' enabled a much faster service of trains to be provided between Southend and Fenchurch Street via the direct line, a feature that we will return to in Chapter 3. Finally, it should be noted that, in addition to the improved services that the LT&SR was able to offer from Fenchurch Street to Southend, connections from London St Pancras via the Tottenham & Hampstead and Tottenham & Forest Gate Railway, together with the GER's own route to Southend — a line opened in 1889 — helped to fuel the rapid growth of the town. The population increased from less than 3,000 souls when the railway arrived, to in excess of 70,000 by the time the LT&SR became part of the Midland Railway in 1912.

The extension from Southend to Shoeburyness had its share of problems. On 5 December 1883 the LT&SR gave one calendar month's notice to the Board of Trade of its intention to open to public traffic the No 2 railway authorised by the LT&SR act of 1882, extending from Southend to Shoeburyness. The Board of Trade responded and appointed Maj-Gen Hutchinson to inspect the new works. Before describing the Maj-Gen's findings I must introduce readers to

Right:
Leigh-on-Sea is between Pitsea and Southend; this early 1900s
picture is facing Southend with the level crossing, signalbox and up
line platform in the distance. *Collection R. J. Essery*

Below:
The picture of Leigh-on-Sea shown here was taken facing Pitsea and
illustrates an Ealing to Southend through eight-coach corridor train
hauled by No 2111, one of the 1923 batch of locomotives built at
Derby. The locomotive is dual fitted and is in the post-1928 black-
lined red livery. The trains employed on the through services were
Westinghouse-only fitted and after the withdrawal of the 4-6-4T
engines were hauled by dual-fitted 4-4-2T locomotives as seen here;
the later Stanier engines were equipped only with the vacuum brake.
Collection T. J. Edgington

Taken on 27 April 1921, this picture of
Pitsea looks east with the station just visible
under the footbridge. Pitsea was the junction
of the original line to Southend via Tilbury
and the direct route from Barking.
Collection R. J. Essery

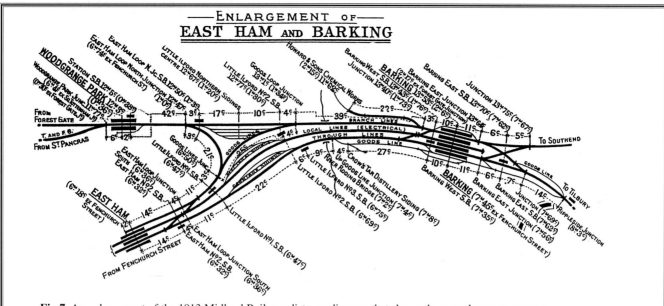

Fig 7. An enlargement of the 1913 Midland Railway distance diagram that shows the complex arrangement of lines between Woodgrange Park, East Ham and Barking.

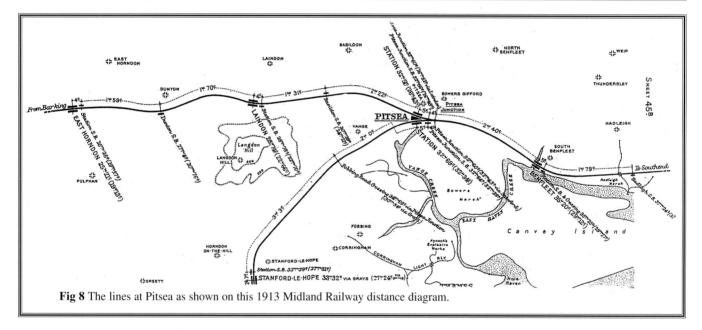

Fig 8 The lines at Pitsea as shown on this 1913 Midland Railway distance diagram.

the Rev Bateman, Rector at Southchurch, Southend. A letter from the Rev Bateman was sent to the Board of Trade drawing their attention to the dangerous state of a footpath crossing the line in his parish. In reply, the Board of Trade said that they had no statutory authority which they could use to impose the construction of bridges at such crossings. However, they told the rector that they called the particular attention of the directors of the LT&SR to this matter etc. In order to provide readers with an insight of how these matters were dealt with more than 100 years ago I have quoted from the rector's letter and the railway company's response.

Unfortunately, not all the correspondence has survived but there is enough to see what happened. Clearly, the Rector wrote to the Board of Trade and they acknowledged this and sent a copy of his letter to the secretary of the LT&SR. This letter was passed to the Engineer & Managers' office and Stride wrote to the rector. This is the substance of what he had to say. *'I beg to inform you that the footpath in question is not, in the opinion of my Directors, of sufficient importance to necessitate the erection of a footbridge over the railway. The*

daily average of passengers [pedestrians would be a better description] over the railway by this path for some weeks past has not exceeded 30 and although it is admitted as probable that in the height of the summer this number may be somewhat increased, it is on the other hand certain that on the opening of the Shoeburyness extension many persons who use this path as a short cut to Southend will travel by railway.' He then went on to deal with the question of a private accommodation work described in the postscript of the rector's letter sent to the Board of Trade, but details were not in the file.

Maj-Gen Hutchinson's report was dated 21 January 1884. He began by describing the railway as *'a double line 3 miles 57 chains long, is a continuation of the railway which has hither terminated at Southend. Southend station has been converted into a through station, and a new station (the only new one) has been constructed at Shoeburyness. The steepest gradient on the line has an inclination of 1 in 100 and the sharpest curve a radius of 80 chains.'*

Other points that he made included confirmation that the permanent way was laid with steel rails 24ft long, weighing

Continued page 33

An undated picture of Pitsea Junction showing the direct line to Barking to the right and the line to Tilbury to the left. *Collection Jack Braithwaite*

An undated picture of Benfleet, looking towards Pitsea. *Collection R. J. Essery*

The end of the line from Fenchurch Street was Shoeburyness and this 27 June 1936 picture shows No 2508, one of the then new Stanier three-cylinder 2-6-4T engines at the head of a train of Midland Railway coaching stock. *H. F. Wheeller 37/45, courtesy Roger Carpenter*

31

Shoeburyness, looking towards the end of the line, with the carriage sidings and the cleaners' walkways prominently in view. In the far distance can be seen the engine sheds to the left and the station in the centre. *Collection V. R. Anderson*

Horwich Mogul No 13064 has just arrived at Southend-on-Sea with an ordinary passenger train. Note that most of the carriage doors are open. The driver appears to be overseeing the uncoupling of his engine from the coaches. The date is given as 21 May 1933 and the photographer recorded that the engine was still painted in red livery. *Collection H. F. Wheeller, courtesy Roger Carpenter*

Some sources suggest that No 59 *Holloway* was originally *Holloway Road* but I am not sure this is correct. George Dow suggests that the date of this picture is c1911 and that seems reasonable. No 59 is at the head of a train made up of Midland coaches from Southend-on-Sea to St Pancras, while No 51 *Tilbury Docks* is for Fenchurch Street. *Collection V. R. Anderson*

Above:
This early 1900s picture shown here illustrates the west end of Southend-on-Sea station. The large hip-roofed brick-based signalbox is prominent in the centre of the picture and the sidings are full of four-wheeled close-coupled five-compartment coaches. *Collection V. R. Anderson*

Right:
Taken at Southend on 2 June 1940, this wartime picture shows children being evacuated from what was expected to be a danger zone at this time. Note the blacked out lamps and the sandbags to protect the windows from shrapnel. *Collection V. R. Anderson*

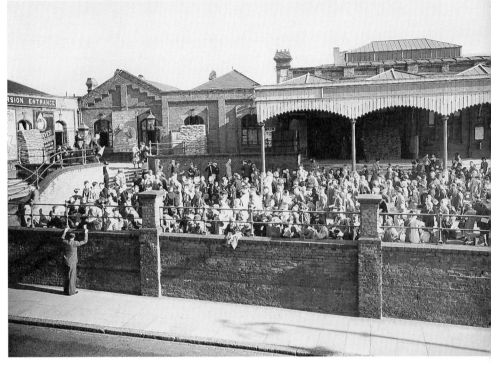

72lb to the yard. Fishplates were used and the dimensions of the sleepers and formation were in keeping with the standards for the period. He described the bridges and confirmed that there were no viaducts, tunnels or public roads crossed. He continued, *'The signal arrangements have been carried out in the existing cabin at Southend, containing 20 working levers and 1 spare lever and in a cabin at Shoeburyness containing 23 working and 3 spare levers. With a few exceptions the interlocking is correct, and instruments have been provided for working the block system.'* There were a number of requirements listed in his report, none was really significant; however, his report concluded with a reference to the rector and the footpath.

He described the conditions, *'Nearly a mile from Southend, the line is in a cutting, but perfectly straight, the piers of an overbridge 300 yards distant should that impede the view, on a gradient of 1 in 120, is much used by visitors and school children etc.'* He concluded, *'Under these circumstances I strongly recommend the erection of a footbridge.'*

The rector wrote, *'Our parish is cut completely in half by the railway extension and we are naturally anxious that the only two footpaths from church and school, to beach, should be preserved. There is a danger attaching to both; but the one about which we wrote is virtually destroyed! We are very glad that Major Hutchinson recommends a bridge and we earnestly hope that the Board of Trade will enforce that recommendation.'* There is nothing else in the file so I am unable to say if the recommendation was implemented. There is an overbridge shown on the 1883 edition of the 1in OS map, (railways inserted to March 1884). The 1897 25in OS plan shows this overbridge leading to Southchurch Hall, also a footpath some 300yd east crossing the line on the level, so presumably the Rector's footbridge was not built. This correspondence does show, once again, that the inspecting officers of the Board of Trade took a very responsible approach to the question of public safety, but lacked the necessary powers, while the attitude of the management of the railway companies was not to spend money if they could get away with it!

Tilbury Docks was opened on 17 April 1886 but the anticipated traffic of 1,000,000 tons per annum did not materialise for many years. Nevertheless in due course, the developing traffic to and from Tilbury Docks, via the Commercial Road goods station with its considerable warehouses at last began to pay dividends to the LT&SR.

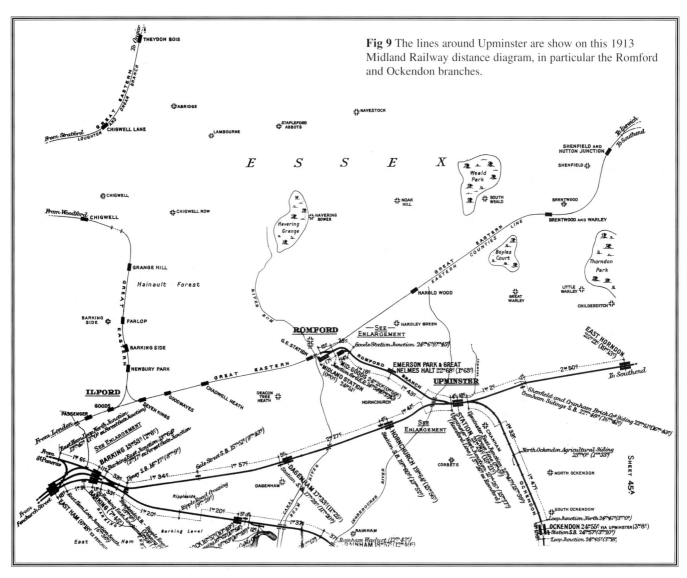

Fig 9 The lines around Upminster are show on this 1913 Midland Railway distance diagram, in particular the Romford and Ockendon branches.

The entrance to Romford station is shown in this Edwardian era picture. The entrance to the LT&SR station was to the right, and to the GER to the left. The covered footway connected both stations. *Collection R. J. Essery*

Romford LT&S station on 11 June 1938 showing the motor train that has just arrived. No 1287 was one of the engines fitted with a vacuum-controlled regulator in order to work the push-and-pull service.
H. C. Casserley 14870, courtesy V. R. Anderson

Romford on 19 June 1954 with No 58054, Midland and LMS No 1341, at the head of three coaches. The line between Romford and Upminster was worked on the electric token block system and the token was used to release the lever in the frame that worked the crossover to enable an engine to run round the train.
Collection R. J. Essery

The next development by the LT&SR was a proposal to link the docks at Tilbury with Romford on the GER's main line. More than one proposal for a railway between these places was made but eventually the LT&SR proposals won the day. This act, which received Royal Assent on 20 August 1883 was for a line from Grays to Romford via Ockendon and Upminster, but having blocked a competitive proposal by the GER, the LT&SR was reluctant to commence construction and this delay was to lead to further applications for additional time to build being made in 1886 and 1888. Finally, in the knowledge that if the powers lapsed, the GER could re-present its own proposals, and if granted, would permit that company to gain access to the 'Tilbury area', the LT&SR decided to proceed. The result was that the section between Grays and Upminster was opened on 1 July 1892, with the final section between Romford and Upminster being completed on 7 June 1893. Unlike most of the LT&SR, these lines were single track with a passing loop at Ockendon, between Grays and Upminster.

The LT&SR gave notice to the Board of Trade that the company intended to open the line between Upminster and Romford for public traffic on 1 June 1893. The Board of Trade responded to that letter, dated 25 April, by appointing Maj-Gen Hutchinson to inspect the line. His report was dated 6 June and began by confirming that the line was single, with sidings at Romford station and '. . . *is 2 miles 56 chains long, from the authorised commencement with the Barking & Pitsea Railway near Upminster station to its authorised junction with the*

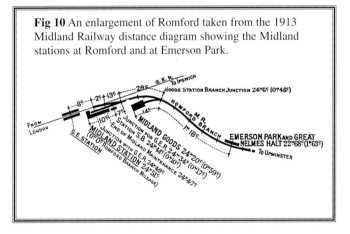

Fig 10 An enlargement of Romford taken from the 1913 Midland Railway distance diagram showing the Midland stations at Romford and at Emerson Park.

Great Eastern railway company's London and Colchester line near Romford'. (These measurements do not agree with the figures on the Midland Railway distance diagrams. For example it is shown as double track on the 1913 edition, but corrected on the 1922/3 amendments. All but two chains of the discrepancy can be accounted for by the extension to the separate platform at Romford and the different point of the junction at Upminster.) *'Instead however of forming a junction with the Great Eastern line at this point it is carried on as a third line, for a distance of 30 chains, to the down end of Romford GE station, where a separate station has been constructed as a terminal station for the new line and a*

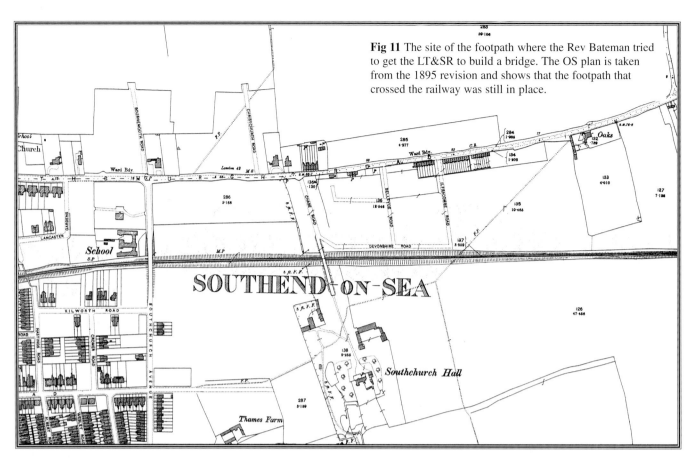

Fig 11 The site of the footpath where the Rev Bateman tried to get the LT&SR to build a bridge. The OS plan is taken from the 1895 revision and shows that the footpath that crossed the railway was still in place.

junction between it and the Great Eastern Railway effected.' He went on to say that the arrangements at Upminster were similar: *'The authorised junction has not been put in, the line has been carried forward for about 18 chains etc.'* The report confirms that *'the new platform at Romford communicates directly with the up platform of the Great Eastern Railway and that a footbridge for giving access to the down platform is now being constructed.'*

He noted *'that land had been purchased and embankments and bridges formed for a double line. The steepest gradient is 1 in 100 and the sharpest curve has a radius of 15 chains.'* His requirements were: 1. A proper detector for the facing points on the Great Eastern Company's down main line at Romford station. 2. The labels on 5 and 16 levers in Romford cabin to have additional releasing numbers painted on them. 3. An alteration to the position of No 28 signal at Romford. 4. An addition to the fencing at the culvert at 0 miles 21 chains. The single line to be worked with the electric staff in accordance with the undertaking given, to the necessary instruments for this mode of working have been supplied. LT&SR Regulation 390 for working railway lines on the electric train staff system stated that 'Only one instrument can be taken from the pillar [this was the instrument] at one time.' He was at pains to point out that a copy of the LT&SR regulations for working the single line with the electric staff did not appear to have been sent to the Board of Trade and should be forwarded.

He made out a separate report about the alterations that he required in the Great Eastern Railway's signal cabin at Romford and gave the LT&SR one month to comply with his requirements, and recommended the Board of Trade to sanction the opening of the line.

Lt-Col Addison, on behalf of the Board of Trade, made a further inspection at Romford on 6 December 1895. I have included this report because it illustrates the method of working sidings on a length of single line. Lt-Col Addison

wrote: *'I have inspected two new sidings on the Romford and Upminster single line of the London, Tilbury & Southend Railway. One, about half a mile from Romford station, has facing points to trains proceeding towards Romford, the other, about ¼ mile from Upminster station, has facing points to trains proceeding towards Upminster. In each case, the points are worked by a lever, which is locked and unlocked by a key on the electric train staff of the section. The facing points are fitted with the usual safety appliances and the arrangements being satisfactory I can recommend the Board of Trade to sanction the use of the new connections.'*

Increasing volume of traffic from the Midland Railway on to the LT&SR required further changes to be made and it is worth recording what the traffic was before describing what new railways were built. Increasing passenger traffic destined for the liners that were now beginning to use Tilbury Docks demanded a through route off the Midland Railway, while the increasing volume of goods traffic destined to carry the products of the factories and industries served by the Midland needed good access to London. The Midland Railway's goods station at St Pancras and Somers Town dealt with much of the company's terminating traffic for the central and northern London areas, but the ability to put wagon loads close to the final consignment point was highly desirable. It was, in part, this kind of thinking which led to the proposal by the LT&SR and Midland companies to jointly promote the Tottenham & Forest Gate Joint Railway, which received approval in 1890. According to Peter Kay in his second volume about the LT&SR, the Tottenham & Forest Gate Railway was originally promoted by Thomas Warner, Lord of the Manor of Walthamstow, and his thorough description of the events that led to the construction of this railway is worth reading. In many respects this new railway, together with the Tottenham & Hampstead Junction Railway, enabled the Midland Railway to obtain direct access to the LT&SR and probably made the

Right:
An early view of Ockendon station taken before the overbridge was built. The photographer was facing towards Upminster. *Collection V. R. Anderson*

Centre right:
This picture, probably taken about 1961, shows the developments that have taken place at Ockendon. The barrow crossing is interesting as there is no trolley access. The line was single with a passing loop through the station. *Collection R. J. Essery*

Below left:
Ockendon station signalbox was at the Grays end of the platform. The box was opened in 1892 and closed on 24 December 1977. *Collection R. J. Essery*

Below right:
Photographed on 15 October 1931, this picture shows 0-6-2T engine No 2231 on a goods train at Ockendon. The train is travelling towards Romford and is probably waiting for an oncoming train to clear the single-line section before it can proceed on its way. *Collection H. F. Wheeller, courtesy Roger Carpenter*

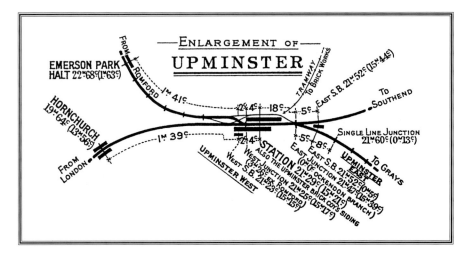

Fig 12 An enlargement of the lines at Upminster and the junction of the branch to Ockendon and Romford.

acquisition of the LT&SR by the Midland Railway a possibility at some future date. Although this book is about the LT&SR and its joint lines, it is impossible to ignore the T&HJR, in particular when considering the traffic flows over the Tilbury line.

The Tottenham & Hampstead Junction Railway was jointly owned by the Midland and Great Eastern railway companies. The line ran from Kentish Town Junction, on the Midland Railway's London and Bedford line, to the North and South Junctions at Tottenham on the Great Eastern Railway's London to Cambridge line, although not all the eastern junctions were opened at the same time. After the railway was opened the already considerable Midland Railway freight traffic bound for the docks was transferred from the North London Railway and travelled over this new route. Later, with the opening of the joint MR and LT&SR Tottenham & Forest Gate Joint Railway, this freight traffic for the docks was diverted again and then ran mostly over lines in which the Midland Railway had a joint interest. The T&HJR is examined in greater detail in Chapter 2.

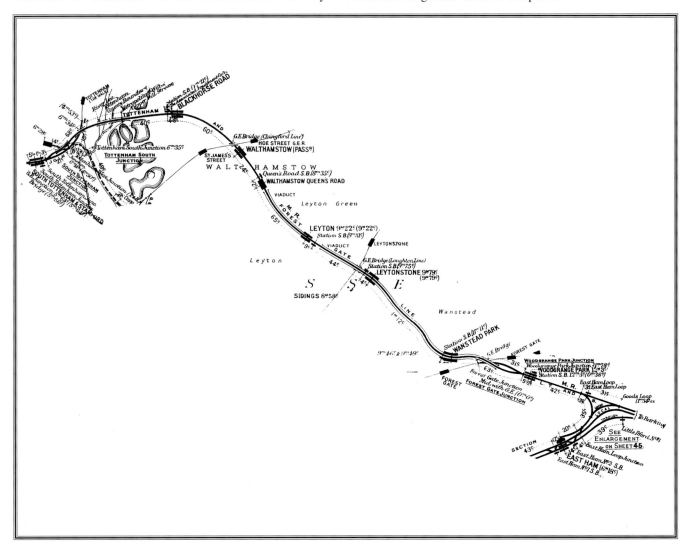

Fig 13 The 1919 Midland Railway distance diagram showing the Tottenham & Forest Gate joint line between the junction of the Tottenham & Hampstead Junction Railway and the beginning of the LT&S lines at Forest Gate Junction.

South Tottenham station was on the T&HJR. The start of the T&FG was just three chains from the end of the platform. This undated Edwardian era picture clearly shows the station with its wooden platform. *Collection R. J. Essery*

Tottenham & Forest Gate Joint Railway

This new line was to run from the terminus of the Midland and Great Eastern's joint railway at South Tottenham and to effect a junction with the LT&SR at Forest Gate. In addition, the LT&SR was to construct a loop, some ½ mile long with the LT&SR main lines near East Ham, this being authorised by an Act dated 5 August 1891.

By the time approval was given to build this new line much of that part of London had recently been built up; therefore some property had to be purchased and then demolished in order to make way for the railway. A considerable part of the line was carried on brick-built viaducts. To assist with the generation of revenue a new station was built at Woodgrange Park, later the name being carried by an LT&SR locomotive of the '37' class. A bay platform was added at East Ham for the benefit of the Midland Railway which operated local services to and from Moorgate and St Pancras and this point.

The new line was inspected by Maj-Gen Hutchinson on 6 July 1894 and he wrote a five-page report. I have quoted the most important sections, beginning with the description of the line. The Maj-Gen said: *'Railway No 1 is a double line 6 miles 9 chains long extending from a junction with the Tottenham and Hampstead at South Tottenham station to a junction with the Forest Gate branch of the London, Tilbury & Southend Railway at a new station called Woodgrange Park.*

'Railway No 2 is also a double line, 30.75 chains long, extending from a junction with the Forest Gate branch of the London, Tilbury & Southend Railway about ½ mile from the termination of railway No 1 to a junction with the branch line of the LT&SR at East Ham station. The steepest gradient on Railway No 1 is 1 in 64, for Railway No 2, 1 in 400. The radius at the sharpest curve (irrespective of the junction curve at South Tottenham, which has a radius of 10 chains) is 20 chains — Railway No 2 is laid on a curve of 15 chains radius.'

He confirmed that the width of the railway at formation level was 25ft in cuttings and 27ft on the embankments, giving 21ft

as the depth of the deepest cutting and 24ft as the highest embankment. *'The permanent way is of the Midland Railway Coy's type consisting of 85lb steel rails in 30ft lengths, fished at the joints, of 50lb cast-iron chairs, secured by outside oak keys. Two spikes and two oak trenails in each secure the chairs.'*

He stated, *'With the exception of a cutting about 1 mile 16 chains long and an embankment amounting to a length of about 1 mile 52 chains the remaining 3 miles 16 chains is carried entirely on viaducts and bridges, and owing to the number of streets and intended roads which are crossed, the works are quite heavy, they are as follows.'* He then went on to

The photographer was slightly closer to the start of the T&FG and this c1909 picture shows the end of the platform. The train is made up of Midland Railway stock and is a St Pancras to Gravesend service, with the final part of the journey for passengers being made by ferry. The locomotive is No 40 *Black Horse Road*, of the 'No 37' class.
NRM/G. W. Tripp Collection

Black Horse Road was the first station on the T&FG after leaving South Tottenham. *H. C. Casserley 92565*

Walthamstow station on 14 September 1957, facing Barking. *R. M. Casserley 86993*

Leytonstone station was 9 miles 79 chains from St Pancras, the distance that the approaching train had travelled. *Collection R. J. Essery*

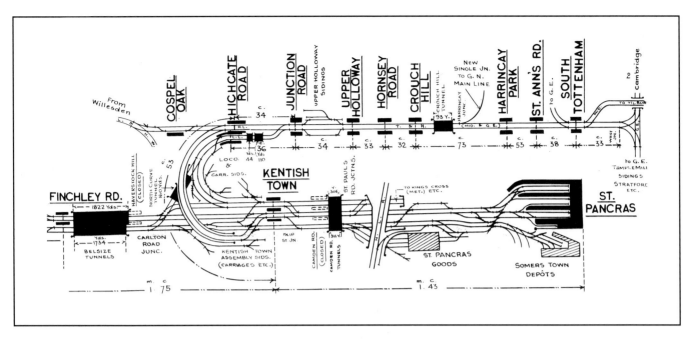

Fig 14 Although not part of the main story, I felt that the inclusion of this diagram would assist readers to understand the route taken by trains from the St Pancras area to the LT&SR.

describe each bridge etc before confirming that there were no tunnels, no public road level crossings and only two occupation crossings and that the fencing was post and rail.

He gave a list of stations beginning with Black Horse Road, Walthamstow, Leyton, Leytonstone and Wanstead Park and said: *'These places have all necessary accommodation, with excellent staircases for reaching and leaving the platforms. Woodgrange Park has been constructed by the London, Tilbury & Southend Railway and has been separately reported on.'* His report of the signalling arrangements can be summarised as: 1. South Tottenham Junction, (reported on separately). 2. Tottenham sidings, 12 working levers and six spares. 3. Black Horse Road station, 14 working levers and six spare. 4. Walthamstow, six working levers and two spare. 5. Boundary Road Depot, 11 working levers and five spare. 6. Leyton station 14 working levers and six spare. 7. Leytonstone station, 13 working levers and three spare. 8. Wanstead Park six working levers and two spare. Woodgrange Park and junction are reported on separately. There was also a three-lever dwarf frame for Copper Mill Stream sidings. He confirmed that the interlocking at these signal cabins was satisfactory.

Then came the list of requirements: 1. Wheel guards to be provided on all bridges of spans exceeding 100ft, where not already fixed and on those portions of the viaduct where they are at present deficient. 2. The handrails of the viaducts at 1 mile 63 chains where they are less than 4½ft above rail level to be increased to that height. 3. The horizontal timbers in the trough girders on the viaduct to be secured in position by hard wood wedges. 4. Outside clocks in suitable positions to be fixed at all stations. 5. At Boundary Road Depot runaway points to be provided in the down line and worked from Black Horse signal cabin. No 10 siding points to be worked by two levers, the normal position of the main line trailing points being for the sidings. 6. At Leyton station No 14 points to be worked by two levers, the normal points of the main line trailing points being for the sidings. 7. At Leytonstone station Nos 7 and 11 points to be freed. A checkrail to be provided for the sharp curve connected with No 10 siding.

The wagon hoist at Leytonstone, photographed on 14 January 1909, was built by the Hydraulic Engineering Company, Chester, to move wagons between the two levels. The necessity for the sign forbidding its use for passengers is somewhat surprising. *Derby Collection NRM DY8968*

His report concluded: '*Subject to requirements Nos 1 and 2 being not within more than two months and Nos 3 to 7 within a fortnight, I can recommend the Board of Trade to sanction the opening for passenger traffic of the Tottenham & Forest Gate Railway. I have requested the Engineer to forward a certificate as to the nature and tests of the steel used in the girders for the under and over bridges. In those cases where the carrying out of the works has been necessary to make alterations in the curves and gradients in excess of those authorised by 8 Victoria Capt Sect 14 the company should apply for a certificate to authorise these deviations. I cannot conclude this report without expressing my opinion of the highly satisfactory manner which the works of this important railway have been designed and carried out.*' Praise indeed from the inspecting officer for the Midland Railway that built most of the line.

A further inspection of the line was made on 12 October 1894 but generally speaking there were no problems. The final report was dated 17 October 1894; this dealt with the new station at Woodgrange Park and East Ham loop. There were some minor requirements set out but everything was generally in order. Before leaving the Tottenham & Forest Gate Railway I must comment on a few developments that took place.

On 17 June 1903, the Midland Railway wrote to the Board of Trade to say that the signalbox at Walthamstow was not now required as a block post. The company submitted a proposal to show how this was to be done. The signalbox was closed on 9 August 1903. The inspecting officer for the Board of Trade, Major Pringle, described the alternative arrangements: '*To protect trains standing at Walthamstow station, a distant and home signal in each direction are retained, which are normally kept at clear, but are put to danger behind trains stopping at the station. The signals are worked from two platform ground frames which each contain two levers properly interlocked. Electrical lock and block working has been introduced between Queens Road and Blackhorse Road signal cabins, and the necessary treadles introduced to control the signals.*' He confirmed that the interlocking changes at Queens Road were in order and recommended sanction for the changes.

Whitechapel & Bow Railway (LT&SR and Metropolitan District Railway)

Other than widening, we come now to the final changes and improvements made by the LT&SR prior to the Midland Railway takeover. The immense advantage that railways have over all other forms of transport is the ability to move large numbers of people quickly between two or more points. The passenger traffic receipts of the LT&S section during the period of Midland Railway ownership of the system was to multiply more quickly than the national average, with many of these passengers bound for or starting their journeys from Fenchurch Street, where it was becoming abundantly clear that the facilities were being outstripped by this rapid growth. However, since many passengers were on journeys which terminated or commenced at points beyond Fenchurch Street it made sense if they could transfer to or from other trains at a point or points that kept them away from that station. I cannot be entirely sure if this was the thinking which led to the construction of the Whitechapel & Bow Railway, authorised by an Act dated 6 August 1897, but that is what happened. The railway was to be jointly owned by the LT&SR and the District Railway and was to be worked by the latter company. Some two miles in length, the line was to run from a junction with the LT&SR at Campbell Road just to the east of Gas Factory Junction in Bow, and to effect a junction with the District Railway at Whitechapel.

Understandably for a railway constructed through a district which had already been built up, major engineering works were required and this was reflected in the cost: some £1,200,000 to construct the line. Opened on 2 June 1902, this link enabled the District Railway to extend its steam-hauled passenger trains from Whitechapel to East Ham with, at that time, a handful of District trains working as far as Upminster. From the passengers' point of view this new line enabled many to journey to and from their destinations without a change of train and to avoid the congested facilities at Fenchurch Street station. One interesting document that came to light during my research was the application made by the Whitechapel & Bow Joint Committee in respect of the Cheap Trains Act 1883. I felt this letter was worth reproducing on the grounds that it shows the letterhead of the two companies.

Within weeks of the Whitechapel & Bow Railway being opened, further powers were obtained on 31 July by the LT&SR to quadruple the line from Campbell Road Junction to East Ham, and this development is dealt with in greater detail later. Suffice to say, the first section between Plaistow and East Ham was opened for traffic on 15 May 1904 with the completion of work dating from 1 April 1908.

Inevitably, one is tempted to ask why the LT&SR sold out to the Midland Railway, and I can only speculate. The company

London, Tilbury & Southend and Metropolitan District Railways.

Whitechapel & Bow Joint Committee.

J.C.88.

41, Trinity Square, Tower Hill,

London, E.C. 18th March 1907.

RECEIVED 1? MAR 1907
No. 3636
BOARD OF TRADE

Sir,

Cheap Trains Act 1883 Urban Certificate.

I regret to find that through an oversight application was not made in due course for a Certificate of the Board of Trade under the provisions of Section 2, Sub-Section 3, of the Cheap Trains Act 1883, for the purpose of classifying this Railway as an Urban District in connection with Passenger Duty.

I now beg to make application for a Certificate, and to state that the following are the Stations on the Railway:-

Whitechapel,
Stepney Green,
Mile End,
Bow Road,

I am, Sir,

Your obedient Servant,

Secretary

The Assistant Secretary,

Railway Department,

Board of Trade, S.W.

Fig 15 I have included this item for two reasons: firstly to show the letterhead for the Joint Committee and secondly to show the bureaucracy that existed at this time.

was well managed even though there was a touch of nepotism! At this point in time I feel that the theory I am about to outline cannot be proved one way or the other; nevertheless it is offered to readers for their consideration. What is known is that in February 1911 Arthur Stride, Chairman of the LT&SR, reported the conclusion of a provisional agreement which would allow the Midland Railway Co to acquire the London, Tilbury & Southend Railway and it has to be said that this statement came as a surprise to both the financial markets and the GER — such was the secrecy which had surrounded the negotiations that had preceded this announcement.

My belief is that the truth lies within the personality of the Chairman and Managing Director, Arthur Lewis Stride. There can be little doubt that he was a father figure, having a paternalistic attitude, and it would be difficult to overstress his service to the company. He arrived in 1875, and during the following 36 years, his efforts transformed it out of all recognition, first as General Manager, later as Managing Director and finally adding the title Chairman in 1906. There would be few employees who had not known Stride as 'The Governor'. Therefore it is not unreasonable to see how he could have achieved a kind of paternal status and as such he may have felt a considerable sense of responsibility for the future of the railway when, in his 70th year, his health began to fail. If this is true then it is understandable why he should either have opened the negotiations with or been responsive to approaches from directors of the Midland Railway company. Without doubt he made a good bargain on behalf of the LT&SR shareholders by ensuring the LT&SR ordinary shareholders received £240 of 2½% Midland Preference Stock for every £100 of Tilbury stock they held. In addition, he agreed terms in respect of transfer and compensation for officers and servants of the company when such arrangements were to prove necessary.

In arranging the sale, Stride secured a good financial deal for the shareholders, made fair arrangements for the workforce (to use a modern term) and was no doubt well satisfied that the line, 'his line', would enjoy a secure future under Midland Railway ownership. As I have said, this is pure speculation on my part, but in the absence of evidence to the contrary I cannot advance a better theory as to why the LT&SR became part of the Midland system.

One interesting document that has survived is the report by the Board of Trade dated 13 June 1912. During the negotiations prior to the Midland Railway takeover of the LT&SR, the Board sought to ensure that the more advantageous LT&SR rates for certain traffic were adopted, for example the amount of luggage that could be taken free by an LT&SR first class passenger was 150lb whereas the Midland Railway only permitted 100lb. They also sought to protect the interests of the Great Northern, Great Eastern and London & South Western railways in respect of either running powers or through traffic to the docks at Tilbury. (It is interesting to see that there were no requirements in respect of the London & North Western Railway.) Needless to say, these Board of Trade recommendations formed part of the purchase arrangements of the London, Tilbury & Southend Railway by the Midland Railway Co.

Meanwhile, if we look at the events taking place at Liverpool Street station, headquarters of the GER, the sale of the LT&SR to the Midland Railway company came as a complete surprise to its officers of the GER and its Chairman, the aristocratic Lord Claud Hamilton, who was not pleased! By the time they became aware of what was happening it was too late to alter events although apparently they tried. When this failed then it is not too difficult to understand why the career of more than one senior officer was blighted and the immediate retirement of the General Manager was forthcoming, such were the happenings within the power game of railway politics in the years immediately prior to World War 1. The LT&S Section was to prove a most valuable asset under both Midland Railway and LMS ownership.

On 7 August 1912, the London, Tilbury & Southend Railway purchase bill received Royal Assent, with its powers being backdated to 1 January 1912. This ended the independence of the LT&SR as a legal entity but it has to be said that the system was to remain as a separate operating division for some time. Between purchase in 1912 and the end of September 1920, it ran with its own management structure, control from Derby not becoming effective until 1 October 1920. Under LMS ownership it was largely to remain as a separate section with its own special operational problems fully recognised by the owning company, even if the LMS was unable to solve all of them.

There appear to be very few pictures of the Whitechapel & Bow Joint Railway and very little has been written about it. The most recent, that also provides source material for further study, will be found in the July 1997 issue of *The London Railway Record*. This picture, taken in 1926, is an interior view of Bow Road station and shows the early style of railway poster boards provided by the Underground Railway for the main line railway companies. The heading was Oxford blue with thin white edging and sans serif letters.
Collection V. R. Anderson

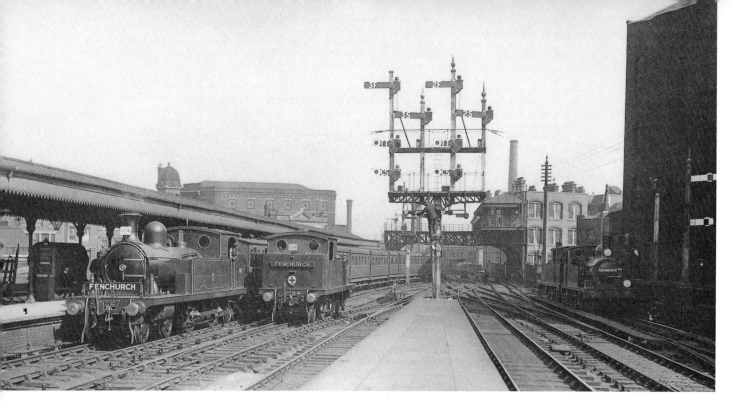

Above:
This *c*1910 photograph at Fenchurch Street shows two 'No 1' class engines, No 27 *Whitechapel* at the head of a train of carriages that have just arrived at Platform 4, and No 34 *Tottenham*. This engine is on the release road between Platforms 3 and 4, which was connected at the concourse end of the platform line by a trailing crossover. There was a short siding with an engine pit and water column at the end of the release road to enable locomotives to be serviced. There is some coal visible in the bunker of No 34 so it is possible the engine will work No 27's train away from the station. *Collection R. J. Essery*

Centre left:
I believe this picture was taken on the same day and shortly after the previous view. No 34 and No 27's train have gone but the latter is now on the engine release road. The train on the right belongs to the Great Eastern Railway and could be an arrival from North Woolwich, Gallions or Blackwall. *Collection Roger Carpenter*

Left:
Here we see the concourse end of the station with LT&SR No 57 *Crouch Hill* carrying a Southend via Upminster headcode. The Great Eastern tank engine is standing on the short siding mentioned above. *Collection Roger Carpenter*

Right:
Taken shortly after the LT&SR became part of the Midland Railway, this picture shows old No 43 *Great Ilford* as MR No 2152 about to depart from Fenchurch Street with a train for Southend. *Collection R. J. Essery*

2. Some Aspects of The Line Described

This chapter examines some of what today is referred to as the infrastructure of the railway, namely the track layouts, junctions, bridges, stations and signalboxes and, in so doing, provides an overview of the railway. What will not be attempted is a 'blow-by-blow' historical analysis of every feature of the line, for the simple reason that probably neither pictures nor all the necessary information to write such a story still exists. Furthermore, if it was available then I suspect that space considerations would make this form of presentation unwieldy. Nevertheless, I hope that what follows will provide readers with a feast of 'Tilbury' material, much of it previously unpublished, or no longer available to the majority of readers.

Fenchurch Street station

The starting point for our journey must be Fenchurch Street station where we would have found the company's general offices, situated inside a building which the company did not own. Fortunately for students of railway stations, *The Railway Magazine* featured an occasional series entitled 'Notable Railway stations & their Traffic' and in the June 1919 issue Fenchurch Street was described. Considerable use has been made of this article whose authenticity was guaranteed by the co-operation of the Great Eastern Railway's officers and staff at the station who, in 1919, were under the control of a Mr A. J. Green, who had been the stationmaster at Fenchurch Street since 1912. Mr Green's service with the GER commenced at Bishop's Stortford in 1877 where he was employed as a telegraph lad and booking clerk. He became a stationmaster in 1897 and his first post was at Limehouse, in 1900. Later, in 1901, he was to move to Burdett Road, with the responsibility for Bow Road being added in 1908; clearly a railwayman with considerable experience.

Fenchurch Street station was opened in 1841 as the terminus and headquarters of the London & Blackwall Railway. With the completion of the Stepney to Bow railway, the station was to be used by the Eastern Counties Railway (later this company was to become part of the Great Eastern railway company) and in due course it became the principal terminus for its suburban train services. Between 1851 and 1866, the station played host to the North London Railway, which used it as its 'City' terminus prior to the opening of the Dalston Junction to Broad Street line in 1865 and its new London terminus at Broad Street. The London, Tilbury & Southend Railway (whose trains were worked by the ECR, GER from August 1862, with rolling stock until 1877 and, until 1880, locomotives also) made the station its headquarters. On 1 January 1866 the GER took over the L&BR under the terms of a 999-year lease. Before the opening of the extension to Liverpool Street, Fenchurch Street was the principal terminus for GER suburban trains in London. Later, more GER services began to run from Liverpool Street so that in GER terms, Fenchurch Street occupied a secondary position for this class of traffic.

The transfer of traffic by the GER away from Fenchurch Street, plus the opening in 1902 of the Whitechapel & Bow Railway, a Metropolitan District and LT&SR joint railway, helped to divert passengers away from the station. This enabled the existing facilities to cope with the ever-increasing volume of residential traffic originating from the Southend line. There was also a considerable increase in passenger traffic from Tilbury Docks. In 1913, the year before World War 1 distorted everything, the figure of 560 trains per day at the five platforms available was quoted (I assume this includes light engine and

Photographed on 29 August 1911, this illustrates the exit from Fenchurch Street station. The unidentified locomotive on the right of the picture is standing on an engine servicing siding. Note the inspection pit. The connection must be a rather sharp curve, as the switchblade to the right has a checkrail. The rebuilt 'No 37' class engine, No 48 *Little Ilford* is probably about to work the train away as empty stock, an assumption made because the destination board has not been moved to the rear end of the locomotive.
NRM GE Collection 900

empty stock movements) and it was stressed that in 1919 the figure was not greatly reduced. A count made one day in October 1913 revealed no fewer than 48,386 passengers and during the same year the total number of passengers booked came to 1,978,124. This total did not take into account either the arriving, through booked or season ticket passengers, to say nothing of other traffic sources, for example passengers using return tickets issued at other stations. The Fenchurch Street station of 1919 remained unaltered until the joint LMS/LNER modernisation was completed in 1934.

With an arched roof covering four of the five platforms and the rail approach on the high level, the station was the subject of a woodcut made in 1857, which is understandably the earliest picture we have of the station. This shows a distinctive building fronting a main thoroughfare, but one that was difficult to photograph in full at that time. Drawing alongside the pavement, into a limited court area that was sheltered by the veranda, was the road approach to the station. Above the veranda were the high-level windows at the rail level area, together with a large circular station clock.

Moving into the station from road level, travellers entered the booking halls that, due to the low-height ceilings, were somewhat dark. The main booking hall had four ticket windows reserved for tickets issued to Great Eastern destinations, while the Tilbury section had three windows for passengers who wished to travel to stations on that line. There was also a side entrance to Platforms 4 and 5 only. A double staircase led from the main hall on the ground floor to the circulating area above. This staircase was on the right-hand side of the building, while to the left there were two single staircases: one ascending directly from the booking hall, the other with an intermediate level that extended directly from

the station yard. Facilities to be found at ground level included left luggage and a cloakroom, and lavatories together with access to a hairdressing salon, a facility that at one time seemed to be almost obligatory at every major railway station. Finally there was the ground floor entrance to the hydraulic lifts for transferring parcels and luggage to the platform level.

Only four platforms were visible from the circulating area, No 5 being a bay off Platform 4. No 1 platform was to the right of a traveller entering the circulating area; this was the shortest, some 360ft in length. It provided rooms for female ticket collectors, porters, lamp rooms, lavatories for the staff, a boiler room for heating footwarmers, accommodation for telegraph linesmen and a hut erected at the end of the platform for women carriage cleaners. Platform No 1 was used by the Blackwall trains, at one time made up of four six-wheelers hauled by either small GER 0-6-0T or 2-4-0T locomotives that were originally 0-6-0T, but with the front section of the coupling rod removed.

No 2 platform was 556ft long and was used mostly by Great Eastern local trains serving the Ilford route. The end of the platform projected well beyond the overall roof, with the final section covered by an umbrella roof. An engine bay, in line with No 1 platform, accommodated spare GER locomotives for both the Blackwall and Ilford trains. The engines from this bay could only back directly on to the short Ilford trains and it was usually necessary for them to run on to No 1 platform first and then to run forward to clear an outer crossover in order to reach platform No 2. This platform was also used before World War 1 for a limited number of GER through trains which ran to Southend conveying excursion traffic.

No 3 platform was the other face of No 2 platform and mostly Loughton line trains used it. No 4 platform was reserved exclusively for the Tilbury line and at 760ft was the longest platform at Fenchurch Street, accommodating 13 LT&SR bogie coaches plus an engine. It was this platform restriction that was the limiting factor for the composition of the heavily loaded Southend trains. No 4 platform was by far the busiest platform at Fenchurch Street and it is worth recording the frequency of evening departures as given in the article. 'For Southend, Leigh and Westcliff alone the evening pressure involved departures at 4.57, 5.6, 5.16, 5.25, 5.38, 5.46, 6.7, 6.17 and 6.26pm with interpolated trains for other destinations at 5.32 and 5.55pm, all dealt with at this platform. Similarly, in the morning, there are arrivals at 8.6, 8.15, 8.24, 8.33, 8.44, 8.53 (at platform No 3), 9.4, 9.10, 9.17, 9.30, 9.34 (at Platform No 3), 9.39, 9.50 and 10.2am.' Not bad for a railway controlled by semaphore signals and worked by steam locomotives!

Platform 4 had a bookstall but little else; however, just beyond the overall roof there was a stairway from John Street that provided passenger access from the road to Platforms 4 and 5 only. This entrance was in a building that also accommodated the offices of the L&BR, and above these were the offices of the LT&SR. Later they became the offices for the London, Tilbury & Southend Section of the Midland Railway and then the LMS. At ground level there was a booking office while at platform level were to be found lavatories together with small general and ladies' waiting rooms.

Between Platforms 3 and 4 was an engine road with crossovers close to the buffer stops. The normal procedure was that on all arrivals the engine ran up to the buffer stops regardless of whether it was going to remain on the middle road, prior to working a train away, or if it was to follow the train out of the station. Platform 3 was also used on a Sunday

The road ahead as seen by the enginemen leaving Fenchurch Street station. Behind the buildings on the right is the Great Northern Railway's Royal Mint Street goods depot and warehouse, and further down the line is the Midland Railway's goods station known as Mint Street (City). To the left is Goodman's Yard that belonged to the GER. Note the servicing area for locomotives with the ash pit, water columns and turntable, and the rather hefty scotch blocks to restrain both locomotives on the turntable and wagons from running away. *NRM GE Collection 895.*

The approach to Fenchurch Street station. The curves are rather sharp — note the number of checkrails that have been used. *NRM GE Collection 903*

Taken from Platform 4, which was set aside for the exclusive use of the LT&SR, this illustrates the elevated station signalbox and No 54 *Mile End. Collection R. J. Essery*

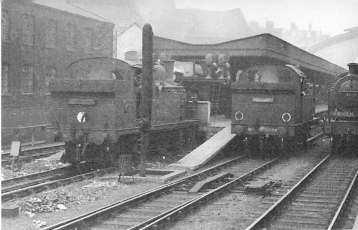

The pictorial coverage of Fenchurch Street is concluded with two pictures taken after the station was enlarged in the 1930s. On 10 July 1937, LNER No 7782 heads a North Woolwich train, while to the right, there is an ex-LT&SR third class coach and another third class vehicle of Midland Railway origin. *Collection H. F. Wheeller 58/6, courtesy Roger Carpenter*

The alterations seen here to the area around old Platforms 1-3 was photographed on 27 June 1936. The locomotives are, left to right: LNER 2-4-2T No 7108, LNER 0-6-2T No 8006 and old LT&SR No 41 as LMS No 2150. *Collection H. F. Wheeller, courtesy Roger Carpenter*

for Woolwich line trains; on weekdays these trains used Platform 5. Some Tilbury section trains that were able to make use of the run-round facility also used Platform 3. The frequency of trains, plus the limited facilities available, meant that the detaching or attaching of carriage trucks or horseboxes was not dealt with at Fenchurch Street. However, there was a considerable amount of 'passenger rated traffic' to be dealt with, such as parcels, luggage, etc.

No 5 platform formed a bay to the outer part of No 4 platform, this lying beyond the overall roof and being 477ft long. It was protected by an umbrella roof and dealt with the North Woolwich and Gallions trains, although the destination board carried on the locomotives was 'Albert Dock'. Just beyond the end of the platform lay the spare engine line that led to a turntable. At some date the table went out of use and was incorporated within the area of Goodman's Yard depot and warehouse complex. *The Railway Magazine* article stated that

it was occasionally useful to employ the turntable to direct engines into the terminus and so release them or enable them to reach the other end of the yard. Finally, it should be noted that close to No 5 platform some additional accommodation for staff was provided.

At the end of the platforms there was a circulating area where the hydraulic buffer stops marked the end of the approach roads. Here there was a bookstall, tearoom and telegraph office together with a refreshment room, general and ladies' second class waiting rooms (an unheard of arrangement today). In addition, the circulating area housed the left luggage rooms and cloakrooms, lift entrance and access to the ladies' first class waiting room, which was described as being a 'notable apartment, with high ornamented ceiling and artistic cabinet work'. This is understandable, perhaps, when it is recognised that at one time this was the boardroom of the London & Blackwall

Taken on 29 August 1911, this shows Goodman's Yard to the right, with part of the outside wall of the Great Northern goods depot and warehouse at Royal Mint Street. *NRM GE Collection 901*

The branch to the left leads to the LNWR goods station at Haydon Square. The goods sidings on the right are part of the Great Northern Railway's depot at Royal Mint Street. *NRM GE Collection 902*

Railway company. The all-important stationmaster's offices were above the refreshment rooms, with the ticket collectors' and inspectors' offices close by.

Fenchurch Street station did, as we have noted, play host to the North London Railway trains as well as those of the LT&SR and the GER. When it was originally laid out the platforms were quite short but extensions were made in an attempt to cope with the increasing traffic requirements and this included improving the track access to the station. At first it was just an up and down road but later an additional up road was laid, to be used by the Loughton, North Woolwich and Tilbury trains that were not scheduled to call at the intermediate stations at Shadwell and Leman Street. These stations did not have a platform face for this line. In 1894/5 this section was widened, and the stations rebuilt, so that there were two slow lines serving Shadwell and Leman Street as well as two fast lines.

The traffic arrangements in 1919 were for the North Woolwich and Tilbury trains to use the fast lines, while the Ilford and Blackwall trains ran over the slow lines. Loughton trains could use either fast or slow lines depending upon traffic circumstances. One remarkable feature of the approach to Fenchurch Street station was the number of goods stations and warehouses in the area. At first this seems surprising in view of the congested nature of the rail approach but not so when the area is considered in a commercial sense. The major railway companies tried to ensure their traffic facilities for the outward despatch or inward delivery of merchandise was as close as possible to their customers. This part of London was, and still is, an area of great commercial importance but undoubtedly more so at this point in time in terms of merchandise distribution. This helps to explain why so many goods stations were there and why they were all connected to this section of line.

A view taken from Leman Street signalbox looking towards Fenchurch Street is shown here, with the sidings at Royal Mint Street on the left. *NRM GE Collection 908*

This picture was taken from the signal gantry in the previous photo and shows the GER station at Leman Street. It was the first station out of Fenchurch Street and was opened in 1877. This view shows the station after it was rebuilt in 1895/96. The junction to the right leads to the GER branch to St Katharine Docks in the Upper Pool just downstream of Tower Bridge. Immediately off this line is the Midland branch to Royal Mint Street City goods station while in the bottom right-hand corner is the connection to the Great Northern depot. The bottom left-hand corner marks the start of the line to the LNWR depot at Haydon Square.
NRM GE Collection 907

Another view taken on 29 August 1911 in the area of Leman Street. This shows the coal drops on this section of the Great Eastern Railway. *NRM GE Collection 912*

Approaching Fenchurch Street from the east the first goods station was at the end of a 27-chain branch owned by the LT&SR; this led to the company's Commercial Road goods depot. This was built by the LT&SR in order to serve the needs of the Tilbury Docks area and to act as the Tilbury's 'London End' marshalling point for wagons being worked away. The access to this line was only from the fast lines. There were also coal drops to be found to the south of the line. Closer to Fenchurch Street station was Leman Street, and three chains beyond was London Docks Junction, which provided the GER with access to its London Docks goods station over a 16-chain branch. This branch also provided access to the Midland Railways City goods station in Royal Mint Street. Reference to the map at Fig 16 will show that the Midland branch left the GER branch just one chain from the junction. The Midland goods station branch was quite short, just 13 chains long. Access to both these depots was only from the slow lines. On the RCH and Midland Railway distance diagrams the MR and GNR goods depots are shown as Mint Street; however, I

believe the Royal prefix is correct. Some official references to the Midland Railway depot describe it as 'City'.

A further junction, some five chains closer to Fenchurch Street station, enabled the Great Northern Railway to reach its goods station at Royal Mint Street. The Great Northern Company's branch was only 16 chains long from the junction that was also connected to the slow lines only. Some four chains closer to Fenchurch Street was the start of yet another branch, Haydon Square Junction, which marked the beginning of the LNWR's 22-chain approach to its City goods station. NLR locomotives and men usually worked this traffic; the NLR and LNWR companies had close ties from the early years of both companies. The final goods station on the approach to Fenchurch Street station belonged to the Great Eastern Railway and was known as Goodman's Yard; it comprised warehouses, bonded vaults, etc.

To control such a complex series of junctions, with the traffic from the various goods stations being 'fitted in' with the passenger traffic, required a number of signalboxes. A signal

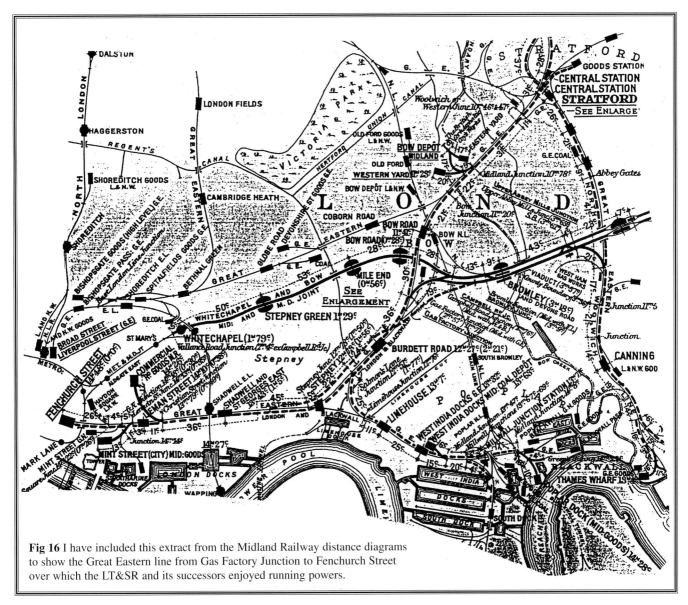

Fig 16 I have included this extract from the Midland Railway distance diagrams to show the Great Eastern line from Gas Factory Junction to Fenchurch Street over which the LT&SR and its successors enjoyed running powers.

cabin with 115 working levers was placed upon an overhead triangular girder structure extending from the end of No 4 platform and was parallel to the up slow line. This box controlled all the station work and presumably Goodman's Yard. The next box, with 45 levers, was the one at Haydon Square Junction, and in conjunction with Fenchurch Street station signalbox took a share in controlling the approaches to the station. Beyond Haydon Square Junction was Leman Street signalbox with 40 levers and beyond that Christian Street signalbox, also with 40 levers. Between them these signalboxes controlled all the traffic to and from the various goods depots plus the through passenger and empty stock trains and light engines to and from Fenchurch Street station.

Campbell Road Junction to Barking

Increasing traffic brought about the need to improve the movement of trains, and this was true of the LT&SR. One of the most important developments to be undertaken was the widening of the line between Campbell Road Junction and Barking, a project that was completed in 1908. During the closing years of the 19th century and the first decade of the 20th, railway expansion continued in order to cope with increasing traffic. With the exception of the London Extension of the Great Central Railway, all the principal main lines had

already been built, but improvements to existing lines continued. The activity during the late Victorian and Edwardian period mostly centred on widening and the laying of additional tracks or similar improvements to enable traffic to flow more freely. A number of companies were engaged in this work in the London area during the early 1900s and along with the London & North Western, London & South Western, South Eastern & Chatham and London, Brighton & South Coast was the London, Tilbury & Southend.

The Railway Magazine, whose two articles provided vital source material for the description that follows, documented this LT&SR project. The other prime sources of material are the surviving reports made by the inspecting officers of the Board of Trade. Indeed, *The Railway Magazine* articles and the Board of Trade reports enable present-day readers to benefit from what was, in effect, on-the-spot reports of developments as they took place. Clearly, any improvements between Fenchurch Street station and the beginning of the LT&SR's own tracks were not really the Tilbury Company's responsibility, so the improvements began 18 chains east of Gas Factory Junction where the Tilbury's metals commenced. The new joint line with the Metropolitan District Railway began at Campbell Road Junction and it was decided to put in an extra pair of lines between this point and Barking station, a distance of 4 miles 39 chains.

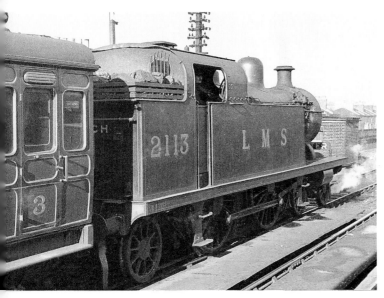

Left:
Four companies are represented in this picture. To the left is the Midland Railway with the notice board proclaiming "Midland Railway City Goods Station, entrance in Royal Mint Street". The wording on the notice board belonging to the Great Northern Railway read "Royal Mint Street Goods Station and Bonded Stores". The third railway was the Great Eastern whose line to Fenchurch Street is in the centre of the picture, with Goodman's Yard to the right and finally, the junction to the fourth company, the London & North Western Railway's branch to its Haydon Square goods depot. *NRM GE Collection 905*

Centre left:
This photograph of 29 August 1911, together with the other official Great Eastern views reproduced here, is facing east and shows the line towards Shadwell & St George's East station that is just visible in the distance, some 36 chains from the junction in the middle of the picture. The lines to the left of the picture go to the LT&SR goods depot at Commercial Road, some 27 chains from the junction at Christian Street, controlled from the Great Eastern Railway signalbox to the right of the picture. *NRM GE Collection 910*

Below left :
Burdett Road was the fourth Great Eastern station from Fenchurch Street before LT&SR trains ran on to their own line at Gas Factory Junction. Both these pictures were taken there on 20 October 1935. LMS-built No 2113 is seen on a passenger train from Fenchurch Street, the first coach being an ex-LT&SR third class vehicle. *Collection H. F. Wheeller 26/32, courtesy Roger Carpenter*

Below right:
Here we see one of the new Stanier three-cylinder 2-6-4T engines, No 2523, on a Southend or Shoeburyness train to Fenchurch Street. *Collection H. F. Wheeller 26/30, courtesy Roger Carpenter*

Taken at Plaistow c1911 this picture shows a train of bogie coaches of the latest type behind rebuilt 'No 37' class No 47 *Stratford*. The headcode confirms this is a Fenchurch Street to Southend train that will run over the direct line via Upminster. A westbound District electric train, showing Car No 124, is on the right. *Collection R. J. Essery*

In order to understand just how congested things were, and how urgently these additional lines were required, I have summarised the traffic flows below.

1. LT&SR passenger and goods trains over the entire section.
2. Metropolitan District Railway passenger trains as far east as East Ham, with three additional daily trains to Upminster and their return workings.
3. NLR local passenger trains from Bow to Plaistow and the return workings.
4. LNWR goods trains (worked by the NLR) to Upton Park, where the LNWR had a goods depot. These NLR trains joined the LT&SR system at Bromley.
5. The GER Gallions trains which travelled over the section between Campbell Road Junction and Abbey Mills Junction.

The requirements for the LT&SR were heavy passenger traffic during the 'rush hours', between say 7 and 10am and between 5 and 8pm. This passenger traffic was a mixture of both short and long distance travel. The short-distance traveller needed to journey between Bromley and Barking and these passenger requirements were met by 'all stations' trains, but this type of service was not suitable for the traveller who wanted an express service to his home in the Southend area. The easiest way to run a railway is where all trains travel at the same speed and stop at the same stations. The classic example is the London Underground system, but when it comes to intermixing fast and stopping trains then the system really needs two separate sets of running lines and this is what the LT&SR planned to accomplish. The plan was that trains running beyond Barking, for destinations such as Grays, Tilbury, Southend, etc, would run on the through or fast lines, while the stopping trains would use the 'local' or slow lines.

The widening was not dissimilar to that carried out today with major trunk roads and motorways: at times the extra width was to one side of the existing lines while elsewhere it was both sides of the original lines. Commencing at Campbell Road Junction, where the railway is built upon brick arches, these were extended and the new junction with the Whitechapel & Bow altered by slewing them towards the north, thus enabling them to parallel the existing LT&SR lines.

The first Board of Trade report to be considered dates from 17 May 1902 and refers to the new works at Campbell Road Junction. Major Pringle was the inspecting officer and his report was straightforward. *'I made an inspection yesterday of the new works at Campbell Road Junction on the London, Tilbury & Southend Railway. These works comprise a double junction with the new Whitechapel & Bow Railway, the joint property of the LT&S and Metropolitan District railways. A new signal cabin (Campbell Road Junction) has been erected and forms a new block post on the first-mentioned railway.'* (This report reads as if the GER/LT&SR junction was at Campbell Road. Both the RCH junction diagrams and the Midland Railway distance diagrams show the junction was at Gas Factory Junction.)

'The frame contains 25 levers, of which eight are spare. The interlocking is correct and the signalling adequate. The new junction has necessitated a reconstruction and extension of the former bridge carrying the LT&S Railway over Campbell Road. I was unable to test the new girder work and arrangements will be necessary to do this at a later date. It will probably be found convenient to carry out the necessary tests at the same time as the reinspection is made of the uncompleted work on the Whitechapel & Bow Railway. Subject to this test proving satisfactory I can advise the Board of Trade to authorise the new works at Campbell Road Junction.'

On 21 October 1904 Lt-Col Von Donop inspected the line between Plaistow and East Ham and his report is largely reproduced in full. *'I have inspected certain widenings which have been carried out between Plaistow and East Ham on the London, Tilbury & Southend Railway. There has been hitherto one set of passenger lines between these two stations. Two additional lines have now been added, one on the north side of the line and one on the south. The two lines on the north now form the up and down local lines, and those on the south side, the up and down through lines.*

'The widening commences at the west end of Plaistow station by a double junction with a facing connection on the down line, and it ends on the east side of East Ham No 2 signalbox by a double junction between the local lines and the East Ham loop lines. The length of the widening is 2 miles 22 chains.

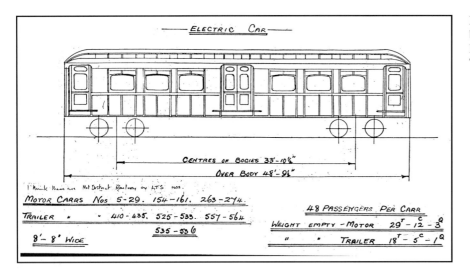

'The gauge of the line is 4ft 8½in and the permanent way is the standard pattern used by the London, Tilbury & Southend Rly; the ballast is of gravel, said to be laid to a depth of 1ft under the sleepers. The drainage is carried out by means of gullies and earthenware drainpipes. There are no gradients, curves, cuttings or embankments calling for mention.

'There are no underbridges, but there are 10 bridges over the line. These consist, with the exception of one brick arch, of steel girders on brickwork abutments, and they vary in span from 15 to 35 feet. They all appeared to be substantially constructed and to be standing well. There are no viaducts, level crossings or tunnels. There are three culverts of 3ft diameter and upwards which appear to be of substantial construction. There are the following stations on the line.

1. Plaistow. Platforms have been provided on the north and south sides of the line, and an island platform between them; the platforms are 600ft long, 3ft high and of ample width. Waiting rooms and all necessary accommodation is provided on all the platforms. The booking offices are on the street level, with steps leading to each platform.

2. Upton Park. This station is almost precisely similar to Plaistow station with the exception that waiting rooms are not provided on the up through platform as very few trains stop there.

3. East Ham is almost precisely similar to Plaistow station, with a bay platform line on the north side of it. At this station also waiting rooms have been omitted on the up through platform.

There are the following signalboxes on the line.

1. Plaistow. A new box and frame containing 120 levers, of which 71 are now spare. Requirements: (a) Lever No 29 to be preceded by No 36.

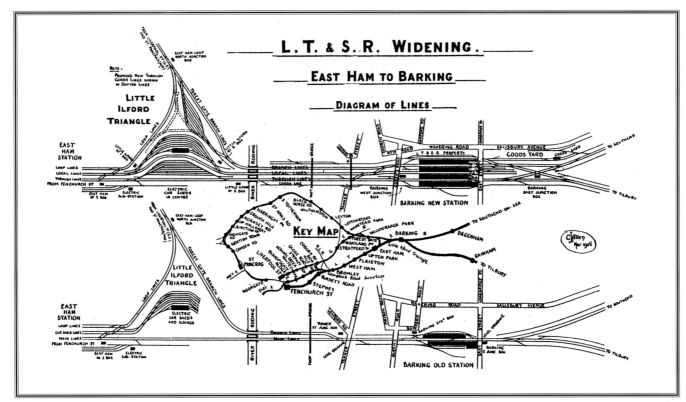

Fig 18 This map shows the extent of the railways in the Barking area in 1904 and the changes that took place following the widening that was undertaken by the LT&SR. *Original by C. J. Allen, courtesy The Railway Magazine*

2. At the east end of Plaistow station, a ground frame of 12 levers, three spare, bolt locked from the station box.
3. Upton Park. A new box, containing a frame of 65 levers, seven spare.
4. East Ham No 1 signalbox at the west end of that station. A new box containing a frame of 65 levers and 9 spare.
5. East Ham No 2 signalbox at the east end of the station. A new box containing a frame of 136 levers of which 20 are now spare.

'All the lines are fitted with Sykes' lock and block apparatus with treadles. The lines appear to be in all respects substantially constructed, and the arrangements are satisfactory, so subject to the one requirement at Plaistow signalbox, I can recommend the Board of Trade to sanction the new works being brought into use.'

Before considering the 20th century improvements we must first record the improvements that took place in the Bromley area in the closing years of the 19th century. On 8 December 1893, the LT&SR wrote to the Board of Trade requesting an inspection of new signalling arrangements at Abbey Mills Junction, but the file is incomplete. Upper Abbey Mills Junction was 43 chains to the east of Bromley station and was the junction of the LT&SR with the Great Eastern's North Woolwich line that passed under the London, Tilbury & Southend Railway. What has survived is the report dated 13 December 1893 by Maj-Gen Hutchinson in respect of the new works at Bromley-by-Bow. This is what he had to say:

'I have inspected an alteration in the position of the junction of a branch of the North London Railway with the London, Tilbury & Southend Railway at Bromley-by-Bow. A new signal cabin and altered signal arrangements in connection with the new station now being erected and the rest of the existing station which is to be abandoned. The new signal cabin contains 34 working levers and two spare ones; the interlocking at this cabin and the other arrangements, so far as they have been completed, are satisfactory.'

Part of the report is not clear but Hutchinson was concerned about falling gradients and the need to install safety points on the up line at or near the junction at Upper Abbey Mills. Provided this work was carried out, he was satisfied.

The widening between Bromley and East Ham was the subject of a letter dated 29 May 1905 from the London, Tilbury & Southend Railway to the Assistant Secretary (Railway Department) Board of Trade. This letter explained the plan that was submitted with the letter in simple terms. 'You are aware that at present this portion of our railway has only two lines of way, and you will observe that it is proposed to provide four lines of way, the two northern lines becoming the down and up local lines, and the two southern lines eventually becoming the up and down fast lines.

'It is necessary for engineering purposes during the course of construction, to divert alter and rearrange the existing lines and bring into use portions of the new lines and provide temporary signalboxes and signals, at varying intervals before the whole work can be completed. In these circumstances I beg to ask for the sanction of the Board of Trade to proceed with the work under those conditions, subject to the following undertaking:'

The writer then sets out the principle of providing plans and submitting the work for inspection. Lt-Col Von Donop inspected the work and his report dated 2 August 1905 has been summarised: 'I have inspected the new works which have been constructed between Bromley and Plaistow stations on the LT&SR which form widening Nos 2 and 3 authorised by the company's Act of 1902. Widening No 2 commences at the down end of Bromley station by an end-on junction with the existing lines from Fenchurch Street and terminates at the west end of West Ham station by an end-on junction with the existing lines towards Plaistow. The total length of this widening, which lies to the south of the existing lines, is 59.7 chains, of which 46.2 chains is double and 13.5 chains is single.

'Widening No 3 commences at a point 14 chains from the up end of West Ham station by an end-on junction with the existing down line and terminates at West Ham station in a similar manner. Length, 14 chains, all single line. At the down end of Bromley station local lines recently passed for passenger traffic have been extended so as to form an end-on junction with the existing lines to West Ham, the connection between the later lines and the existing lines from Fenchurch Street having been removed.' His remarks about the permanent way, ballast and fencing, were similar to other reports in this chapter.

This report gave 1 in 90 as the steepest gradient and 60 chains as the radius of the sharpest curve. All the lines were on an embankment with a maximum height of 7ft 6in. He reported four underbridges, one over a canal the others over roads; he was satisfied with their construction. The report confirms no viaducts, tunnels or level crossings and only one culvert. There were no new stations but he said: 'The company has submitted for inspection a new platform on the north side of Bromley station. This platform is 600ft long, 3ft high and of ample width; overbridges are provided at each end, giving access to the existing platforms and to the booking office, which is on a higher level. The new platform is provided with waiting rooms and all suitable accommodation.'

He confirmed that there were two new signalboxes. Bromley station signalbox contained a frame of 75 levers with seven spare and the other was Abbey Mills with a 90-lever frame containing 15 spare levers. He had one locking requirement for Abbey Mills, otherwise he was satisfied, but pointed out, 'As the existing lines are still in use, it is not possible to complete the final connecting up until the new lines are actually brought into use. But subject to this being done and to the fulfilment of the above mentioned requirements, I can recommend the Board of Trade to certify the lines as fit for passenger traffic.'

A further inspection by Lt-Col Von Donop took place on 3 March 1908. His report covered the new works between Little Ilford and Barking — a continuation of the widening authorised by the 1904 Act. The advantage of these reports is that they describe the line with considerable clarity. However, in order to remove undue repetition I have edited the report somewhat. 'The new lines, which are 68 chains in length, commence nearly opposite Little Ilford No 3 signalbox by an end-on junction with the existing Forest Gate branch lines, which have been diverted slightly to the north of their original position. From this point the new lines run eastwards through Barking station, terminating on the east side of it by means of junctions with both the lines to Southend and those to Tilbury. On the west side of Barking station, a double junction is provided between the new lines and the existing Tilbury lines, and at Barking station an additional platform loop line has been provided on the north side of the new lines.' He said that the rail weight was 80lb but that in the stations the weight was 90lb. This was the first time that I have seen this rail weight variation mentioned in a Board of Trade report.

Boundaries were mostly brick walls, the steepest gradient was 1 in 187 and the sharpest curve was 15 chains. His report said that the line was mostly in a cutting, with a maximum depth of 17ft. There were no viaducts, level crossings or tunnels and only one culvert of upwards of 5ft in diameter. The only underbridge carried the line over the River Roding; it consisted of three openings, each of 50 feet span. There were two overbridges carrying public roads and two public footpaths over the line.

The report continues: *'The only station on the new line is Barking. On the north side of this station two new platforms have been provided for three additional lines; these platforms are 700 ft long and they are connected by an overbridge. The more northerly of the two has a shelter, waiting rooms and all the necessary accommodation; the other has only a shelter and a lavatory for men. The company states that waiting rooms have not been provided on this platform, as they do not anticipate that they will be needed, but it is not clear why this should be so. I would recommend therefore that this platform be only accepted on the understanding that the company will at a future date provide additional accommodation if in the opinion of the Board of Trade it is desirable.*

'The points and signals are worked from the following signalboxes:

Little Ilford No 2: a new box containing a frame of 84 levers, of which 74 are spare. [These and the ones below are the figures given in the report.]
Barking West: a new box containing a frame of 160 levers of which 95 are at present spare.
Barking East: a new signalbox containing a frame of 125 levers of which 98 are now spare.
Rippleside: an existing box containing a frame of 25 levers, six spare.
Upney: an existing box containing a frame of 20 levers, three spare.

Construction of the line appears to be in all respects satisfactory, so, subject to the understanding stated above, I can recommend the Board of Trade to sanction these new works being brought into use.'
During the next ten days, many signals and points were connected up and spares became working levers. An inspection of the new works between East Ham and Little Ilford took place on 13 March. Lt-Col Von Donop reported his findings and said these works, together with those described on 3 March, comprised the whole of the widening authorised by the company's 1904 Act.

He said that there were no gradients calling for mention, the lines were mostly on a slight embankment with a maximum height of 8ft 6in. The only new bridge was an underbridge and he was satisfied with the construction. He referred to the signalboxes including East Ham No 2, an old box with 136 levers, but said that it was not yet complete and that a further inspection would be required. He made some requirements at Little Ilford No 1 signalbox. This was a new box with 60 levers, of which nine were spare. There were also minor requirements requested at Little Ilford No 2, a new box with 84 levers, seven spare, and Little Ilford No 3, another new box with 34 levers, which included six spare. There were also requirements at Barking. The new West signalbox contained a frame of 160 levers including 21 spare and, finally, the new East Ground Frame that contained 24 levers of which six were spare.

The report found the work was satisfactory and, subject to the requirements that were of a minor nature, a provisional sanction could be given. His final remarks were to the effect that the company should advise when the above-mentioned signalbox was complete so that an inspection could be made. The LT&SR wrote on 10 June to confirm that all the requirements had been complied with, but said, *'We are, however, contemplating further alterations at East Ham to allow for additional facilities for shunting at that station, and as these will necessitate further alterations in No 2 signalbox, I beg to suggest that the inspecting officer's final visit be postponed until such time as they are completed.'* The letter confirmed that a plan showing these alterations would be sent to the Board of Trade shortly.

The final inspection was made and the report dated 2 September confirmed that the arrangements were satisfactory at East Ham No 2 signalbox. The report concluded: *'At the west end of East Ham station a new crossover road has been provided between the up and down local roads and two new draw-ahead signals have been provided on the same lines. The points and signals are worked from the East Ham No 1 signalbox containing a frame of 65 levers, of which four are now spare. The interlocking is correct so I can recommend the Board of Trade to sanction the new works being brought into use.'*

This final report completes the official description of this most important development; we will now look at what *The Railway Magazine* had to say. In presenting extracts from the articles I have endeavoured to avoid duplication as much as possible but inevitably readers will see that some developments appear in both the Board of Trade reports and the magazine articles.

The *Railway Magazine* Summary

A new bridge was built where the LT&SR line crossed the NLR's Poplar branch at Bow and a concrete retaining wall was erected on the north side of the existing line of railway, being continued to the east end of Bromley station which required reconstruction. East of Bromley the new works lay to the south of the original tracks. New bridgework carried the railway across the River Lea bringing the work to Abbey Mills Junction. From this point to West Ham the new works were on both sides of the existing railway.

Further bridgework was required across public roads together with one across the GER branch from Stratford to Canning Town. At Plaistow the station was almost entirely rebuilt and a new signal cabin was commissioned. Continuing east from Plaistow to East Ham the railway ran in a shallow cutting. The new works were completed in 1908 and opened for traffic on 1 April. This new construction enabled the electric trains to run through to Barking over their own tracks that were equipped with conductor rails (referred to at this early date in the development of electric trains as 'current rails'). Other changes included the replacement of the two level crossings, one by a footbridge, the other by an overbridge. An Act of Parliament in 1904 was required for this improvement. It was intended from the outset to continue the electric service from Wimbledon, Hammersmith, Ealing and other stations on the Metropolitan District Railway from their temporary terminus at East Ham to Barking. This length of railway would have six running lines: the two centre lines were for the electric trains, and the two other pairs were for steam trains.

At this date, overseas travel was by sea and there was considerable passenger traffic, often conveyed by special train, to and from the docks at Tilbury. Other sea passenger traffic was for summer pleasure coasting steamers that went

A magnificent picture of the new 84-lever signalbox, Little Ilford No 2. The position of the box can be seen in Fig 18. *Collection A. E. Overton*

from the London termini to Tilbury & Southend and beyond to Herne Bay and Margate.

The sidings at the Little Ilford triangle were to serve the Tilbury for many years and the centre of the triangle contained seven sidings that held Metropolitan District electric trains when they were not in use. These sidings had replaced the temporary terminal at East Ham and were used following the opening of the Whitechapel & Bow line. In addition, there was a car shed, spanning two tracks, which was used for the examination and repair of the electric stock. Attached to this building was the necessary administrative office. The triangle was bounded to the east by the running lines from Liverpool Street, GER and St Pancras, MR. The GER trains came via Forest Gate Junction while the approach from St Pancras over the Tottenham & Forest Gate joint line was from Woodgrange Park Junction. Trains from both companies approached the triangle from the north and at East Ham Loop North Junction signalbox they could either turn west for East Ham or east for Barking station. Connected to this Forest Gate branch were sidings used for both the exchange and marshalling of goods traffic from the GER and MR systems.

The changes at Barking were considerable and later we will tell the story of the level crossing at East Street that does not appear in either the contemporary Board of Trade or *The Railway Magazine* reports. I have used an extract taken from the May 1908 *Railway Magazine* that shows the changes that took place between the years 1904 and 1908. These included a new goods yard, new bridges of both the over and under types including one over the River Roding. The work required the acquisition of property and its demolition to make way for the enlarged railway system, and the signalling changes were substantial.

I cannot be entirely sure of what traffic changes took place after 1912, but I suspect that there were very few. The Victorian steam railway changed slowly as far as established traffic patterns were concerned. Midland Railway goods trains from the company's City goods station at Mint Street could travel via the loop lines direct from the Tilbury lines on to the Tottenham & Forest Gate joint line before joining the Midland lines at Kentish Town Junction. On the other hand, traffic could be exchanged at Little Ilford Northern Sidings although how much is open to speculation. The most likely answer would be that these sidings were used for traffic originating on,

consigned to, or travelling over the MR and GER lines bound for or coming from Tilbury Docks. These sidings would be the most logical point at which to sort such traffic. At the south of the triangle, lying between the new local and existing through lines, were further sidings used by the LT&SR for storing steam-hauled coaches.

The new works at Barking were for an entirely new station with four island platforms that carried eight faces numbered from north to south. No 1 served the GER local trains from Liverpool Street and Barking together with local LT&SR trains when required. In 1910 there were eight weekday trains and four on Sunday, but the 1922 Bradshaw does not show any. Nos 2 and 3 were from the Midland line for Southend and for any other through service beyond Barking which ran on the Forest Gate branch lines. Nos 4 and 5 served the local line electric services while Nos 6 and 7 were for the LT&SR principal trains routed via the Tilbury lines. Platform 8 still served the 'local' LT&SR services between Tilbury and Barking although it could also be used for through Tilbury-Fenchurch Street trains when so required. Finally, it should be noted that provision was made for a number of short engine sidings to accommodate engines required to work forward sections of trains which were divided at Barking. For example, a number of LT&SR trains were 'express' between Fenchurch Street and Barking, where they were divided into 'fast' and 'slow' portions prior to working forward.

Before we continue with the description there is the story of the level crossing to be told. It is a tale of how the LT&SR, or perhaps I should say Stride, procrastinated about the need for a bridge at Barking to replace the level crossing. It began when the clerk of the Barking Local Board wrote to the Secretary of the Railway Department at the Board of Trade on 28 October 1885 with a complaint about the LT&SR train line that crosses over a main street with great inconvenience to locals. The level crossing was at East Street. There is nothing else in the file for that year; however, the clerk wrote again in 1887, and on 19 May, the Board of Trade wrote to the LT&SR and forwarded a copy of the clerk's letter. There is an interesting note on the internal BoT correspondence to the effect that 'the Board of Trade have the necessary powers to order the bridge to be built but unless the company agrees the powers could not be enforced.'

On 12 August, Arthur Stride replied, signing the letter as,

The LT&SR lines went over the North London Railway's line from Bow to Poplar Docks and this picture shows the bridge that was built as part of the work entailed with the Whitechapel & Bow Railway at Campbell Road Junction. The electric lines are to the left of the picture; the photographer was facing east. *L&GRP 8016*

Engineer and Manager. His defence was that the line was originally constructed under the powers of the Act of 1852 and crossed East Street on the level. East Street was an important street and the property fronting it was of considerable and increasing value. He continued by pointing out that the nature of the ground was such that 'it is impossible to affect any adjustment of levels which would enable the road either over or under the railway without altering its gradient in such a way as would practically destroy the access of many houses to the road on both sides of the level crossing.'

Stride then played his trump card and said, 'In the Session of 1882 the railway company when applying to Parliament for powers to construct the Barking & Pitsea Extension Railway sought authority to close the level crossing and substitute a route for traffic by means of a road which it was proposed to construct.' He then explained the proposals to construct a new road that would have overcome the problem of the level crossing but pointed out why it failed to become part of the

powers conferred on the company. It appeared that the Vestry of Barking, on behalf of the inhabitants, opposed the plan at the Committee stage at the House of Commons and the powers were withdrawn in consequence of this opposition. He also pointed out that before the powers required for the purchase of the land expired, the railway company made overtures to the Local Board for the construction of the new road at the joint expense of the railway and the ratepayers. But as the Local Board was prepared to subscribe only £500 towards the estimated cost of £6,000 nothing came of it. He concluded that 'the responsibility lay with the past action of that body and its predecessors'.

This letter produced a spirited reply from C. E. Wilson, clerk of the Barking Town Local Board. Dated 27 September 1887 the essence of his letter can be summarised thus. He began by suggesting how the levels could be altered to enable a bridge with a gradient of 1 in 40 on the approach roads to be built, without affecting any buildings on the east side of the crossing. He refuted some of Stride's statements about overtures and the refusal of the railway company to accept the offer of £500. He also gave details of a traffic survey between 24 October and 13 November 1884, a period of 18 days. He said that between the hours of 9am and 6pm the average time that the gates were closed was for a total of 4¾ hours and that they were frequently closed for between 10 and 15 minutes at a time and on occasions for more than 30 minutes. The reason was largely due to the shunting of trains. Correspondence then took place with the result that the gates were replaced but the new ones took much longer to open. He also complained about the siting of the footbridge, its condition and the fact that a footpath was diverted as part of these changes and that the railway company declined to restore the footpath. He also pointed out that there was no lighting, which meant that many people did not use the bridge. He concluded by expressing the view that when the new docks at Tilbury came into full working order a bridge at this point was really indispensable.

Stride's response to the Board of Trade on 23 November was short and to the point. 'We have been in touch with the Local Board and we cannot agree. Road traffic is increasing and has occasionally been delayed by shunting operations which have been necessary in consequence of the want of siding accommodation at the station.' He went on to say that the directors had given approval for the construction of a new

The level crossing at East Street, Barking, the subject of much correspondence between the various parties as described in this chapter. *Collection R. J. Essery*

station and the rearrangement of the station yard, 'which will entirely do away with any obstruction to the level crossing except during the time a train is actually crossing'. He said that the work should be completed by June of the following year and suggested that matters should be deferred until then.

The file contains a press cutting from the *Essex Times* dated 18 February 1888 that tells the story of a narrow escape to a porter who closed the gates just before an express train ran through. A horse that took fright and bolted had opened the gates by trying to jump over them. I presume that the Local Board had sent this cutting to the Board of Trade.

On 8 June the Barking Town Local Board wrote to the Board of Trade to point out that the suggestion of completion by the end of June was unlikely since the tenders for the work had only just been sent to the railway company. They pointed out that because the company was exempt from the Public Health Act they had no idea what the company planned for the new station.

Maj-Gen Hutchinson visited Barking on 31 January 1893 and wrote a long report about the problem. His solution was to place the control of the gates in the direct hands of the signalman rather than a gateman who had to contact the signalman before the gates could be opened etc. The Maj-Gen paid a further visit later in the year and his report is dated 10 July. This was in connection with a fatality that took place on the crossing but no conclusions about solving the problem of East Street were reached.

By 1900, the reports and letters were typed rather than hand-written but no other progress had been made. A letter dated 9 October to the Board of Trade restated the position and painted a gloomy picture of delays and frustration and bitter complaints from the public. The shunting continued and he put it to the Board that 'It would almost appear in practice that the railway company had a monopoly of the public highway and that the public were seeking leave to cross the company's line rather than the reverse.' The letter concluded by asking if the

This slightly misty view shows the new bridge at East Street with the station buildings above. The electric sidings, with the electric stock visible, ran beyond the end of the station and the warning sign made their position clear. This picture was probably taken shortly after the new work was completed. Finally, this picture shows the 1907 permanent way with the chairs secured by four fixings, probably two coach screws and two spikes, using 45ft rail. *Collection A. E. Overton*

A later picture, taken on 7 October 1938, illustrates the platforms and the station entrance. The eastbound train appears to be made up of Midland or early LMS stock, while a westbound electric train with an Ealing destination board is about to depart. *Collection V. R. Anderson*

Board would receive a small deputation from the Council to discuss the subject. On 13 October a further letter was sent together with details of traffic during the week ending 22 September 1900. A detailed survey was taken between the hours of 8am and 6.30pm that showed the gates were closed for 34 hours 8 minutes and open for 28 hours 52 minutes. A total of 2,863 vehicles had to wait while 1,894 vehicles were able to cross without waiting. The gates were closed between 80 and 92 times on the days in question.

Stride waited until 5 February 1901 before replying and began by rejecting much of the survey. His solution was: 1. calling-on arms and 2. some possible alteration in the locking between two signalboxes, and he confirmed the matter was now with the signal inspector. There did not appear to be any immediate improvement; a letter from the new clerk to Barking Urban District Council, E. H. Lister, dated 12 July, said in effect, there was no improvement and the delay and inconvenience were getting worse.

There was a meeting between the Board of Trade and members of the Council on 23 October 1901 at which the Board told the Council that it was illegal for a railway company to shunt over a level crossing. On 11 January 1902, Lister wrote to the Board of Trade pointing out that notwithstanding the assurances given to the Council, that the Board would oppose further powers being given to the company over this crossing, the LT&SR was promoting a bill in the next session of Parliament and they wanted to know what powers they sought.

Then, on 20 February, Stride wrote to the Board of Trade and submitted a plan for new signals and other works then being constructed in the neighbourhood of Barking. It was not a bridge, but it was the company's response to the problem. However, after many years, matters were at last drawing to a close. A press cutting, dated 26 April 1902, stated that the Committee of the House of Commons had been considering a new bill that would finally deal with the problem of East Street. The final note in the file is dated 29 April, to the effect that a new clause would be inserted. In place of the existing level crossing in (East Street) the company would, within two years from the passing of this act, carry the road over the railway by means of a bridge, and none of the powers conferred upon the company by section 10 of this Act would be exercised until the Board of Trade had certified that such bridge had been completed, or substantial progress had been made in the construction thereof. The cost was to be borne by the Urban District of Barking and the company and in default of an agreement, the Board of Trade was to appoint an arbitrator.

So ended the saga of the East Street level crossing and the bridge to replace it. I have dealt with this at some length if only to show that railway history goes much deeper than trains and concerns such things as local politics.

But to return to the developments in the area. Beyond the station the electric trains, which used the local lines, ran on to dead-end sidings terminated by buffer stops. These sidings were about 400ft long and there was also a short siding some 300ft long that allowed stowage of 'half-trains' during the times of the day when traffic was slack and the trains could be reduced in both length and passenger accommodation. Just to the east of the station area was the Barking East Junction signalbox and at this point the Southend and Tilbury lines separated at a fairly complex junction which permitted trains to run from either the through or branch lines on to either the Tilbury or Southend lines. This meant that all traffic from either Fenchurch Street or off the Forest Gate line could go in either direction once the road had been set.

The local goods and mineral needs for the area were served by a goods yard connected at the west end to the Forest Gate branch line and at the east end to the Southend main line. It is worth noting that considerable alterations were made to the signalling arrangements, which in 1908 between Fenchurch Street and Barking, were of the mechanical pattern on the lock and block system. Finally, it should be mentioned that the LT&SR was justifiably proud of this major development, carried out to the designs and under the supervision of Mr J. R. Robertson, MInst CE, the Chief Engineer of the company. The staff under the supervision of Mr H. W. Stride, MInst CE, District Engineer, who was almost certainly related to the Chairman, carried out the whole of the earthworks and permanent way work that was required.

Lt-Col Von Donop was required to inspect the new works at the western end of the Forest Gate branch where a new double junction had been installed. His report dated 2 September does not call for further comment; he was satisfied with what he found, noting that the new signalbox contained a frame of 60 levers of which 19 were spare. The inspection report for Little Ilford was dated 28 June 1911 and once again it was Lt-Col Von Donop who was the inspecting officer.

The LT&SR had written to the Board of Trade on 16 March 1911 to say that it had been found necessary to make certain alterations in the electrical sidings at Little Ilford. In consequence, certain signalling alterations are shown on the accompanying plan etc. Von Donop's report was quite brief and he said: 'At this point, slips have been added to an existing through connection, forming a facing connection on the down local line leading to a new traffic siding; an additional draw-ahead signal has also been provided on the down local line, to facilitate shunting operations.' The points and signals were worked from an existing box and all the interlocking was correct, so he concluded his report by recommending that the work be sanctioned.

New Stations

During the final years of the LT&SR's existence some new stations were opened and although I give a full list of the stations on the line in Appendix 1, some Board of Trade reports have survived that describe the arrangements at the time of opening. We begin with Dagenham Dock. Lt-Col Von Donop's report was dated 1 July 1908 and he said: 'I have inspected the new works at Dagenham Dock. At this point, which is situated between Barking and Rainham stations, the company has constructed a new station. This consists of up and down platforms, each of which is 600ft long, 20ft wide and 3ft high, and which are connected by an overbridge. Each platform is provided with waiting rooms, booking office, shelter, and all necessary accommodation.

'No alterations of any sort have been made to the permanent way, but a few additional signals have been provided and the gates of an occupation crossing, which were formerly worked by hand, are now interlocked with the signals and are worked from the signalbox. The points and signals are worked from an existing signalbox [Dagenham Dock signalbox opened on 16 December 1901] containing a frame of 42 levers of which five are now spare. The additional interlocking has been correctly provided and the arrangements are satisfactory, so I can recommend the Board of Trade to sanction the works being brought into use.'

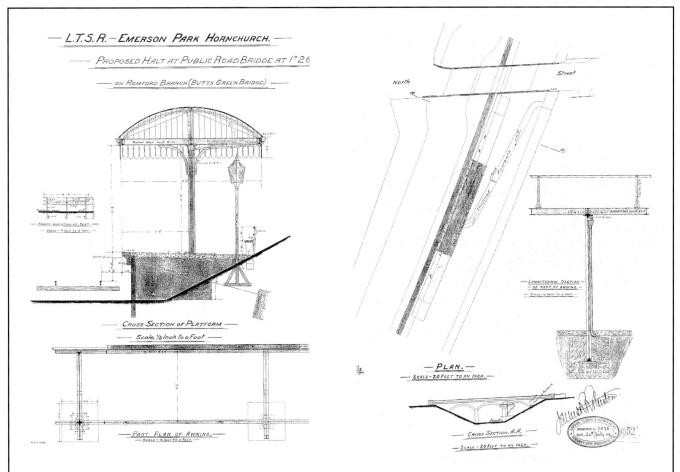

— L.T.S.R. — EMERSON PARK HORNCHURCH. —

— PROPOSED HALT AT PUBLIC ROAD BRIDGE AT 1*26 —

— ON ROMFORD BRANCH (BUTTS GREEN BRIDGE) —

— FRONT ELEVATION OF SEAT. —
— SCALE - ½ INCH TO A FOOT. —

— CROSS SECTION OF PLATFORM —
— Scale, ½ Inch to a Foot —

— PART PLAN OF AWNING. —
— SCALE - ½ INCH TO A FOOT. —

North

Street

— LONGITUDINAL SECTION —
— OF PART OF AWNING. —
— SCALE - ½ INCH TO A FOOT. —

— PLAN. —
— SCALE - 20 FEET TO AN INCH. —

— CROSS SECTION. A.A. —
— SCALE - 20 FEET TO AN INCH. —

Fig 19 I have included this drawing of the shelter at Emerson Park station described on the drawing as Butts Green Bridge. It was, to use a modern expression, 'a low budget affair'.

On 2 September 1909, the LT&SR wrote to the Board of Trade and enclosed a plan of a halt that was on their single-line branch halfway between Upminster and Romford. The halt had been requested by the residents on the housing estate which had been built in the neighbourhood and was to be known as Emerson Park, and the company wished to bring it into public use on 1 October of that year. This small halt often features in pictorial form in books about the LT&SR so I felt it would be of interest to include it in the drawings reproduced here, together with the inspecting officer's report. The company's letter was interesting and said: *'As the local train service between Upminster and Romford is only composed of short trains and is not particularly frequent, and the trains are worked by Webb's electric train staff block system, I shall be glad if the Board of Trade will give permission for the halt to be opened for traffic on the 1st prox, subject to subsequent inspection. There will be no signals provided at the halt, the platform being simply placed alongside the running line, the train being controlled by the driver having possession of the electric train staff.'* The use of the word, 'worked' is interesting; 'controlled' would be a more accurate description.

Lt-Col Von Donop's report was dated 10 November 1909 and this is what he had to say. *'At this point, which is situated on the single line between Upminster and Romford, a new loop has been provided; it consists of a single platform, 200ft long, 14ft wide, and 3ft high; it is provided with a shelter, booking office, lamps, and a footpath approach from the neighbouring road.'* Once again we encounter an interesting use of words by the inspecting officer. There was both a loop and a platform, which is not entirely clear from the report.

'The arrangements are satisfactory, and I can recommend the Board of Trade to sanction the use of this halt for trains, the length of which does not exceed that of the platform. At the same time I inspected, at the request of the company, a loop which has been constructed on the single line about a quarter of a mile on

The platform at 'Emerson Park and Great Nelmes' lay to the east of the line. The nameboard is prominent in this picture which shows 0-6-0 No 50 on a goods train heading for Romford. Although the station nameboard displayed the name in full it was, as far as I can see, only described as Emerson Park in official documents. *Ken Nunn/LCGB*

Now known as Emerson Park Halt, this view dated 24 January 1971, is looking towards Romford and shows the BR-style nameboard. *J. M. Rickard/Ian Allan Library*

the down side of the above halt, for the purpose of enabling [the engines that had worked up trains], which do not proceed further than the halt, to run round their trains. The points and signals are worked from a ground frame of four levers, which is controlled by the key on the electric staff of the section.

'The only requirement noted was that a clearance bar should be provided on the running line at the up end of the loop, similar to that at the down end and the company has agreed to provide. The company informs me that the loop will only be used for the running round of engines, and that no vehicles will, under any circumstances, be allowed to stand on it.

'Subject to this understanding, and to the fulfilment of the above mentioned requirement, I can recommend the Board of Trade to sanction these new works being brought into use.'

The final inspection report to be included in this chapter deals with Purfleet Rifle Range station in 1915, when the

LT&S was part of the Midland Railway. The station was in use in 1910, but it was not inspected until June 1911 and it did not become a public station until 1921. Prior to that date the traffic was military; however, some changes were recorded in 1915, no doubt due to the Great War. Lt-Col Druitt made an inspection on 3 March 1915 and reported that an old siding has been converted into an up bay platform, running alongside the south side of an existing up platform. He also reported that an additional connection had been made for the War Department tramway nearby. The new connections and necessary signals were worked from a new ground frame, containing eight levers, all in use, which was bolt locked from the signalbox that contained 27 working and 13 spare levers. The interlocking and other arrangements were satisfactory and he recommended that the work be sanctioned by the Board of Trade.

'No 51' class engine No 61 *St Pancras* was outstationed at Kentish Town and worked over the Tottenham & Hampstead Junction and Tottenham & Forest Gate railways before joining LT&SR lines with the St Pancras trains that it worked on a regular basis for a number of years. This splendid picture shows the engine at St Pancras station. *L&GRP 25952*

Tottenham & Hampstead Junction Railway

We come now to the one of the two joint railways that connected the Midland Railway to the LT&SR system. While the T&HJR has already been mentioned, it is examined in greater detail here. The physical connection with the Midland Railway's London extension, or as the company called it, London & Bedford, was effected at Kentish Town Junction, just to the north of the station bearing that name and in order to avoid conflicting movements the traffic arrangements were somewhat complex. This should be clear from the accompanying map, Fig 14 on page 41.

The joint line was owned by the Midland and Great Eastern railways, its full title being Tottenham & Hampstead Junction Railway, although from 1st July 1902 it was known as the Tottenham & Hampstead Joint Committee, I will refer to it as the T&HJR as indeed I have done so previously. The T&HJR ran through stations at Highgate Road, Junction Road, Upper Holloway, Hornsey Road, Crouch Hill, Harringay Park, St Ann's Road and South Tottenham where, at South Tottenham Junction, it joined the second joint line, which was known as the Tottenham & Forest Gate Railway. As I have already said in Chapter 1, the original owners of this joint line were the Midland and London, Tilbury & Southend Railway companies. On post-1912 RCH maps it is shown as being of Midland Railway origin. The RCH was only interested in the current position and used green for the Midland Railway and yellow for the former LT&SR lines following the Midland Railway's purchase of the company.

The history of the T&HJR was slightly complex and began with the passing of the Tottenham & Hampstead Junction Railway Act on 28 July 1862. For a number of years various proposals had been put forward to link the western districts of London with those railways whose lines were to form the Great Eastern Railway. The formal creation of the Great Eastern was on 7 August 1862 although it had been effective from 1 July. At first this line was not planned to connect with the Great Northern Railway at Harringay, under whose line it passed just to the south of that company's Harringay station. A junction was made a few years later but the final connection was not put in. The rails that had been laid were removed in 1885 and they were replaced during World War 1. Following the end of the Great War the junction was taken out again but reinstated once more during the 1939-45 conflict and is still there.

The eastern end of the T&HJR commenced at Tottenham North Junction, leaving the Great Eastern Railway some 24 chains south of Tottenham station. The railway took six years to build and because it ran through a rural area, no intermediate stations existed when the line was opened for traffic in 1868. The initial service provided was from Fenchurch Street to Highgate Road, a somewhat roundabout route that was made worse by the need to reverse all trains at Tottenham station. Not surprisingly this service ceased to run in 1870 and in an attempt to improve matters a south-west curve was opened, thereby forming the west and south junction. The westward extension, which helped to justify the line's name, was opened on 4 June 1888 and ran from Highgate Road Junction to Gospel Oak, a single platform situated behind the LNWR station of the same name, where it terminated. This enabled the GER service from Chingford to Highgate Road, which had commenced in the summer of

1885, to be extended, thus enabling passengers to join the LNWR Hampstead Junction line and for local residents, who so wished, to reach the delights of Hampstead Heath.

The T&HJR did not enjoy a happy beginning and was soon in financial trouble, with the GER declining to work the line for passenger traffic from 31 January 1870. However, shortly afterwards the Midland Railway was to enter the scene and from 1 July 1870 it commenced running a service of passenger trains from Moorgate to Crouch Hill. This was made possible by using the connection from Kentish Town Junction to Highgate Road Junction that had been opened on 3 January 1870. By now the Midland Railway had obtained running powers for its goods and mineral trains to work over the GER to the company's various dockland area goods depots. These running powers were obtained at the same time that the GER obtained powers to work over the Midland Railway and to run into St Pancras station, which in effect gave the Great Eastern Railway a London terminal station that was closer to the West End.

Signalling

The story of LT&SR signalling begins with a line that was opened at a time when signalling practice was extremely basic. Signals were few and signalboxes in the sense that we understand were non-existent. At first they were no more than signal platforms, in effect small elevated platforms with a hut to provide some cover. The interlocking of signals and points was in the future. Peter Kay, in his book, gives a list of locations and names — Upper Abbey Mills Junction, Barking Junction, Tilbury West Junction, Tilbury East Junction and Thames Haven Junction — as the original signal platforms.

Shortly after the LT&SR began to run its own affairs a programme of improvements began and Stevens & Sons undertook the work. Later, Easterbrook and finally the Railway Signalling Company were responsible for the London, Tilbury & Southend Railway Company's signal installations. According to Kay, until the 1890s the signal posts were of the slotted type and the distant signals were, as indeed elsewhere in the kingdom, red. The LT&S distinguished them from stop signals with a horizontal stripe.

With the growth of traffic it became necessary to 'shorten the block' by the introduction of additional block posts at Basildon, Hadleigh, Dunton and Gale Street. However, it was the introduction of semi-automatic signalling that was so interesting. There are three reports that have survived and they describe the semi-automatic signals the LT&SR installed between Pitsea and Benfleet, Dagenham and Hornchurch, and Leigh and Westcliff. The installations were, in the words of the inspecting officer, 'precisely similar' at each location. Therefore I have chosen to describe only the first location in detail. Lt-Col Von Donop inspected each location, Dagenham and Hornchurch and Leigh and Westcliff at the end of August 1912, and his first report was dated 8 March 1912.

'I have inspected the new semi-automatic signalling arrangements which have been provided on both the Up and Down lines, between Pitsea and Benfleet signalboxes, on the London, Tilbury & Southend Railway. The distance between the above-mentioned boxes is 4,585 yards, and the object is to shorten the block section.

'The arrangements on the down line are as follows: a new intermediate 'stop' signal, with a distant signal 800 yards behind it, has been erected at a distance of 1,749 yards ahead of the Pitsea down advance signal, both these new

The instructions that were published by the LT&SR for their staff as referred to in the Board of Trade report shown on page 65.

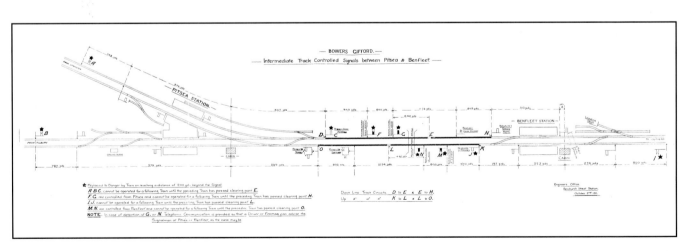

signals being worked from one lever in the Pitsea signalbox. Two sections of track circuit have been provided; the first extends from Pitsea down advance signal to a point 440 yards ahead of the new intermediate Stop signal, and this portion of track circuit prevents the Pitsea down advance starting Signal and its two distance signals being lowered for a following train, until the preceding train has cleared the circuit. The second section of track circuit extends from the termination of the first section up to the Benfleet Down Home Signal, and this section similarly prevents the two new signals being lowered until the preceding train has cleared this second section. Each of all the above mentioned signals is automatically replaced at danger when the train reaches a point situated at a distance of 200 yards beyond each of them. Indicators are provided in the signalbox to show the signalmen whenever there is a train standing on the first section of the track circuit, and also to show him the position of each of the two intermediate signals.

'The mode of working is as follows; provided the indicator in the Pitsea signalbox shows 'track clear', the signalman asks for line clear for the train in the usual way, and on receiving it, he lowers the Pitsea advance starting signal and the two intermediate stop signals. Immediately the train passes the Pitsea down advance starting signal the indicator will show 'track occupied' and the Down Advance Starting Signal after having gone to danger automatically will be held in that position until the train has cleared the first track section, when it will be electrically released and the track indicator will again show 'line clear'. The 'train entering section signal' will then be sent and the lever working the intermediate signals will be replaced in the danger position. If a down train arrives at Pitsea before 'line clear' can be obtained from Benfleet, it may be allowed to proceed to the intermediate stop signal; as soon as 'line clear' is received from Benfleet, the intermediate

stop signals may then be lowered, but the 'train entering section' signal must not be sent to Benfleet until the indicator shows 'line clear', and the lever for the intermediate signals will then be replaced at danger.

'Precisely similar arrangements are provided on the up line, and trains from Benfleet to Pitsea will be worked in a precisely similar manner to that described above.

'The Pitsea signalbox contains a frame of 32 levers of which five are now spare, and the Benfleet signalbox contains one of 40 levers of which three are now spare. I attach herewith a copy of the instructions issued by the company with reference to the working of these new signals.

'The arrangements appear in all respects satisfactory, and I can recommend the Board of Trade to sanction the new works being brought into use.'

These three, for the period, modern approaches to signalling had been planned prior to the Midland Railway purchase of the LT&SR. McKenzie Holland & Westinghouse Power Signal Company carried out the installation. It is interesting to note that, as far as I am aware, similar schemes were not introduced on the Midland Railway and developments of this nature had to wait until the Midland became part of the LMS.

Above:
Plaistow became the principal engine shed on the LT&SR system and this undated but early 20th century picture shows the enlargement that took place when the new running shed was built and the works were enlarged. Although the classes of locomotives can be identified, the individual engines cannot. Probably the most interesting to be seen is the Metropolitan District Railway 4-4-0T engine. *Collection R. J. Essery*

Right:
Photographed late in 1909, this view of the shed shows No 79 *Rippleside* in lavender grey livery and confirms the pre-1910 date when the engine was repainted in standard LT&SR green. The other engines on shed whose numbers can be seen are, left to right: Nos 81, 58, 77 and 21. *Collection V. R. Anderson*

Engine Sheds and Locomotive Works

The locomotive works at Plaistow were opened in 1880. Prior to the LT&SR owning its own engines, repairs to locomotives working on the railway would have been the responsibility of

the Great Eastern Railway and before that the Eastern Counties Railway. Plaistow Works was closed for locomotive repair work in 1925 and for carriage and wagon work c1932.

During the independent life of the company engine sheds were first established at Tilbury and Southend and these were probably the only depots in being and owned by the company

The coaling stage with Baltic tank engine No 2102. Clearly, this was a posed photograph; there is not a person in sight. *Derby Collection NRM DY14369*

during the time it was run on a lease basis. The precise details are unclear and the only reference available to date, Hawkins and Reeve, *LMS Engine Sheds*, Volume 4, has many gaps as far as the London, Tilbury & Southend Railway is concerned.

The London, Tilbury & Southend Railway directors approved the preliminary plans drawn up by the General Manager A. L. Stride, but told him to consult with William Adams of the GER. This led to Adams's involvement in a number of areas, in particular with the design of the 'No 1' class of engines and the design and layout of Plaistow Works. During the independent life of the LT&SR, the company's locomotives were maintained at Plaistow but after 1912 Derby Works played an important part by supplying material and undertaking repairs, while after 1923, the old North London Railway's works at Bow undertook a considerable amount of work for locomotives stationed at depots on the LT&S Section.

The earliest order that I can trace following the Midland Railway's purchase of the LT&SR is number 4316 dated 9 August 1913 that gave instructions for the production of cylinder patterns, one right-hand and one left-hand for LT&S engines Nos 2110-2179. The drawing numbers quoted were made in 1913 and were for both 17in and 19in cylinders. On 3 October 1913 orders for three spare boilers for engines of the 2110-2145 class were placed (order No 4326) and two spare boilers for engines of the 2146-2157 class (order No 4327). The order referred to two new drawings that the Derby Works locomotive drawing office had made. On 7 October, to order numbers 4329 and 4330, repair work to engines Nos 2142 and 2178 was authorised. Thereafter there was a steady flow of works orders for repairs to LT&S Section engines.

The renumbering of the LT&S boilers was authorised by order No 4353 dated 31 October 1913. The numbers were to be applied to the boilers which were either fixed or allocated to engines. The order stressed that a careful record must be kept. The plates were to be made at Derby and fixed at Plaistow.

Four orders, Nos 4430-3 dated 13 March 1913, were for the production of patterns for various wheel centres. The 5ft 3in wheel used with the 0-6-2T engines was to be the Midland Railway standard wheel centre with a slight alteration to the inside of the boss. Order No 4483, dated 15 May 1914, was for cylinder relief valves for engines Nos 2100-2107.

Engines Nos 2149/53 were rebuilt at Derby with new 3A class boilers to order No 4554 dated 4 September 1914. The following year, the first order was placed on Derby Works to replace copper fireboxes on LT&S engines, 4 October 1915, for engine No 2173. Steam heating of LT&S trains using the Johnson & Bain steam heating system was authorised by order No 4595 dated 29 December 1914. The locomotives were Nos 2112/4/6/22/3/32/4/5 and 2140. Order No 5735 dated 31 May 1922 was interesting; it said: 'Two sets of safety valves to drawing 22-9635. The safety valves to drawing 13-8912 are not to be proceeded with.' I am unsure what the differences were.

By 1925, LT&S engines were being repaired at the old NLR works at Bow. Order number 6491, dated 29 July 1925, was issued to cover any work done at either Derby or Plaistow for LT&S engines that were repaired at Bow. There were a number of orders issued during the 1930s in connection with the Hudd ATC equipment that was installed at this locomotive works.

The opening of an engine shed at Plaistow in 1880 provided the company with a depot at the London end of the line, while the extension from Southend to Shoeburyness saw the new shed at the latter location replace the old depot at Southend, probably in 1884. The final new work was to construct an engine shed at Upminster that opened in 1893. While I am unsure how much use, if any, was made of the Midland Railway's London sheds at Kentish Town and Childs Hill, later known as Cricklewood, during the pre-1912 era, I suspect that after 1912 ex-LT&SR engines would have been serviced at both depots.

A document at the PRO Kew suggests that the allocation of locomotives, in terms of accommodation, in the final years of the company was: Plaistow, in shed 48 engines, in lifting shop two engines, Upminster four engines, Tilbury 16, Shoeburyness 12 in the shed and five in the 'lean-to'.

There was little change for a number of years after 1912 when the company became part of the Midland Railway. Locomotive allocations were shown as LT&S Section without the individual shed being shown, although as Hawkins and Reeve point out, a March allocation list does refer to P.T.S. or U. A list that appeared later in the year gave the sheds

Right:
Old No 15 now running as LMS 2091 at the coaling stage with the bunker of old No 25 (LMS No 2076) just visible. *Collection R. J. Essery*

Lower right:
No 1344 0-4-4T was one of several ex-Midland Railway locomotives to be allocated to the shed on the LT&S Section. This late 1930s picture shows the motor-fitted engine at Plaistow. *G. Y. Hemingway*

Below right:
No 2948, in Midland ownership, was a single-frame goods engine. By the time of this picture, in the mid-1920s, it was classified as a No 2 goods engine. A steam brake only engine, it is taking on coal and appears to have just had the fire cleaned. *Collection R. J. Essery*

numbers. Plaistow became 34, Tilbury 35, Upminster 36 and Shoeburyness 37. In 1935, the LMS reorganised its shed codes and the LT&S depots were renumbered within the 13 district. The main depot, Plaistow, became 13A, Tilbury 13C, Shoeburyness 13D and Upminster 13E. The missing number 13B was given to the old North London Railway shed at Devons Road.

As far as the actual locomotives were concerned, a copy of the Midland Railway allocation list for 30 April 1914 in my collection does not show any District numbers for LT&S section locomotives. The 30 November 1920 list of engines and the Districts to which they are allocated does give some details, although no reference is made to an LT&S District in the section that gave the various District Nos between 1, Derby, and 33, Carlisle. However, it does show that a number of engines were allocated to the LT&S which is how they were shown in the document. The locomotives were: 2-4-0 Nos 3, 44, (127 is shown crossed out and transferred to 16, Kentish Town), 134, 136, 137; 0-4-4T Nos 1405, 1406, 1416; 0-6-0T Nos 1667, 1786; 0-6-0 double-frame goods engines Nos 2454 (2589 is shown as ex-LT&S, now at 16, Kentish Town); 0-6-0 single-frame goods engines Class 2 Nos 3035, 3102, 3513 and 3528. All the original LT&S engines are shown, or it can be inferred from the list, as being stationed on the LT&S Section, with the exception of the 4-6-4T engines. On 30 November Nos 2100-2 and 2107 are shown as LT&S and Nos 2103-6 as 15, Cricklewood, but a list dated 13 January 1922 giving the position as at 30 November 1921, shows Nos 2100-2 and 2107 as being transferred from 15 (Cricklewood) to the LT&S Section.

I conclude this section about allocations by giving details contained in the LMS Locomotive Stock Book dated 8 April 1944. However, it must be remembered that the LT&SR engines had been subject to a degree of renumbering by that time. By this date none of the old 'No 1' class was still in service and the oldest engines were old 'No 37' class onwards. The Midland and LMS-built engines were included and the list is set out below.

2092-2109 LT&S 4-4-2 2PT
2110-2160 LT&S 4-4-2 3PT
2180-2193 LT&S 0-6-2 3FT

The allocations were: Nos 2092 19C Canklow; 2093 16D Mansfield; 2094/5 17B Burton; 2096 18C Hasland; 2097 13A Plaistow; 2098 16D Mansfield; 2099 16A Nottingham; 2100 13C Tilbury; 2101 16A Nottingham; 2102 18C Hasland; 2103/4 16A Nottingham; 2105 13A Plaistow; 2106 13D Shoeburyness; 2107 13C Tilbury; 2108/9 16A Nottingham; 2110 13A Plaistow; 2111 13D Shoeburyness; 2112-2117 13A Plaistow; 2116-2122 13D Shoeburyness; 2123/4 13A Plaistow; 2125 13C Tilbury; 2126/7 13A Plaistow; 2128 13D Shoeburyness; 2129/30 13A Plaistow; 2131-2139 13C Tilbury; 2140 13A Plaistow; 2141-2145 13C Tilbury; 2146-2156 13D Shoeburyness; 2157-2160 13A Plaistow; 2180 13C Tilbury; 2181-90 13A Plaistow, 2191/2 13D Shoeburyness; 2193 13A Plaistow; 1287 13E Upminster; 1290, 1360 13A Plaistow; 2500/1 13D Shoeburyness; 2503/7/14 all 13A Plaistow; 2526/32/5 all 13D Shoeburyness; 3035 13C Tilbury; 3358/85 13A Plaistow; 3478 13C Tilbury; 3559 13A Plaistow; 4259 13C Tilbury; 4297, 4530/80 all 13A Plaistow; 7235/47 7311/51 and 7458, all 13A Plaistow.

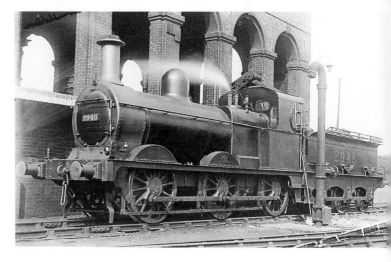

Continued page 70

Above left:
This final picture at Plaistow engine shed shows the front of old No 78 *Dagenham Dock*, an 0-6-2T engine now running as No 41989 in this *c*1950 picture. *Collection R. J. Essery*

Above:
This is the only photograph known to me that shows the original timber-built engine shed at Tilbury; the photographer of this 1890s picture was looking north-west. The most noteworthy aspect is the absence of trap points at the exit from the engine shed, suggesting this may be the original connection made in 1854, and the shed erected by the lessees. *Collection R. J. Essery*

Left:
Old No 30 as LMS No 2060 at Tilbury shed, carrying a Broad Street destination board. *Collection J. A. G. H. Coltas*

Shoeburyness was at the eastern end of the railway and supplied the motive power for the Southend to St Pancras trains. Most of the locomotives that can be seen are passenger tank engines but in the distance there are two Class 4F engines. It is possible that in this 27 June 1936 picture they have arrived on the shed after working excursion trains to Southend. *Collection H. F. Wheeller, courtesy Roger Carpenter*

Right:
Taken in April 1954, this picture shows both the brick-built shed at Shoeburyness and the 'lean-to', as it was sometimes called. Both the engines are 2-6-4Ts, one is three-cylinder No 42509 and the other a British Railways Standard, No 80076. *Photomatic/NRM*

Below:
In keeping with the work undertaken by this depot these three locomotives, seen at Shoeburyness on 14 June 1958, are all passenger tank engines, Nos 42500 and 42503 being visible. *Collection R. J. Essery*

In comparison with the other sheds on the LT&SR, Upminster was small. The original shed was replaced in 1931 when the station was enlarged, and this c1950 view shows the replacement that was built for the few engines stationed there. *Collection R. J. Essery*

Photographed on 11 June 1938, this picture shows motor train-fitted 0-4-4T engine No 1287 on a Romford service at Upminster. The shed dealt with the local branch passenger services and was the home of the motor-fitted tank engines working on the two branch lines. *H. C. Casserley 14874*

The hard water in this part of England caused considerable problems for the operating staff on the LT&S Section and order No 5900, dated 4 April 1923, was for a hot water washing out plant for Plaistow engine shed. This was followed by order No 5951 dated 21 June 1923. This order was the authority to fit engines Nos 2100-2107, 2120-2179 and 2200-2209 with adapters for blow-off cocks, to drawing No S-4016. Engines Nos 2180-2193 and 2898/99 were to be fitted with MR blow-off cocks for the firebox to drawing No S-4024. The material was to be prepared at Derby and sent to Plaistow for fitting.

The best source of pictures of LT&SR coaches is the book by R. W. Rush. Details are given in the Bibliography, but they are largely official side elevations. Therefore I have included a few pictures of LT&SR coaches in service, some during their final years and carrying their allotted British Railways prefixed and suffixed numbers.

Taken at Tilbury in September 1932, this picture shows the saloon that was built in 1912 to Diagram 43 and originally numbered 4 by the company. The saloon was 9ft wide and 47ft 8in long over the body. The Midland Railway renumbered the vehicle 2799 and the LMS renumbered it 817 in 1933. Withdrawal from service was in December 1945. *Photomatic/NRM*

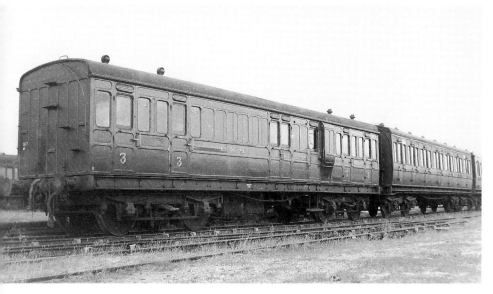

LT&SR Diagram 26 was a bogie brake third 8ft wide, 46ft long over the body with seating for 40 passengers. There was a large central luggage compartment. In total, 15 vehicles were built between 1906 and 1911. This coach began life in 1906 as LT&SR No 67, becoming MR 4305 in 1912 and LMS 2677 in 1923 and then 22854 in 1933. It was withdrawn in June 1939. There was some movement in carriages on the LT&S Section; some of the Midland Railway close-coupled sets that were originally used in the Birmingham District were sent to the LT&S Section and old coaches moved elsewhere. This picture was taken at Deganwy in Wales and was an example of the 'cascading down' that took place. *L&GRP 23659*

It was not unusual to reclassify coaches from first to third class and No M10497 is one such example that was photographed at Upminster c1949. Built in 1910 to Diagram 6 the carriage was 8ft wide, 48ft over the body and seated 36 passengers. A total of 20 was built between 1901 and 1911. This coach was originally LT&SR No 73. The Midland Railway renumbered it 2486 and in 1933 it became No 10497. Withdrawal came in November 1955. *Collection R. J. Essery*

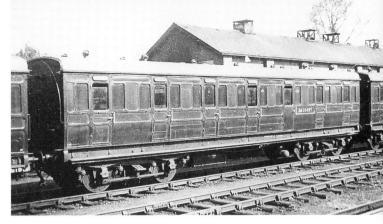

Carriages

Other than references in photographs, I do not propose to cover the subject of coaches that ran over the LT&SR. Two books have dealt with the vehicles owned by the company and both are still in print. The first was the second volume of the work by R. E. Lacy and George Dow, the second was by R. W. Rush, and details are given in the Bibliography. Both provide details of the company's stock that passed to the Midland and later to the London, Midland & Scottish Railway companies. A further source is the work of David Jenkinson and myself that is now under the OPC imprint; this contains details of the coaching stock that was built by the LMS for use on the LT&S Section.

The only other point that I would make is that although drawings for both Midland Railway and LMS coaches have survived and are at the NRM, no drawings of LT&SR coaches are known to exist. It is possible that some drawings are in private collections but model makers should treat drawings generated from LT&SR diagrams with caution.

Above right:
The roof end profiles of LT&SR coaches can be clearly seen in this picture. The coach on the right is the end of No M10497, described above; the brake third No M22863 is another example of Diagram 26. This coach was built in 1911 as LT&SR No 76 and became Midland Railway No 4314 and in 1923 LMS No 2715. The LMS renumbered the vehicle 22863 in 1933 and it was withdrawn from service in February 1955. *Collection R. J. Essery*

Centre right:
LT&SR Diagram 10 was an 8ft wide, 48ft long composite coach that carried 16 first and 60 third class passengers. Some of the 21 coaches allocated to this diagram were 8ft 4in wide, including the example shown here, but the seating remained the same. Beginning life as LT&SR No 44, it was built in 1911 and was renumbered 3841 by the Midland Railway the following year. In 1933, the coach became LMS No 17316 and it was withdrawn from service in August 1955. I am unable to explain the 96-seat branding; there were six third and two first class compartments at five per side, which equals only 80, so the intention must have been to carry six per side, including the old first class that would have been reclassified as thirds. *Collection R. J. Essery*

Bottom right:
This brief look at LT&SR coaches is concluded with this picture, taken at Shoeburyness on 11 March 1956 of a restored third class vehicle, No 283. Built in 1910 to Diagram 18, which totalled 70 vehicles, the coach became Midland Railway No 2300 and in 1933 LMS No 14035. The width was originally 8ft and the length 46ft over the body. They carried 80 passengers in eight compartments. Some, including No 283, were 8ft 4in wide, while others were equipped with lavatories which reduced the seating to 66 passengers.
T. J. Edgington

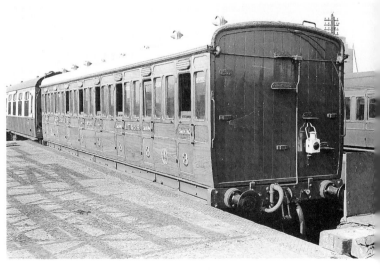

Freight Stock

Other than sketches of individual wagons the only information on LT&SR wagons will be found in two sources, *Midland Wagons* Volume 2 by myself, and by R. W. Rush. The latter based his book on my original research so both books can be considered as one. To the best of my knowledge no drawings of LT&SR wagons have survived. I published the diagrams in my book, while Rush has made drawings based upon the diagrams.

Ferry Steamers

During the early years of the company the ferry traffic at Gravesend and Tilbury was of great importance and no examination of the London, Tilbury & Southend Railway can ignore this aspect of the 'railway'. For my part, I have chosen to represent this aspect pictorially by use of these pictures with extended captions and timetable details of ferry services.

Hudd Automatic Train Control

No description of the LT&S Section would be complete without a reference to the Hudd system of automatic train control. The first LMS experiments took place on the Buxton branch at Ashwood Dale in 1932 and by 1935 the Ministry of Transport had given provisional sanction to a major installation. In addition to fitting the equipment at the lineside and signals, the locomotives had to be fitted with the necessary receiving equipment. The LT&S Section was the area selected for the installation and all the engines stationed at the sheds in the Section, together with those engines stationed in the London area that could work over the LT&S lines, were also equipped. The work begins with Derby Works order number 9161, dated 3 July 1935. The locomotives were fitted with the equipment at Bow Works. World War 2 hindered progress and it was not until the end of 1947 that the Hudd ATC system was finally brought into use on the LT&S Section.

The development of Hudd ATC is a subject that has, to the best of my knowledge, never been described by any railway historian to date. While it would be possible to give full details of all the LT&SR engines that were so equipped, the entire subject is too large for the space available here.

Fig 22 The Rates and Conditions make interesting reading; I wonder how many corpses were conveyed at 10s (50p) per trip?

This is a series of views of the Gravesend, Tilbury and the ferry steamers. The oldest ferry steamer illustrated was the TSS *Rose* built by A. W. Robertson of London in 1901; it was withdrawn in 1961. Others in the 20th century fleet were:

TSS *Catherine* built by A. W. Robertson, London 1903, withdrawn 1960;
TSS *Gertrude* built by A. W. Robertson, London 1906, withdrawn 1932 (sold to New Medway SP Company);
TSS *Edith* built by A. W. Robertson 1911, withdrawn 1961;
TSS *Tessa* built by Lytham Shipbuilding & Engineering Co. Ltd 1924, withdrawn 31.12.1964;
TSS *Mimie* built by Ferguson Bros (Port of Glasgow) Ltd 1927, withdrawn 31.12.1964;
TSMV *Edith* (ii) built by White's Shipyards (Southampton) Ltd 1961, laid up 1992;
The *Edith* (ii) had two sister ships, the *Catherine* (ii) and the *Rose* (ii), built by White's Shipyards (Southampton) Ltd.
The *Catherine* went to the River Tyne in 1961 and the *Rose* to the River Clyde in 1961, where it was renamed *Keppel* in 1967.
The *Tessa* and *Mimie* were vehicle and passenger ferries, the others were passenger-only ferries.
(TSS — twin-screw steamship; TSMV — twin-screw motor vessel; PS — paddle steamer.)

The information about the earlier ferries is less complete but I believe they were as below.

PS *Tilbury/Sir Walter Raleigh* 1855-1905
PS *Earl of Essex* 1855-?
PS *Earl of Leicester* 1855-?
PS *Cato* 1849-? Acquired 1873
PS *Thames* 1868-1913
PS *Tilbury* (ii) 1883-1922
TSS *Carlotta* Built by A. W. Robertson, London, 1893, withdrawn 1930
(*Information courtesy John Edgington*)

Above Left:
This view of Tilbury, taken in 1922, is looking downstream and shows the station before the LMS built the Riverside terminal. The ships alongside are believed to be the *Rose* and *Catherine*. Note the vessel on the slips behind the pier. *Derby Collection NRM DY12420*

Top Right:
Taken in February 1922, this illustrates the TSS *Rose* approaching the passenger pier at Gravesend. *Derby Collection NRM DY12414*

Above right:
TSS *Gertrude* at the Gravesend West Pier in February 1922. *Derby Collection NRM DY12417*

Lower right:
TSS *Catherine* at the Gravesend passenger pier, February 1922. *Derby Collection NRM DY12413*

Left:
TSS *Edith* in February 1922, the picture showing the ferry off Gravesend. *Derby Collection NRM DY12415*

Above:
Gravesend West Street Pier with TSS *Gertrude*. A wagon on the London, Chatham & Dover pier is just visible on the original print, to the right of the chimneys and to the left of the ferry. Although the LT&SR had ceased to exist ten years before this photograph was taken, the legend on the end of the building still reads London, Tilbury & Southend Railway Goods & Cattle Station. *Derby Collection NRM DY12411*

Ten years separate these two pictures of the road entrance to the Gravesend passenger pier. The February 1922 picture is interesting. The London, Tilbury & Southend legend remains in place ten years after the company became part of the Midland Railway, but understandably, all the posters are examples of Midland Railway advertising. Judging by the poster that advocated travel by rail and 'Get your Christmas shopping done early', this 1932 view was taken towards the end of the year. The LMS has made some changes; its notices are bolder and more prominent. On the 1922 picture the information about the goods and cattle station in West Street had been inscribed on the stone pillar, but the LMS replaced this with a notice board that was clearer but gave no new information. I can only presume this was part of the attempt to create a corporate image for the company. *Derby Collection NRM DY12409 & DY17718*

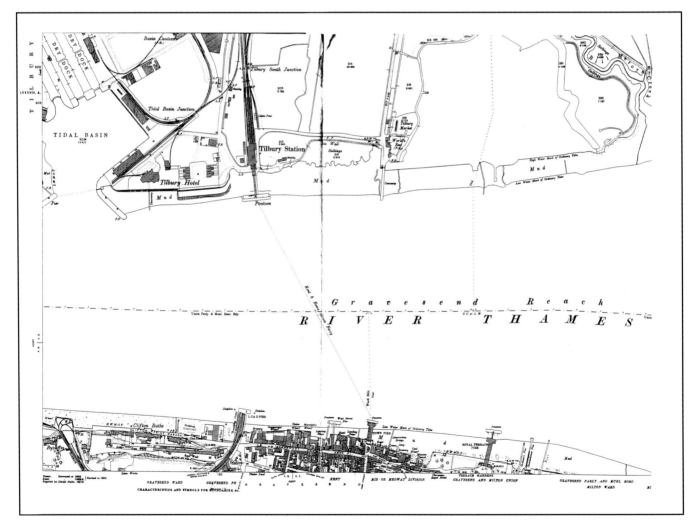

Fig 23. I have included this section of an 1895 OS map in order to show the station and ferry at Tilbury, together with the facilities at Gravesend. At Tilbury there was a single pontoon but at Gravesend there were four. To the west there was the London, Chatham & Dover Railway's station and pier, with the West Street pier to the east. Further east lay the Town Pier, which was used for passengers and, finally, the Royal Terrace Pier. The volume of passenger traffic that came downstream to Gravesend explains the abundance of piers there.

FERRY STEAMERS

Will run as under, weather and other circumstances permitting.

GRAVESEND TO TILBURY.

WEEK DAYS.

Rosherville dep. A.M.	West St. dep. A.M.	Town Pier dep. A.M.	Tilbury arr. A.M.
...	5 30	...	5 35
...	6 30	...	6 35
...	...	7 5	7 10
...	...	7 25	7 30
...	...	7 58	8 3
...	...	8 10	8 15
8 32	...	8 40	8 45
...	...	9 15	9 20
...	...	9 30	9 35
...	...	10 0	10 5
...	...	10 8	10 13
...	...	10 48	10 53
...	...	11 13	11 18
...	...	11 28	11 33
P.M.		**P.M.**	**P.M.**
...	...	12 0	12 5
...	...	12 28	12 28
...	...	12 38	12 43
...	...	12 48	12 53
...	...	1 30	1 35
...	...	1 48	1 53
...	...	2 30	2 35
...	...	2 53	2 58
...	...	3 15	3 20
...	...	3 43	3 48
...	...	4 5	4 10
...	...	4 33	4 38
...	...	4 52	4 57
...	...	5 3	5 7
...	...	5 35	5 40
...	...	6 10	6 15
...	...	6 25	6 30
...	...	6 45	6 50
...	...	7 13	7 18
...	...	8 5	8 10
...	...	8 43	8 48
...	...	9 40	9 45
...	...	10 35	10 40

SUNDAYS.

West St. dep. A.M.	Town Pier dep. A.M.	Tilbury arr. A.M.
...	9 0	9 5
...	9 30	9 35
...	10 5	10 10
...	10 30	10 35
...	11 50	11 55
	P.M.	**P.M.**
...	1 0	1 5
...	2 55	3 0
...	4 30	4 35
...	5 30	5 35
...	6 0	6 5
...	7 0	7 5
...	7 55	8 0
...	8 40	8 45
...	9 28	9 33
...	10 10	10 15

TILBURY TO GRAVESEND.

WEEK DAYS.

Tilbury dep. A.M.	Town Pier arr. A.M.	West St. arr. A.M.	Rosherville arr. A.M.
6 15	...	...	...
7 3	7 8	...	...
7 21	7 26	...	...
8 8	8 13	...	...
8 48	8 53	...	...
8 50	8 55	8 20	...
9 28	9 33	...	...
10 0	10 5	...	...
10 15	10 20	...	...
10 48	10 53	...	...
11 23	11 28	...	...
11 40	11 45	...	...
P.M.	**P.M.**		
12 0	12 5	...	...
12 35	12 40	...	...
12 50	12 55	...	...
1 15	1 20	...	...
1 41	1 46	...	...
2 41	2 46	...	...
3 5	3 10	...	...
3 37	3 42	...	...
3 55	4 0	...	...
4 25	4 30	...	...
4 45	4 50	...	...
5 2	5 7	...	...
5 27	5 32	...	...
6 5	6 10	...	6 15
6 20	6 43	...	...
6 38	6 43	...	...
7 0	7 5	...	...
7 25	7 30	...	...
8 15	8 20	...	...
8 53	8 58	...	...
10 0	10 5	...	...
10 50	10 55	...	...

SUNDAYS

Tilbury dep. A.M.	Town Pier arr. A.M.	West St. arr. A.M.
...	9 15	...
9 40	9 45	...
10 18	10 23	...
10 40	10 45	...
P.M.	**P.M.**	
12 8	12 13	...
1 10	1 15	...
3 10	3 15	...
4 40	4 45	...
5 37	5 42	...
6 15	6 20	...
7 10	7 15	...
8 5	8 10	...
8 53	8 58	...
9 35	9 40	...
10 48	10 53	...

* These Boats do not run in connection with Trains and the times are subject to alteration during the month.

SHIP PASSENGERS.

TILBURY DOCKS.

Passengers to and from Ships lying in the Tilbury Docks are conveyed direct by Express Train from and to Fenchurch Street Station.

PASSENGERS FOR THE

PENINSULAR & ORIENTAL STEAM NAVIGATION CO.'S STEAMERS

ARE CONVEYED by EXPRESS TRAIN from LIVERPOOL ST. STATION to TILBURY, and Embarked on board their Ships lying in the River off Gravesend by Steam Tender.

PASSENGERS FOR THE

Ships of the BRITISH INDIA STEAM NAVIGATION Co., the NEW ZEALAND SHIPPING Co., and the SHAW, SAVILL and ALBION and other Companies.

Are also conveyed direct to the Ships from FENCHURCH STREET STATION.

Passengers arriving at Gravesend by Homeward-bound Ships not going into Tilbury Docks are conveyed by Steam Tender to Tilbury, and thence by Special Train to London when the arrival ot the Ships does not meet the departure of the Ordinary Trains. For further particulars apply at the Offices of the Shipping Companies.

By the time this picture was taken in 1932 the LMS had marked the change of ownership at West Street Pier, Gravesend. *Derby Collection NRM DY17722*

Left:
Fig 24 The service between Tilbury and Gravesend was very good, as this 1889 timetable confirms.

Above:
Gravesend Goods & Cattle Station from the road entrance in February 1922. *Derby Collection NRM DY12410*

Below:
This view shows TSS *Catherine* at the Town passenger pier in February 1922. *Derby Collection NRM DY12412*

3. The Traffic Worked

Any description of the various traffics carried by the London, Tilbury & Southend Railway in the years prior to the 1923 Grouping must take account of two factors, beginning with growth of the LT&SR system. My interpretation of the word 'system' means lines owned by the company, together with those lines over which the LT&SR exercised running powers, which may or may not have been exercised in full. In addition, some account must be taken of other companies' running powers over the LT&SR. These connections provided the basis for the development of the traffic flows and they are examined below.

The other factor was the development of what can best be called 'traffic generators'. For example, the opening of Tilbury Docks in 1886, which in time became a major source of traffic, was one, while the ferry between Tilbury and Gravesend, that had existed prior to the opening of the railway, was another. The ferry was a prime reason for the railway being constructed and for many years it was a major source of passenger revenue. Furthermore, since the revenue from freight was, as we have seen, minimal prior to the opening of the docks at Tilbury, the revenue from passenger traffic was vital for the well-being of the company.

This chapter looks at a variety of subjects using, where possible, prime source material. I begin with a comparison of the LT&S and Midland railways' traffic returns for the year

immediately prior to the LT&SR becoming part of the Midland Railway; later, by use of some 1915 material, we can examine the passenger coaching stock and locomotive diagrams at that time. I do not think that similar material has been published before and, with the LT&SR being such a compact railway, it is possible to work out what happened without too much guesswork. A number of other sources have been consulted including the 1890 working timetable and later editions of Midland and LMS public and working timetables.

Following the opening of the line between Barking and Pitsea in 1888, the company was to have in effect two routes to Southend. The most southerly one was via Tilbury and was known as the main line, the distance from Fenchurch Street to Southend being about 42 miles. The direct route, which in effect bypassed Tilbury, saved six miles and was 36 miles in length. In mileage terms the LT&SR route from London to Southend was 5½ miles less than the competing GER route. The Gravesend to Tilbury ferry service, which became a company monopoly at an early date, was another important source of traffic.

The connection with the GER over the Tottenham & Forest Gate Railway and via Forest Gate Junction enabled through carriages to be attached or detached at Barking as well as assisting the movement of GER goods trains, although as far

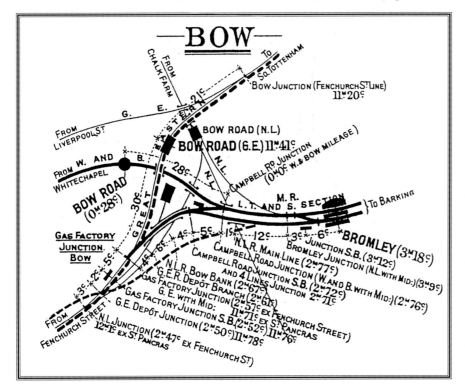

Left:
Fig 25 The complex system of railways in the Bow area is shown on this extract of a Midland Railway distance diagram dated 1919 which helps to show the route being taken by No 31 seen in the photo at the top of p.81.

Right:
Fig 26 A comparison of the working expenses, net receipts and rolling stock of the Midland Railway and the London, Tilbury & Southend Railway as at 31 December 1911

as goods traffic is concerned, its importance was probably less than the NLR's Poplar branch. This line gave an exit and entry for the 'northern companies' to the London docks, in particular for the LNWR and Midland Railway, although in the case of the latter company, it was the joint construction with the GER of the Tottenham & Hampstead Junction Railway that enabled Midland trains to gain direct access to the LT&SR system. In passenger traffic terms it was the joint venture with the Metropolitan District Railway, in the form of the Whitechapel & Bow, which opened in 1902, that was to be in the long term the most important development undertaken by the LT&SR for passenger traffic. This gave the company a number of London starting and terminating points for passengers, a statement that requires some qualification.

The use of the London & Blackwall Railway station at Fenchurch Street provided the company with its headquarters and principal London terminus or, in traffic terms, the destination or starting point for passenger traffic. Another starting point was Liverpool Street, with Barking acting as the junction for passengers to change trains, while St Pancras also provided a further valuable traffic source. However, the Whitechapel & Bow was rather different. The developing London Underground system was able to move people quickly and in large numbers. As we have seen over the years, without it London's traffic would have ground to a halt. The connection that was made between the LT&SR at Bow and the eastward development of the electrified lines, in parallel with the LT&SR to Barking, which was reached in 1908, transformed the travelling time for passengers who lived near stations further to the east. They were able to begin their journey at an LT&SR station, travel west and then change trains and join the Metropolitan District Railway system. By using this route they could journey to the various London stations best suited to their needs, rather than be set down at one City terminal and then have to make their way on again by road, foot or as may be, because Fenchurch Street had no direct connection to the Underground system.

As the London Underground system developed so the potential for additional traffic increased. Although they are perhaps slightly outside of the terms of reference that I have set, I cannot but note some of these developments that have affected the railway's ability to handle the ever-increasing passenger traffic. In 1930, an LMS programme provided for two additional tracks to be laid between Barking and

Fig 26

The Midland and London, Tilbury & Southend Railways Compared: Working Expenses, Net Receipts and Rolling Stock as at 31 December 1911
(Source: Railway Returns 1911)

	MR	LT&SR
Length of line open at 31.12.1911 (miles)	1,532	79
Maintenance of way, works, etc	£1,220, 655	£61,610
Locomotive power, including stationary engines	£2,316,000	£103,934
Repairs and renewals of carriages and wagons	£778,421	£32,274
Traffic expenses: coaching and merchandise	£2,738,827	£118,201
General charges	£272,494	£35,553
Rates and taxes	£442,910	£40,783
Government passenger duty	£16,606	£1,446
Subscriptions or donations to hospitals, schools etc, not under direct control for the exclusive benefit of company servants	£1,447	£287
Compensation to employees under Workmen's Compensation Acts1897 and 1906	£22,048	£930
Compensation for personal injuries	£3,331	£211
Compensation for damage and loss of goods	£53,549	£1,074
Legal and parliamentary expenses	-	£4,433
Steamboat canal and harbour expenses	£121,688	£12,350
Misc work expenses not covered in foregoing	£651,318	£1,870
Total working expenses	**£8,665,191**	**£415,510**
Total receipts	**£13,809,395**	**£695,643**
Net receipts	**£5,144,204**	**£280,093**
Proportion of expenditure to total receipts	**63%**	**60%**
Locomotives	2,800	82
Rail motor carriages — steam	2	-
Rail motor carriages — electric	3	43
Passenger coaches	3635	559
Non-passenger coaching stock	1,849	45
Wagons of all types, goods, mineral and brake vans	117,571	1,844
Service stock	*	62
Total number of vehicles	**123,060**	**2,553**

Notes Midland Railway figures do not include any returns for its Irish operations.
*Not shown as a separate figure. Included within 117,571.

Upminster together with the upgrading of Gale Street from halt to station status. New stations were opened with additional carriage sidings, and other facilities were added to help cope with the increased number of trains. District Line trains commenced running to Upminster from 12 September 1932. The Elm Park housing estate, claimed to be the largest single private housing enterprise built in Britain to that date, added further to the traffic potential. I could continue, but as I have said, the post-1923 developments are largely beyond the scope of this work and interested readers are referred to the Bibliography of published works about the company. Here, the reader will find the story of the more recent developments of the Tilbury section.

As we have seen, the LT&SR was a passenger line. A statement, which can easily be proved by referring to the annual returns for the company and comparing them with the results from other British railway companies. In order to illustrate this I have included extracts from the Railway Returns of 1911, the last complete year of the company's independence. Additional information has been extracted from the *Railway Yearbook* and I begin by setting this out below. The company was owned by 1,200 Debenture and 3,750 Preference and Ordinary shareholders and it is worth noting traces of nepotism within the organisation!

The *Railway Yearbook* is a fascinating document and below are extracts from the 1911 edition. The entry starts with a concise history of the line and it goes on to say, 'For further information reference may be made to the following articles in *The Railway Magazine*' and then quotes three references. Needless to say, these have been used in this book; however, it is worth pointing out that *The Railway Magazine* and *The Railway Yearbook* were owned by the same company, namely the Railway Publishing Company. Such is the historical importance of this information that it is reproduced in the same format even though some information is not strictly related to the subject of traffic.

LONDON, TILBURY AND SOUTHEND RAILWAY
GENERAL OFFICES
FENCHURCH STREET STATION

DIRECTORS

ARTHUR LEWIS STRIDE, Esq., (Chairman and Managing Director), Bush Hall, Hatfield, Herts.

JAMES ROLLS HOARE, Esq., (Deputy-Chairman), 48, Mount Street, W.

CECIL BROWN. Esq., 9, Ennerdale Road, Kew Gardens, S.W.

FRANCIS CLAUGHTON MATHEWS Esq., Bradbourne Park House, Sevenoaks.

CAPTAIN HERBERT MERTON JESSEL, MP, 50, Mount Street, W.

RT. HON. JAMES ROUND, Birch Hall, Colchester.

FREDERICK WHINNEY, Esq., 85, Avenue Road, Regent's Park, N.W.

CHIEF OFFICERS
(Unless otherwise stated, the addresses of the Officers are at the General Offices as above)

Secretary and Accountant—H. CECIL NEWTON, 41, Trinity Square, Tower Hill, E.C.

Manager—B. BULLOCK.

Goods Manager—E. CHALK, 137, Leman Street, E.

Engineer—JAS. H. ROBERTSON. Mem. Inst.C.E.

Auditors—ARTHUR FRANCIS WHINNEY, 411, Frederick's Place, Old Jewry, E.C., and BASIL HUGH STRIDE, 18 and 19, Ironmonger Lane. E.C.

Solicitors—F. C. MATHEWS & CO., 151, Cannon Street, E.C.

Locomotive, Carriage, Wagon, and Marine Superintendent—ROBERT H. WHITELEGG, Locomotive Works, Plaistow, E.

Bankers—LONDON COUNTY AND WESTMINSTER BANK, LTD., Lothbury.

There were no Changes in the Directorate and Official Staff during 1911.

Telegraphic Addresses and Telephone Numbers of Principal Departments

Managing Director and Manager …	Letser, London …	4376 Avenue
Secretary …	Cecinimus, London …	4375 '
Goods Manager …	Goods, c/o Letser, London …	2195 '
Engineer …	Engineer, c/o Letser …	4376 '
Locomotive Superintendent …	London …	693 Stratford

From the statistical information shown in the table reproduced here it will be seen that these were, size notwithstanding, very different railways. In many respects the financial results achieved by the LT&SR, expressed in percentage terms, were better than those of the Midland Railway. However, we look at this aspect in greater detail below.

Number of Passengers Conveyed

First Class: LT&SR	322,278	Midland	897,764
Third Class: LT&SR	34,077,660	Midland	49,639,853
Season or Periodical Tickets: LT&SR	34,400,238	Midland	50,539,617

(The passenger totals for season tickets are probably based upon 313 per annum x 2 per ticket.)

Goods Traffic in Tons

Minerals: LT&SR	682,641	Midland	41,780,500
Merchandise: LT&SR	547,685	Midland	9,481,053

Number of Miles Travelled by Train

(Train miles per annum in modern terms)

	Passenger	*Goods & Mineral*	*Total*
LT&SR	2,235,921	293,208	2,529,129
Midland	22,441,551	26,394,922	48,836,473

Gross Receipts From Passenger Traffic

	First Class	*Third Class*	*Season Tickets*	*Total*
LT&SR	£30,943	£349,384	£110,621	£480,994
Midland	£214,305	£2,705,914	£335,009	£3,255,228

Other Sources, Excess Luggage, Parcels		*Mails incl Receipts for Carriage of Mails Belonging to Other Coys, Carriages, Horses and Dogs*	
LT&SR	£26,486	LT&SR	£884
Midland	£821,335	Midland	£82,005

Grand Total From All Forms of Passenger Rated Traffic

LT&SR	£508,568	Midland	£4,158,568

Gross Receipts From Goods Traffic

	Merchandise	*Livestock*	*Minerals*	*Total*
LT&SR	£111,458	£313	£36,025	£147,796
Midland	£3,680,230	£102,331	£4,898,723	£8,681,284

Receipts from steamboats, canals, harbours, docks, etc	LT&SR	£15,331	Midland	£105,658
Misc rent, tolls, hotels, etc	LT&SR	£24,148	Midland	£863,885

Total Gross Receipts From All Sources

LT&SR	£695,643
Midland	£13,809,395

Before we begin to look at the train services in greater detail, it is worth noting a few comparisons between these two companies. The income from the LT&SR in its final full year amounted to approximately 5.04% of that generated by the new owners or, as we would say today, the acquisition of the LT&SR by the Midland Railway gave it a 5.04% increase in turnover. However the source of these earnings or receipts, as they were described, was very different. While the Midland Railway generated 30.11% of its income from passenger rated traffic, the LT&SR achieved 73.07%. The Midland Railway's great strength was its income from goods and mineral traffic that made up 62.87% of the total earnings or, in comparative terms, almost three times as much as the percentage achieved by the LT&SR.

Miscellaneous receipts from sources such as hotels, rent tolls and various maritime activity saw the Midland generating, again expressed in percentage terms, almost twice the LT&SR's 3.48%, at 6.23%. It should be noted that the sums

Bethnal Green was the junction of the Great Eastern's lines from both Bishopsgate and Liverpool Street, one going north through Cambridge Heath, the other to Bow, Stratford and Forest Gate. This undated picture shows a 'No 1' class engine with four-wheeled coaches at Bethnal Green; the photographer was looking east. *Collection R. J. Essery*

expressed above do not equate with the grand totals and reflect only traffic income — there were other income sources — but I felt that the figures given above show a clear picture of the variation between the LT&SR and the Midland Railway.

In order to examine the story of the traffic conveyed over the LT&SR we need to begin by summarising the principal changes that took place over the years to see how the railway was enlarged to respond to the changes in the traffic patterns. These are expressed in simple chronological order.

All Opened by 1856
A passenger service from London using Fenchurch Street and Bishopsgate as the termini with combining or separation of trains at Stratford for services to and from Tilbury and Southend.

All Opened by 1858
Thames Haven branch — becomes goods only in 1880 apart from some special passenger trains and workmen's trains.

Direct line from Barking to Gas Factory Junction enables the Stratford arrangements of combining or separating trains to cease, with no further use made of Bishopsgate as a London terminus by the LT&SR.

Effective by 1869
Connection made with the NLR Bow to Bromley branch. NLR starts to run excursion trains to Southend. LNWR and NLR now have running powers over entire LT&SR system.

Effective by 1888
Tilbury Docks complex and Commercial Road goods station opened. A direct line to Southend between Barking and Pitsea open. Line extended from Southend to Shoeburyness in 1884.

Completed by 1892/3
Branches between Romford and Upminster and Upminster and Grays opened throughout.

Effective by 1894
Tottenham & Forest Gate, joint railway with Midland Company.

Effective by 1902
Whitechapel & Bow, joint railway with the District Railway.

Effective by 1908
Track widening between Campbell Road Junction and Barking.

Effective by 1912
Running powers granted to GNR for goods trains to Tilbury Docks, (part of the terms included in the act that allowed the MR takeover of the LT&SR).

Post-Midland Takeover and Grouping Developments

Although not strictly part of the LT&SR story, I have recorded the following:

Purfleet Rifle Range Halt opened in 1911 as a private halt and was made a public station in October 1921. LMS trains to the Southend area started to run to and from Broad Street station (ex-North London Railway) via Bow from Monday 1 January 1923. Clearly, negotiations between the various offices concerned were in progress before the Grouping came into effect. This service ceased on 28 February 1935 when the Fenchurch Street remodelling was almost completed. Gale

Taken at Bow, North London Railway on 25 June 1912, this shows No 31 *St Pancras*, when the locomotive was working the 7.28am from Southend to Chalk Farm. The photographer was looking south and the footbridge is part of the passage linking the NLR station to the Great Eastern's at Bow Road.
Ken Nunn/LCGB

Both the LNWR and the North London Railway enjoyed running powers over the LT&SR. This picture, taken at Cranham on 5 August 1913, shows a NLR 4-4-0T engine now running as LNWR No 29 at the head of a Chalk Farm to Southend excursion train.
K. A. C. R. Nunn

Street opened in 1926, followed by Southend East in 1932, Chalkwell in 1933, Elm Park in 1935 and East Tilbury in 1936.

Industrial units began to appear on the north bank of the Thames, including the arrival of the Ford Motor Company in 1924. There were other industries in this area, notably chalk quarries, and some of this traffic was rail connected.

Modernisation of Fenchurch Street, a joint LNER/LMS project to cope with increased traffic, was completed in April 1935.

Miscellaneous Traffic Information, Pre-1890 Services

The first trains to Tilbury commenced or terminated in London at either Fenchurch Street or Bishopsgate and these trains were combined on the outward or down direction at Stratford, or divided at this point when working in the up direction. This practice ceased on 31 March 1858 whereupon all LT&SR traffic commenced or terminated at Fenchurch Street. According to K. A. Frost, writing in *Railways South East*, the April 1856 timetable showed only three down trains, which ran as follows: 9.22am departure from Fenchurch Street arriving at Tilbury at 10.30. This train then departed at 10.35am for Southend, arriving at 11.28am, a journey of 2hr 6min. The next train, the 2.7pm, arrived at Southend at 4.13pm.

The final down train of the day left Fenchurch Street at 5.37pm and did not stop at Rainham, Purfleet or Grays, reducing the journey time to 1hr 53min. The time of arrival at Southend was 7.30pm. The up trains took 2hr 7min or 2hr 5min for the journey and the respective departure and arrival times were: 8.43am/10.50am; 1.45pm/3.50pm; 5.33pm/7.40pm.

The same source gave details of an early up morning express in December 1865 from Southend. The times for this train were: Southend depart 8.20am, Tilbury arrive 8.50, depart at 8.57, with a Fenchurch Street arrival at 9.40. It is not possible to say how long this service ran, but there was a train with a similar timing in the 1890 working timetable. After the LT&SR became independent and responsible for its own train service the same source records that the directors set about improving train services, revising fares and adding third class carriages to all trains. However, from the working timetable it can be seen that some services in 1890 were express services that carried first and second class passengers only. For example, trains 101 (5.5pm dep Fenchurch Street to Shoeburyness, arr 6.4pm) and 110 (6.8pm dep Fenchurch Street to Shoeburyness, arr 7.15pm) in the down direction did not carry third class passengers. The non-third class passenger trains in the up direction were trains 16 (7.43am Shoeburyness to Fenchurch Street, arr 8.50am) and 28 (8.55am Shoeburyness to Fenchurch Street arr 10am).

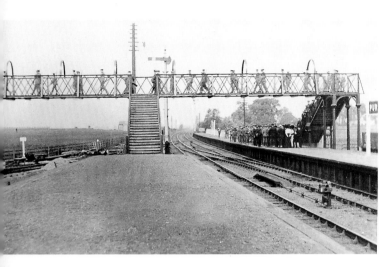

The pricing policy for the LT&SR was such that authorisation was obtained, due to the low fares currently in being, for services over the shorter direct line to be at the same mileage cost as those over the longer distance via Tilbury. It was said that this was done in order to help to recover the high construction costs of the direct line. Frost also records that two days after the formal opening of Tilbury Docks on 17 April 1886, the LT&SR introduced a service of two trains per hour to London between 9am and 7pm, one of which was to be an express. The traffic from the docks was slow to develop and in 1887 a receiver for the dock company was appointed, which helps to explain why the service declined, so that by 1890, the trains were departing from Tilbury at 8.50am, 9.40am, 10.18am, 11.23am and 12.33pm etc with a running time of between 45 and 58 minutes to Fenchurch Street.

The earliest authoritative working timetable known to the author is dated January 1890. This appeared after the opening of the direct line and the Tilbury Docks complex but before the completion of the Romford branch, or more importantly from the traffic standpoint, the connection with the Midland Railway via the Tottenham & Forest Gate joint line. This timetable has been summarised, and I hope that all the essential information has been included.

Before turning to the 1890 timetable I should briefly mention the early freight services which, prior to the opening of Tilbury Docks in 1886, were sparse. It would be very helpful if a copy of a c1885 or earlier working timetable was available, but in the absence of any firm evidence to the contrary I can only agree with the statements made by other writers that suggest it was the development of Tilbury Docks, the opening of Commercial Road goods station, and the post-1900 industrial developments along the north side of the Thames which helped to increase the freight business, the 1911 balance sheet of which is provided in the table shown here.

I have already referred to the January 1890 working timetable; at that date only 30 of the 'No 1' class were in service. I also have a copy of the October 1889 public timetable so between them it is possible to examine the train services at that time. The 1889 timetable begins with a summary of the Fenchurch Street to Southend and Shoeburyness services via both Tilbury and the direct line via Upminster.

The first train of the day from Fenchurch Street was the 6.18am, stopping at Stepney, Bromley, Plaistow, Upton Park, East Ham, Barking, Rainham, Purfleet, Grays, Tilbury Docks and Tilbury, with an arrival time of 7.16am. The departure time from Tilbury was 7.19am and the train stopped at Low Street,

Continued page 87

Southend East station was opened in 1932 and the name was changed to Southend-on-Sea East on 1 May 1949. Twenty years later, in 1969, the station became Southend East again. *Collection V. R. Anderson*

Taken on 23 July 1931, this shows the new work being undertaken at Upminster. The brake coach furthest from the camera is possibly to Diagram 21, a four-wheel brake third; the others appear to be six-compartment thirds to Diagram 17. *Collection R. J. Essery*

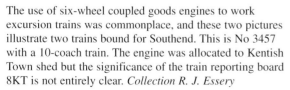

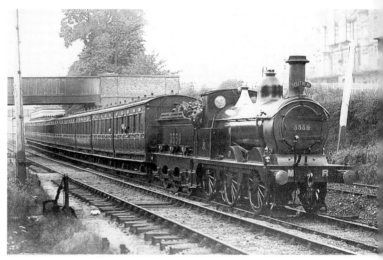

The use of six-wheel coupled goods engines to work excursion trains was commonplace, and these two pictures illustrate two trains bound for Southend. This is No 3457 with a 10-coach train. The engine was allocated to Kentish Town shed but the significance of the train reporting board 8KT is not entirely clear. *Collection R. J. Essery*

Leigh-on-Sea was a favourite place for photographers and the dip beneath the road bridge is clearly marked by the coach roofs. The locomotive is, to use the Midland Railway classification for when the picture was taken, a standard single-frame goods engine. The train of four-wheel coaches appears to be largely made of third class Diagram 495. These had five compartments, with six per side, the vehicles weighing just over 10 tons, but carried 60 people when every seat was filled. *Collection R. J. Essery*

The use of goods engines on excursion, or special passenger trains as the LT&SR called them, is shown in this undated picture. No 71 *Wakering* was one of the 1903 batch of locomotives seen at the head of a train heading for Southend. It appears to be made up of two sets; the leading vehicle is a brake third, probably to Diagram 21, followed by five, five-compartment third class vehicles to Diagram 15. The seventh coach is another brake third. The rest of the train could be a similar formation; unfortunately it is not possible to be sure. *Collection R. J. Essery*

I am not entirely sure of the precise location, but it was between Benfleet and Upminster and was favoured by a photographer who captured a variety of trains that show certain LT&S Section train formations. Old No 8 is in Midland Railway livery as 2207, its 1923 LMS number. The locomotive retains the MR on the buffer beam but there is no other sign of identity to be seen. The leading vehicle is a brake third to Diagram 19; the rear brake is probably to Diagram 21. The second, fourth, sixth and seventh are third class to either Diagram 11 or 15; the other two coaches are four-compartment vehicles and could be composites to Diagram 7 or firsts to Diagram 2, or one of each. *Collection A. G. Ellis 15348*

No 2128 began life as No 19 and in this picture the engine is in full pre-1928 LMS passenger engine livery heading a train for Barking. The leading vehicle is a third brake to Diagram 21 and the next three coaches are five-compartment third class vehicles. The next two are four-compartment, but I cannot be sure if they are first class or composites. Two more five-compartments third class follow and then there is a brake van; the remainder of the train cannot be identified. *Collection A. G. Ellis 15345*

'No 37' class No 47 *Stratford* heads an up passenger train of Midland Railway coaches for St Pancras near Upminster. *L&GRP 21303*

No 44 *Prittlewell* was a 'No 37' class engine that was rebuilt in 1911. This undated but prior to rebuilding picture shows the locomotive at the head of a train for Southend. The leading carriages are six-compartment six-wheel vehicles to Diagram 17 headed by a brake third to what appears to be Diagram 22. *L&GRP 21132*

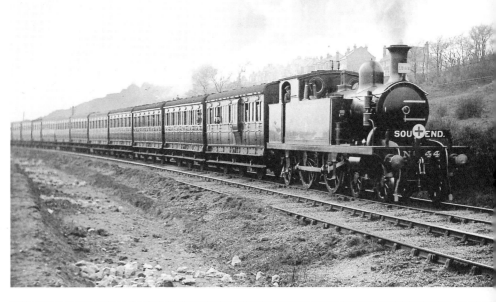

The eight-carriage Ealing to Southend trains would have been a splendid sight and compared very favourably with the austere four-wheel coaches that the LT&SR also operated. This picture was taken c1924 and shows one of the Baltic tank engines at the head of the train; the absence of a destination board makes it impossible to decide if it is bound for Southend or Ealing. The coaches were built in 1911 and the service ran until the outbreak of World War 2. The stock was only Westinghouse fitted, so either a Baltic or a dual-fitted 4-4-2T engine worked the train from Southend to Barking; in this case it is 4-6-4T No 2101. Between Barking and Ealing the motive power consisted of two of the District Railway's bogie electric locomotives. *Collection R. J. Essery*

This picture shows one of the 4-4-2T engines at the head of the Ealing to Southend train. The train engine is No 2149 that was originally No 40 *Black Horse Road* but was renamed *Benfleet* in 1910 when it was rebuilt as seen here. *L&GRP 5564.*

Thorpe Bay is the scene of this picture and the through train from Ealing to Southend is made up of LT&SR bogie stock. 'No 37' class rebuild, No 46 *Southchurch*, was given the original name of the station. Note the variation of the destination nameboard, with the addition of the 'Through Train Daily' to the Southend to Ealing branding.
Ken Nunn/LCGB

These two pictures were taken from the same place, which I believe is between Benfleet and Upminster. The locomotives are in pre-1928 LMS passenger livery, but note that the LMS emblem is on the bunker side of No 2121 and on the tank side of No 2154. The trains are Southend or Shoeburyness to Fenchurch Street and the composition varies. No 2154 has a train of LT&SR coaches, while that of No 2121 contains a number of Midland Railway vehicles. *Collection A. G. Ellis*

Fast Through Trains between DISTRICT RAILWAY and SOUTHEND-ON-SEA.

THE SHORTEST AND QUICKEST ROUTE FROM THE WEST END.

DOWN.	WEEK-DAYS.							SUNDAYS.			UP.	WEEK-DAYS.							SUNDAYS.		
				Not Sats.								‡		‡		‡					
	a.m.			p.m.		p.m.		a.m.	p.m.			a.m.		a.m.		p.m.			p.m.		
Ealing Broadway	8 5	...	...	8 36	...	1042	...	1026	9 54	...	Southend-on-Sea	5 0	...	7 15	...	8 5	...	...	7 40	...	...
Ealing Common	8 7	...	...	8 38	...	1044	...	1028	9 56	...	Westcliff-on-Sea	5 3	...	7 18	...	8 8	...	...	7 44	...	...
Acton Town	8 10	...	...	8 41	...	1047	...	1031	9 59	...	Leigh-on-Sea	5 7	...	7 23	...	8 13	...	...	7 50	...	...
Chiswick Park			...	8 43	...	1049	...	1033	10 1	...	Bow Road										
Turnham Green	8 14	...	...	8 45	...	1051	...	1035	10 4	...	Mile End	6 0	...	...	...	...	...	...			
Stamford Brook											Stepney Green										
Ravenscourt Pk.	...	...		...	...	...		...	...	...	Whitechapel			...	...	...			8 51	...	...
Hammersmith	8 18	...		8 50	...	1055		1040	10 9	...	Aldgate East	6 5	...	8 20	...	9 15	...	...	8 57	...	...
Barons Court	8 19	...		...	...	...		...	...		Mark Lane	6 7	...	8 22	...	9 17	...	...	8 59	...	...
West Kensington		...		8 53	...	1057		1042	1012	...	Monument	6 9	...	...	...	9 18	...	...			
Earls Court		...		8 56	...	11 0		1045	1015	...	Cannon Street	6 10	...	8 25	...	9 19	...	...	9 1	...	...
Gloucester Road				8 58	...	...		...	...		Mansion House	6 11	...	8 26	...	9 21	...	...	9 3	...	...
South Kensington	...			9 1	...	...		...	...	...	Blackfriars	6 12	...	8 27	...	9 22	...	...	9 4	...	...
Sloane Square	8 27	...		9 3	...	11 5		1051	1020	...	Temple	6 14	...	8 29	...	9 24	...	...	9 6	...	...
Victoria	8 29	...		9 5	...	11 7		1053	1022	...	Charing Cross	6 16	...	8 31	...	9 26	...	...	9 9	...	...
St. James' Park	8 31	...		9 7	...	11 9		1055	1024	...	Westminster	6 18	...	...	...	9 27	...	...			
Westminster	...					1110		1057	1025	...	St. James' Park	6 19	...	8 34	...	9 28	...	...	9 12	...	...
Charing Cross	8 34	...		9 10	...	1112		1059	1027	...	Victoria	6 21	...	8 36	...	9 30	...	...	9 14	...	...
Temple	8 35	...		9 11	...	1113		11 0	1028	...	Sloane Square	6 23	...	...	...	9 32	...	...			
Blackfriars	8 37	...		9 13	...	1115		11 2	1030	...	South Kensington	6 25	...	8 40	...	9 35	...	...			
Mansion House	8 39	...		9 15	...	1117		11 4	1032	...	Gloucester Road	6 27	...	...	...	9 37	...	...			
Cannon Street	8 40	...		9 16	...	1118		11 5	1033	...	Earls Court	6 30	...	8 44	...	9 39	...	...	9 22	...	...
Monument	...			9 17	...	...		11 6	1034	...	West Kensington	6 31	...	8 46	...	9 41	...	...	9 24	...	...
Mark Lane	8 42	...		9 19	...	1120		11 8	1036	...	Barons Court	6 33	...	...	...	...	...	...			
Aldgate East	8 44	...		...	...	1122		1110	1038	...	Hammersmith	6 35	...	8 48	...	9 43	...	...	9 26	...	...
Whitechapel				...	...	1124		1113	1042	...	Ravenscourt Pk.	6 36	...	...	...	...	...	...			
Stepney Green				...	...	...		1115	1043	...	Stamford Brook	6 38	...	...	...	...	...	...			
Mile End				...	...	...		1117	1045	...	Turnham Green	6 40	...	8 52	...	9 47	...	...	9 30	...	...
Bow Road	...			...	...	...		...	...		Chiswick Park	6 42	...	8 55	...	9 49	...	...	9 32	...	...
Leigh-on-Sea	9 48	...		1035	...	12†16		1219	1141	...	Acton Town	6 45	...	8 57	...	9 51	...	...	9 34	...	...
Westcliff-on-Sea	9 53	...		1039	...	12†20		1223	1145	...	Ealing Common	6 47	...	8 59	...	9 53	...	...	9 36	...	...
Southend-on-Sea	9 58	...		1044	...	12†24		1228	1150	...	Ealing Broadway	6 50	...	9 2	...	9 56	...	...	9 39	...	...

‡ Will not run on Bank Holidays. † 10 minutes later on Saturdays. There are many additional trains by changing, see pages within.

Fig 27 This undated copy of the through train timetable shows the extent of the weekly trains between Southend and Ealing.

Stanford-le-Hope and Pitsea, where it arrived at 7.40am. Passengers travelling beyond Pitsea had to wait for the 6.45am departure from Fenchurch Street that had also called at Stepney, Bromley, Plaistow, Upton Park, East Ham and Barking, but the 6.45am went by the direct route, stopping at Dagenham, Hornchurch, Upminster, East Horndon and Laindon. Arrival at Pitsea was at 7.48am, and departing at 7.49am, this train then stopped at Benfleet, Leigh, Southend and Shoeburyness, where it arrived at 8.23am.

The passenger train departures from Fenchurch Street can be summarised thus: 7.23am to Barking, 7.45am to Tilbury for Gravesend, 8.23am to Pitsea, 8.38am to Upminster, 8.57am to Shoeburyness via Upminster, 9.13am to Tilbury and 9.45am to Tilbury for Gravesend. The next train was the 10.28am to Pitsea via Upminster, then the 10.45am to Shoeburyness via Tilbury, 11.13am to Tilbury for Gravesend, followed by the 11.45am to Pitsea via Tilbury. The first afternoon departure was the 12.8pm to Shoeburyness via Upminster, then there were two trains to Tilbury for Gravesend, the 12.38pm and 1.38pm. The timetable also contains some interesting details including information about Saturday workings. The 2.8pm train was Saturday-only from Fenchurch Street to Shoeburyness via Upminster. The WTT contains a note, 'Cord communication to be provided'. The 2.15pm ran to Pitsea via Upminster on Monday to Friday, but on Saturday it was shown as running to Tilbury for Gravesend. Another Saturday-only train was the 2.33pm from Plaistow to Pitsea, but the carriages for this train started as part of the 2.15pm, appearing in the WTT as, 'Carriages for this train to be detached from the 2.15pm from Fenchurch Street'.

The 2.32pm from Fenchurch Street ran to Tilbury for Gravesend and the note in the WTT states, 'Carriages from Liverpool Street to be attached to this train at Barking and transferred to 3.8pm at Tilbury for Shoeburyness'. The 3.8pm was the next LT&SR train to depart from Fenchurch Street for Shoeburyness via Tilbury. The time of arrival at Tilbury was 3.51pm with five minutes being allowed to attached the carriages. This was rather more than the three minutes allowed at Barking to attach the carriages from Liverpool Street to the 2.32pm train.

The 3.28pm was a Saturday-only train from Fenchurch Street to Purfleet, then came the 3.50pm to Pitsea via Upminster, followed by the 4.25pm to Tilbury for Gravesend, this train attaching carriages from Liverpool Street at Barking, three minutes being allowed for this. The 4.48pm ran to Barking where it terminated. I have already mentioned the evening express trains that conveyed first and second class passengers only. The first down train was shown as train 101 in the WTT and departed at 5.5pm. There is a note that states, 'Cord communication to be provided'. This was in connection with the requirements of the Regulation of Railways Act, 1889. The 5.15pm, with carriages for the Upminster line to be detached at Barking, was the next departure and this train ran non-stop to Barking. The carriages were worked forward at 5.40pm, seven minutes after the 5.15 had arrived, the 5.15 continuing to Tilbury, with arrival times at Gravesend and Rosherville shown in the WTT.

There was a 5.22pm from Fenchurch Street to Rainham followed by a Saturday-excepted train to Pitsea departing at 5.45pm. The 5.53pm to Shoeburyness was due to arrive at Upminster at 6.33pm and to depart at 6.46pm, being required to shunt at Upminster for the 6.8pm express from Fenchurch Street to Southend. This train was the second of the evening express trains that carried only first and second class passengers. Whereas the 5.5pm ran non-stop to Southend and then to Shoeburyness, the 6.8pm stopped at Stepney,

Taken at Hornsey Road, this 1898 picture shows Midland Railway 2-4-0 No 1081 at the head of a St Pancras to Southend train. *Collection R. J. Essery*

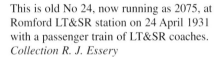

This is old No 24, now running as 2075, at Romford LT&SR station on 24 April 1931 with a passenger train of LT&SR coaches. *Collection R. J. Essery*

Although the train engine cannot be seen, it was ex-Midland Railway 0-4-4T No 1261. The train was the 3.55pm from Romford to Upminster and Tilbury and the vehicle closest to the camera is an LMS standard driving trailer used for motor train work. *W. A. Camwell*

Upminster, East Horndon, Southend and Shoeburyness. The Monday-Friday evening business train that followed was the 6.22pm that ran to Tilbury. However, on a Saturday this train was extended to run to Shoeburyness, where it arrived at 8.21pm.

Later in the evening there was a departure at 6.53pm to Rainham and 7.15pm to Upminster. The 7.48pm, which attached through carriages from Liverpool Street at Barking, ran to Shoeburyness. Other evening trains were the 8.13pm to Barking, 9pm to Shoeburyness, 9.45pm to Tilbury for Gravesend, attaching carriages at Barking from Liverpool Street, 10.28 and 11pm to Barking, and finally the 12am to Tilbury. This train would set down passengers at Rainham and Purfleet upon notice being given to the guard at Barking.

In the up direction the first train was the 5am from Barking to Fenchurch Street, followed by the 6.10am. Then came the 6.50am from Upton Park, 6.53am from Barking and 6.36am from Laindon, all for Fenchurch Street. The 7.45am from Upton Park was followed by the train connection from the 7.25am ferry from Gravesend (Town Pier). The first up train from Southend was the 7.43am due to arrive at Fenchurch Street at 8.50am. This train stopped at Leigh, Upminster, Hornchurch, Dagenham and Stepney. The first up train from Shoeburyness was the 7.45am which stopped at all stations to Tilbury, then at Grays, Barking and Fenchurch Street, arriving at 9.35am. However, there were other up trains, the 8.35am from Barking, and 8.10am from Gravesend and Tilbury. The morning trains continued with the 8.43am from Pitsea, which ran non-stop to Laindon then all stations to Fenchurch Street where it was due to arrive at 9.51am. Hard on its heels was the 8.55am express from Shoeburyness, stopping only at Southend, with 50 minutes allowed to reach Fenchurch Street at 10am. The headway between these trains closed so that at Stepney it was 10 minutes. The 8.55 was first and second class only and the WTT contained the cord communication note mentioned previously. Other morning trains were the 9.40am from Upminster, and the 9.30 and 10.8am from Gravesend and Tilbury. The 10am from Shoeburyness was due to arrive at Fenchurch Street at 11.41am, with the 10.55am from Pitsea due at 12.21pm. The 11.50am from Shoeburyness conveyed through carriages for Liverpool Street, to be detached at Barking.

The afternoon departures began with the 12.12pm Pitsea to Barking, followed by the 12.48pm Gravesend and Tilbury to Fenchurch Street. There was a daily 1.56pm train from Barking to Fenchurch Street, then a 2.30pm from Gravesend and Tilbury. The next arrival in Fenchurch Street was the 2pm from Shoeburyness, again with through carriages for Liverpool Street to be detached at Barking. There was a 3.2pm from Pitsea to Fenchurch Street, a 4.5pm from Gravesend and Tilbury and a 4.53pm from Barking to Fenchurch Street.

The 3.47pm from Shoeburyness was retimed to start at 3.57pm on Saturday. Both trains ran via Tilbury and the difference in the arrival time at Fenchurch Street was 30 minutes: 5.30 and 6pm. The slower running Saturday train is explained by the fact that the Saturday train made a number of additional stops at Leigh, Benfleet, Low Street, Purfleet, Rainham, East Ham, Upton Park and Bromley. There was also a Saturday-excepted train from Gravesend and Tilbury at 5.2pm from Rainham at 6.10pm and Shoeburyness at 5.10pm via Upminster.

The 5.52pm from Pitsea to Fenchurch Street conveyed carriages for Liverpool Street that were to be detached at Barking; the next up passenger train was the 7.57pm from

Rainham that preceded the 7pm from Shoeburyness via Upminster into Fenchurch Street. The following up arrival was the 7.47pm from Pitsea, this train conveying carriages for Liverpool Street via Barking. The final trains of the day were the 9.36pm from Upminster and the 9.40 and 10.35pm trains from Gravesend and Tilbury. This completes the overall weekday Fenchurch Street to Shoeburyness service via Upminster and Tilbury.

The Sunday service from Fenchurch Street began with the 9.15am to Shoeburyness via Tilbury. There were trains at 9.45 and 11.40am from Barking to Pitsea. The Fenchurch Street to Tilbury for Gravesend service continued with the 11.5am. The 9.45 arrived at Pitsea at 10.27am, enabling passengers to connect with the 9.15am from Fenchurch Street; this train arrived at Pitsea at 10.39am and went forward to Shoeburyness at 10.40, where it was due to arrive at 11.14am. The 11.5 from Fenchurch Street was the second departure from this station on a Sunday; the train went to Tilbury and Gravesend, the arrival time at Tilbury being 12.3pm. There was also a train from Barking at 11.40am to Pitsea.

The afternoon down Sunday trains were the 12.55, 6.15 and 11pm from Fenchurch Street to Barking; the 11pm was the last train of the day. The service to Shoeburyness via Tilbury was provided by the 2.7 and 7.48pm trains, while stations between Barking and Pitsea were served by departures at 2.37 and 8.30pm. The afternoon and evening trains to Tilbury and Gravesend were the 4.30 and 9.45pm. Finally there were trains at 6.15 and 10.15pm from Fenchurch Street to Upminster.

The Sunday up train service began with the 8.30am from Barking to Fenchurch Street. The first service from Shoeburyness was the 8.35am. The next through service was the 2pm, with the 7pm the last through train of the day; all three trains were via Tilbury. The Pitsea to Barking service was at 9.22am, 2.47, 7.42 and 9.20pm. There was an 11.32am train from Pitsea to Fenchurch Street. The Gravesend and Tilbury trains were at 11.50am, 5.30 and 9.28pm with a booked arrival time of 10.38pm; this was the last train to arrive at Fenchurch Street. Other Sunday trains were the 5.35 and 9pm Barking to Fenchurch Street and the 7.20pm Upminster to Fenchurch Street.

I have not dealt with the light engine or the empty stock movements. However, I must mention that there were some workings between Southend and Shoeburyness that were either empty stock or shown as passenger trains and were balancing movements required to meet operational needs. In addition to the LT&SR trains, the public timetable provides details of train services from Liverpool Street to Shoeburyness via Barking. There were daily departures from Liverpool Street at 8.5, 11.37am, 2.20, 4.11, 7.38 and 9.31pm. The Sunday service was at 9.3am, 1.55 and 7.31pm. All trains provided a service to Tilbury; only the 4.11 and 9.31pm did not also provide a service to Shoeburyness. In the up direction the times of departure from Shoeburyness were 7.45, 11.30am, 2.0, 5.10 and 7pm. There was also a 9.40pm train from Tilbury and three trains on a Sunday at 8.35am, 2pm and 7pm.

I believe these were GER trains that worked to Barking in the down direction with the coaches being attached to LT&SR trains to be worked forward. The reverse applied in the up direction. In addition, it is possible that some workings were LT&SR trains that worked to and from Liverpool Street. Finally, the London & North Western and North London services were quite intense and the public timetable shows the various connecting services with the LT&SR already described.

The LT&SR goods services in 1890 are taken directly from the 1890 timetable, which is not as clear as I would wish. The first entry in the down direction was at 5.5am for a goods train from Abbey Mills Junction to Stanford-le-Hope. The train arrived at 8.25am after spending 30 minutes at Barking, 15 minutes at Rainham, seven minutes at Purfleet, 10 minutes at Tilbury Docks, 15 minutes at Low Street and 12 minutes at Thames Haven Junction. There was a 6.55am departure from Commercial Road goods depot to Tilbury. The arrival times are shown as 'When required', and there is a note in the WTT to the effect, 'To be shunted if necessary to prevent delay to passenger trains'.

There was a path in the timetable for a goods train to depart from Thames Haven Junction at 8.50am arriving at Thames Haven at 9.2am. This train is shown as departing from Stanford at 8.35am. The 8.30am goods from Plaistow to Tilbury arrived at 9.38am and the WTT states 'Engine only from Tilbury Docks to Tilbury'. The 10.59am from Commercial Road worked to Tilbury, the timetable note reading 'To Dock Co's siding'; the arrival time was 12.5pm.

The 12.58pm from Commercial Road goods depot was due to arrive at Shoeburyness at 5.40pm. The WTT note states: 'To shunt at Rainham for the 1.38pm and on Saturday only, at Grays for 2.15pm Fenchurch St. to Tilbury passenger trains; and at Stanford for 3.8pm Fenchurch St. Passenger trains — trucks for Tilbury to be detached at Tilbury Docks station and worked thence by the Tilbury pilot engine. Trucks from Tilbury to be worked to Low Street by the Tilbury pilot engine.'

There was a 3pm goods from Plaistow to Pitsea that was required to shunt at Barking for the 3.8pm passenger train from Fenchurch Street. The next departure from Commercial Road was the 3.59pm to Tilbury and there was another Commercial Road departure at 6.38pm to Southend where it was due at 11.30pm. This train was to shunt at Tilbury Docks station for the 7.48pm Fenchurch Street to Shoeburyness passenger train. The final down goods working was the 11.15pm goods train from Barking to Upminster.

The up goods trains began with the 4.45am from Plaistow to Abbey Mills Junction. Then there was a train from Tilbury at 5am to Commercial Road. There was a departure to Thames Haven from Stanford at 8.35am. This train is also shown in the down timetable. The train was booked to be at Thames Haven Junction for 10 minutes. The 10.53 goods train arrival at Commercial Road was booked to pass Tilbury Docks North Junction at 9.47am but the actual departure time was not given. The return service from Thames Haven was at 10.20 and the train was due at Plaistow at 1.53pm. The WTT note states 'To shunt at Grays for 10.55am Pitsea to Fenchurch Street passenger train; at Rainham for the 11.30am passenger train from Shoeburyness, at Barking for the 12.42pm Tilbury Docks to Commercial Road goods train and at Plaistow for 12.58 Tilbury to Fenchurch Street passenger train. Will call at Tilbury Docks North Junction Siding when required.'

There was a 9.40am goods train from Southend to Commercial Road, where it was due to arrive at 2.37pm. This train ran via Upminster and shunted most stations between Southend and Barking. The 12.42pm train mentioned above is shown in the timetable as passing Tilbury Docks North Junction at 12.41, so obviously there is an error in the WTT. There was a 5.25pm goods train from Tilbury to Plaistow, where it was due to arrive at 7.12pm. There were two other goods trains during the day. One, the 6.15pm from Pitsea, ran to Plaistow via Tilbury, arriving at 9.23pm. The other was the

6pm from Shoeburyness to Commercial Road via Upminster. This train was booked to stop at most stations and ran via Upminster. The arrival time at Commercial Road was 11.15pm. There were no goods trains on a Sunday.

In order to examine the developments that took place following the opening of the Tottenham & Forest Gate Railway I have set out some details of the train services advertised in the July-September 1897 public timetable. This shows a variety of trains that ran from either St Pancras or Moorgate to make connections on the LT&SR, including a number of through trains. The majority of these services ran from Moorgate Street and, other than the through trains, all terminated at East Ham, where the Midland Railway had a bay platform on the north side of the station. In addition to the Southend services, the public timetable shows trains for Tilbury for Gravesend that included connections with pleasure steamers for Margate and Boulogne. There was also a reasonable Sunday service that included three through trains to Southend and one through train to Tilbury.

The July to September 1915 public timetable combined the London terminal stations to destinations on the LT&S Section in a single timetable, which must have been helpful to travellers. The weekday down trains from Fenchurch Street to Shoeburyness were at 5.5, 5.45, and 6.52am (both via Tilbury), 7.20, 7.32am (to Southend via Tilbury), 8.20, 9.5am (via Tilbury), 9.26, 10.17am (via Tilbury), 10.45, 11.45am (via Tilbury to Southend). The afternoon trains were 12.15, 1pm, 1.5pm (Saturday-only), 1.15 and 1.25pm (both Saturday-only to Southend), the 1.15pm (via Tilbury), 1.48pm (to Southend via Tilbury weekdays, to Shoeburyness via Upminster Saturday-only), 1.56pm (Saturday-only to Southend), 2.6, 2.26pm (Saturday-only). The 2.25pm Monday to Friday train was retimed to start at 2.30pm on Saturday. The Saturday 3.8pm train arrived at Shoeburyness six minutes later than on weekdays. There was a 3.25pm to Southend via Tilbury, a 4.7pm (the Saturday arrival time at Shoeburyness was three minutes later), 4.16pm (via Tilbury), 4.27pm (on Saturday the arrival time at Shoeburyness was 18 minutes later at 6.6pm), 4.57pm, (Saturday-excepted to Southend), 5.6pm (Saturday-excepted), 5.16, 5.25pm (Southend only via Tilbury; on Saturday this train terminated at Tilbury); 5.38pm (Saturday-excepted), 5.46 and 5.55pm (both Saturday-excepted to Southend; the weekday train ran via Tilbury, the Saturday service was via Upminster), 6.17, 6.26pm (the Saturday service had altered timings), 6.38pm (Saturday-only, via Tilbury), 6.53pm (Saturday-excepted), 7.20pm (arrived at Shoeburyness three minutes later on Saturday), 8pm (Saturday-excepted), 8.41, 9.25 and 10.15pm (the 9.25 and 10.15 via Tilbury) and the last train was the 12.10am, arriving at Shoeburyness at 1.22am.

The Tilbury service was largely made up of through trains but some ran only to Tilbury. In addition to those mentioned above, were trains for either Southend or Shoeburyness. There were departures at 5.50am from Plaistow and Fenchurch Street at 8.11, 8.29, 9.39, 11.13am, 12.25, 2.40, 4.46, 6.53 (Saturday only) and 7.41pm (Saturday-excepted).

The timetable also shows some trains that terminated at Pitsea and there were some through trains from Ealing to Southend and Shoeburyness. The Midland Railway timetable does not give the Ealing starting times but it does show the time at Mark Lane. For example, the first through train was shown as 10.10am at Mark Lane, then 10.38am at Barking, 11.17 at Leigh, 11.21 at Westcliff-on-Sea, 11.26 at Southend, 11.34 at Thorpe Bay and 11.38am at Shoeburyness. The last through train of the day was 11.20pm at Mark Lane and 12.24am at Southend.

Other services over the LT&S Section shown in the timetable include some excursion trains that ran only on Saturday and a few District trains that terminated at Upminster. The Sunday service was very good indeed. However, the inclusion of the section on engine and carriage working that follows should provide readers with a very clear idea of the Tilbury line services at this time, before the effects of the Great War took their toll.

Engine Workings

This is a subject close to the author's heart and one that provides a rich feast for study. We reproduce at Appendices 1 and 2 the engine and carriage workings for June 1915. However, the diagrams refer only to those turns which included passenger work. For example, Plaistow 5 and 6 are duties that included both passenger and goods train activity. Unfortunately the goods element of these trains is not recorded on the diagrams and this, plus more importantly, the lack of any goods engine diagrams or even the 1915 working timetable, makes it totally impossible to tell the full story. However, I will try to put as much flesh as possible on to the bones.

At this date there were 42 daily turns plus one Saturday-only working (Plaistow 10). They comprised Plaistow 9, Upminster 3, Tilbury 10, Shoeburyness 18 and Kentish Town 2. The company's engine stock consisted of the following motive power units:

4-6-4T: '2100' class — 8
4-4-2Ts: '79' class — 4; '51' class — 18;
'Rebuilt 37' class — 12; 'No 1' class — 36
0-6-2T: '69' class — 14
0-6-0: '49' class — 2

These could be divided into:
Top link passenger — 16 engines from the '79' and 'Rebuilt 37' classes.
Almost equal to top link — 18 engines of the '51' class.
Freight engines — 16.
This left the 36 engines from the 'No 1' class relegated to goods, shunting and secondary passenger work, plus the eight engines of the '2100' class which were something of a white elephant in view of the fact that they could not be used between Fenchurch Street station and effectively Barking. We will consider them first, since, as we will see, the more '2100' class engines that could be employed, the less 'No 1' class engines would be needed on a daily basis for passenger work.

Kenneth Leech tells us that No 2107 was always at Plaistow and so what follows is no more than guesswork. It is possible that employment for two other '2100' class locomotives could have been Shoeburyness Turn No 18. For the sake of this hypothetical exercise we will assume that one was spare at Plaistow with three others in daily use, which meant that the other four were either standing spare, in works under repair or employed upon the Midland system. Readers will note that Plaistow 9 was a possible turn that, in theory, could have employed a '2100' class locomotive but more likely this was a job covered by a locomotive of the 'No 1' class. Before leaving the '2100' class I would like to draw attention to the quick dash made by the crew of Shoeburyness 18 from Southend to Shoeburyness in order to effect a change of engine men, where upon the morning shift men were relieved by the afternoon shift men.

One thing, which is unknown to the author, is the daily availability of locomotives, and we are going to assume 80%. If this was correct we would have a daily basis, to cover the remaining 39 turns, the following locomotives.

Top Link Passenger	Nearly Top Link	'No 1' Class	
13	14	28	= 55 locomotives
Less	39 turns	16 surplus	

This provides, in theory, 16 'No 1' class engines available on a daily basis to cover any special or excursion trains (one would be required for the Saturday-only train), with the balance joining the 16 freight engines of the '49' and '69' classes.

Kenneth Leech records that not all members of this class were regularly employed but it is possible that when he made this observation there were other reasons to explain this downturn in traffic requirements, because the first of the class was not withdrawn until 1930. By this time the LMS had added further 4-4-2Ts to the stock of the Tilbury section. I have said that we will probably never know and it is all guesswork on my part, but just suppose some other working diagrams came to light or we were able to confirm, with greater accuracy, the daily availability of locomotives and special workings, this may help to explain pictures of goods tank engines on passenger work.

I will now consider in greater detail some of the turns, but readers should not lose sight of the fact that at this time the normal working day for enginemen, before overtime applied, was 10 hours.

The diagram variations between daily and Saturday working are to be noted and in particular there was only one extra Saturday turn which could not be covered by engines already in traffic — Plaistow No 10. This was a Saturday engine job that took empty coaches from Plaistow to Fenchurch Street, comprising the bogie stock which made up train No 23 that was to form the 7.20pm Fenchurch Street to Shoeburyness. After being released the engine worked the 7.35pm from Fenchurch Street to Upminster, which comprised B stock in train No 11. Upon arrival, after disposing of the stock, the locomotive was booked to return light engine to Plaistow shed; its work was over and this diagram poses two questions at least. Was this locomotive a pilot duty at Plaistow or was it a turn booked to a passed fireman? In addition, reference to the carriage diagram poses yet a further question. If the coaches are left at Upminster on Saturday night, how do they get to Tilbury by Monday in readiness to start the week? The most probable answer would lie in their employment on Sunday, but I don't have the Sunday diagrams to confirm what happened.

Some turns were in effect two shifts with a lengthy lay over during the day; Plaistow No 3 provides a good example of such duty. The crew probably booked on at around 3.45am, prepared their engine before running light to Little Ilford sidings in order to collect train No 6 and work it to Barking, whereupon the empty stock became the 5.37am to Fenchurch Street. The engine, upon release at Fenchurch Street, was then available to work the 6.52am Fenchurch Street to Tilbury with train No 9 (this train arriving by Tilbury No 1 locomotive turn), prior to returning to Fenchurch Street with the 8.44am departure from Tilbury. The final working was empty coaches from Fenchurch Street to Plaistow with train No 29, whereupon the engine stood on the shed until it was required

Photographed on 11 September 1908, this picture shows the 12.50pm Tilbury Docks to Commercial Road Express goods train at Grays. The locomotive is No 75 *Canvey Island*. I suspect that it is the fireman on the running plate and that there may be a problem; the signals are in the clear position. *Ken Nunn/LCGB*

to work the 6.55pm empty coaches from Plaistow to Fenchurch Street and so on.

It would not be difficult to indulge in further speculation and to comment about most if not all of these diagrams, but the temptation will be resisted and it is left to readers to 'tie together' the various workings. However, a few final remarks may be helpful before we move on to consider other traffic matters.

Plaistow No 6: Almost certainly it was a 'No 1' class engine that ran light from Plaistow to Upminster in order to work the 7.55pm Upminster to Hammersmith, train No 21. This was an interesting service, running as far as Barking where the District Line took over. The remainder of the shift was spent on shunting or goods work, almost certainly diagrammed, but not shown on the sheet.

Tilbury No 7: Note how the goods shunting work during the weekdays was replaced with additional Saturday passenger workings. These diagrams provide an invaluable insight into how it was possible to work an intensive service with what were in effect set trains and separate motive power units. While there are, as we have noted, some errors in these diagrams, it is possible to piece together an almost

complete picture of what happened. One possible explanation for the possible errors was that it was a wartime period and this may help explain why they were printed. However, it was not unusual for a timetable to be issued and then for it to be quickly followed by amendments. These were distributed in one form or another and it is just possible that these timetables were drafts made prior to issue and were corrected before being given to the staff. We will probably never know.

Romford and Ockendon Branches

There was little change to the train services over this section of line following the Midland Railway takeover. K. A. Frost, in his book, *The Romford-Upminster Branch*, published in 1964, covers the story quite well where he sets out in considerable detail the July to October 1934 passenger timetable. In that year the LMS introduced the motor trains, sometimes referred to as push-and-pull or 'reversible trains'. For my part, I outline in the table below the earlier, 1925, train services that were typical of the train times in use during the Midland and early LMS years.

There was a seven-day service over the lines and while most trains ran between Romford and Upminster others started or terminated at Grays and Tilbury. The 13 July 1925 Working timetable of passenger trains gives the following train movements.

Down Trains
Weekdays

12.6 MX Pass.	Upminster to Emerson Park. Arrive 12.10.	
12.31 MX Pass.	Upminster to Emerson Park. Arrive 12.35.	
5.50 Pass.	Upminster to Romford. Arrive 5.58.	
6.28 Pass.	Upminster to Romford. Arrive 6.57.	
7.1 Pass.	Upminster to Romford. Arrive 7.10.	
7.12 Empty	Upminster to Emerson Park. Arrivé 7.17. To be propelled.	
7.38 Empty	Upminster to Romford. Arrive 7.45.	
7.47 Empty	Upminster to Emerson Park. Arrive 7.52. To be propelled.	
8.12 Empty	Upminster to Emerson Park. Arrive 8.17. To be propelled.	
8.31 Pass.	Upminster to Romford. Arrive 8.39.	
8.41 Empty	Upminster to Emerson Park. Arrive 8.46.	
9.17 Pass.	Upminster to Romford. Arrive 9.25.	
9.49 Pass.	Upminster to Romford. Arrive 9.57.	
10.55 Pass.	Upminster to Romford. Arrive 11.4.	
11.0 Pass.	Grays to Romford. Arrive 11.37.	
12/44 SO Pass.	Upminster to Emerson Park. Arrive 12/48.	
12/40 Pass.	Grays to Romford. Arrive 1/9.	
1/57 SO Pass.	Upminster to Romford. Arrive 2/6.	
2/5 Pass.	Grays to Romford. Arrive 2/32.	
2/58 Pass.	Upminster to Romford. Arrive 3/7.	
3/40 Pass.	Upminster to Romford. Arrive 3/49.	
4/13 Pass.	Upminster to Romford. Arrive 4/22.	
5/0 Pass.	Upminster to Romford. Arrive 5/9.	
5/33 Pass.	Upminster to Romford. Arrive 5/42.	
6/4 Pass.	Upminster to Romford. Arrive 6/13.	
6/17 Pass.	Upminster to Emerson Park. Arrive 6/21.	
6/50 Pass.	Upminster to Romford. Arrive 6/59.	

7/25 Pass.	Upminster to Romford. Arrive 7/33.
7/35 Pass.	Tilbury to Romford. Arrive 8/15.
8/34 Pass.	Upminster to Romford. Arrive 8/43.
9/26 Pass.	Upminster to Romford. Arrive 9/34.
9/57 Pass.	Upminster to Romford. Arrive 10/6.
11/4 Pass.	Upminster to Emerson Park. Arrive 11/8.

Sundays

12.6 Pass.	Upminster to Emerson Park Arrive 12.10.
12.31 Pass.	Upminster to Emerson Park. Arrive 12.35.
8.0 Empty	Upminster to Romford. Arrive 8.7.
8.30 Pass.	Upminster to Romford. Arrive 8.39.
9.48 Pass.	Grays to Romford Arrive 10.16.
12/12 Pass.	Tilbury to Romford. Arrive 12/51.
1/59 Pass.	Upminster to Romford. Arrive 2/8.
3/15 Pass.	Grays to Romford. Arrive 3/49.
6/5 Pass.	Upminster to Romford. Arrive 6/14.
7/37 Pass.	Tilbury to Romford. Arrive 8/13.
9/52 Pass.	Grays to Romford. Arrive 10/18.
10/43 Pass.	Upminster to Romford. Arrive 10/52.

Up Trains
Weekdays

12.17 MX Empty	Emerson Park to Upminster. Arrive 12.21.
12.43 MX Empty	Emerson Park to Upminster. Arrive 12.47.
6.3 Pass.	Romford to Upminster. Arrive 6.12.
6.44 Pass.	Romford to Upminster. Arrive 6.53.
7.19 Pass.	Emerson Park to Upminster. Arrive 7.23.
7.28 Pass.	Romford to Upminster. Arrive 7.37.
7.53 Pass.	Emerson Park to Upminster. Arrive 7.57.
8.2 Pass.	Romford to Tilbury. Arrive 8.53. Changes engines at Upminster.
8.22 Pass.	Emerson Park to Upminster. Arrive 8.26.
8.48 Pass.	Emerson Park to Upminster. Arrive 8.52.
9.2 Pass.	Romford to Upminster. Arrive 9.10.
9.30 Pass.	Romford to Upminster. Arrive 9.39.
10.2 Pass.	Romford to Grays. Arrive 10.31.

11.12 Pass.	Romford to Upminster. Arrive 11.21.
11.43 Pass.	Romford to Grays. Arrive 12/19.
12/55 SO Pass.	Emerson Park to Upminster. Arrive 12/59.
1/15 Pass.	Romford to Grays. Arrive 1/56. at Upminster between 1/24-1/40.
2/12 Pass.	Romford to Upminster. Arrive 2/20.
2/40 Pass.	Romford to Tilbury. Arrive 3/21.
3/55 Pass.	Romford to Tilbury. Arrive 4/37.
4/45 Pass.	Romford to Grays. Arrive 5/25.
5/18 Pass.	Romford to Upminster. Arrive 5/27.
5/48 Pass.	Romford to Upminster. Arrive 5/57.
6/28 SX Pass.	Romford to Emerson Park. Arrive 6/32.
6/38 Pass.	Romford to Tilbury. Arrive 7/14.
7/6 Pass.	Romford to Upminster. Arrive 7/15.
7/38 Pass.	Romford to Upminster. Arrive 7/45.
8/20 Pass.	Romford to Grays. Arived 8/52.
9/7 Pass.	Romford to Upminster. Arrive 9/16.
9/39 Pass.	Romford to Upminster. Arrive 9/48.
10/40 Pass.	Romford to Upminster. Arrive 10/49.
11/16 Pass.	Emerson Park to Upminster. Arrive 11/20.

Sundays

12.17 Empty	Emerson Park to Upminster. Arrive 12.21.
12.43 Empty	Emerson Park to Upminster. Arrive 12.47.
8.15 Season Excursion.	Romford to Upminster. Arrive 8.24.
8.44 Season Excursion.	Romford to Grays. Arrive 9.13.
10.25 Pass.	Romford to Tilbury. Arrive 11.16.
12/56 Pass.	Romford to Upminster. Arrive 1/4.
2/26 Pass.	Romford to Grays. Arrive 2/55.
4/55 Pass.	Romford to Upminster. Arrive 5/4.
6/42 Pass.	Romford to Upminster. Arrive 6/51.
8/38 Pass.	Romford to Upminster. Arrive 8/47.
10/24 Pass.	Romford to September. Arrive 10/32.
11/0 Pass.	Romford to Upminster. Tilrive 11/10.

At Emerson Park there was a run-round loop that was to become redundant when the motor trains were introduced.

According to K. A. Frost, there were old LT&SR six-wheel coaches still in service on the branch in 1934 so it seems reasonable to assume these carriages had been in use since the branch was opened. In the days of the motor fitted trains he records that Midland 0-4-4Ts Nos 1261, 1287, 1290 and 1344 were in regular use on the line. The first three locomotives were fitted with vacuum control regulator gear to order number 8612 dated 5 January 1934, specifically for work on this line. The order stated that they were to be equipped with quick starting gear, but whistle cords were not required.

Freight Train Working

I have chosen to use a 1930 LMS working timetable as the model for freight train services over the LT&S Section in the post-1923 period; it is very different from the 1890 timetable described above.

Working timetables are extremely complex and provide a variety of details about both train and light engine workings. Rather than set out each service, I have attempted to summarise the principal traffic flows at this point in time. I hope this approach will be helpful in understanding how the freight train traffic had developed during a 40-year period.

Some freight train services were local and operated within the LT&S Section while other trains began their journeys beyond the boundary of the old London, Tilbury & Southend Railway. We will begin with the long-distance arrivals as described in Section 10 of the 7 July to 21 September 1930 working timetable. This section covered the freight service between Commercial Road, Plaistow, Tilbury and Shoeburyness, and branches.

In 1930, I believe that the old North London Railway depot at Devons Road was still part of the Western Division and if this is correct it could explain the numerous references to Western Division engines and men that appear in the details that follow.

Notes

Generally, during both the LT&SR and Midland Railway periods, I have shown the times as am or pm but for the LMS period freight timetable I have used the method employed by the company. A . (dot) was used to show am, and a / for pm.

MX	Monday excepted
MO	Monday only
WX	Wednesday excepted
SX	Saturday excepted
SO	Saturday only
Q	Runs when required
St Pancras	This was the goods, not the passenger, station
LE	Light engine

Down Direction Trains

Brent

There were a number of mineral trains that started from Brent. They ran over the T&HJR and the T&FGR to Woodgrange Park and are listed below.

MX	10/35 Mineral to Shoeburyness
	4.15 Mineral to Little Ilford Northern Sidings
	5.40 Stopping freight to Little Ilford Northern Sidings (started from West End sidings)
	7.30 Mineral to Little Ilford Northern Sidings
	9.40 Mineral to Little Ilford Northern Sidings
	11.40 Mineral to Tilbury
	12/15 Mineral to Little Ilford Northern Sidings
	1/55 Mineral to Little Ilford Northern Sidings
	2/55 Mineral to Thames Haven
	3/50 Mineral to Little Ilford Northern Sidings
	5/45 Mineral to Little Ilford Northern Sidings
	6/53 Mineral to West Thurrock Sidings

Commercial Road

The principal goods depot was at Commercial Road. The down line originating trains were:

MX	12.30 Through freight to Plaistow Sidings
	3.45 Express freight to Tilbury Docks
	10.40 Express freight to Tilbury Docks
SO	11.30 Mineral to Little Ilford Northern Sidings
SX	12/30 Mineral to Little Ilford Northern Sidings
SX	3/45, SO 3/59 Express freight to Tilbury
SX	9/8 Express freight to Tilbury. SO. This train ran as a through freight and terminated at Plaistow.
SO	9/55 Mineral to Little Ilford Northern Sidings
SX	10/30 Mineral to Little Ilford Northern Sidings

Taken on 3 May 1909, this picture shows the 9am Romford to Tilbury Docks train at Romford hauled by No 70 *Basildon*.
Collection R. J. Essery

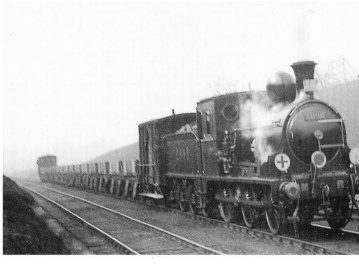

Above left:
The location of this short train hauled by No 46 *Southchurch* is not known to me, but the locomotive carries an Upminster destination board. Note the open-ended goods brake van, a most unusual design.
Ken Nunn/LCGB

Above right:
Old LT&SR No 49 now running as Midland Railway No 2898 has a ballast train with brake vans at each end of the train.
Ken Nunn/LCGB

'No 69' class engine No 77 *Fobbing* heads the 5.30am Plaistow to Pitsea goods train near East Horndon on 10 June 1912.
Collection R. J. Essery

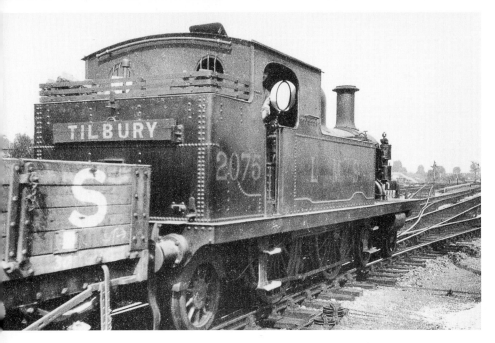

The 'No 1' class 4-4-2Ts were often used on goods trains, and this undated but early 1930s view shows old No 24 at work. The picture also provides a good rear view of one of these engines, together with the swivelling cab front windows in the open position.
Collection R. J. Essery

The 0-6-2T engines were in regular use on freight trains, and this picture shows No 2225 passing Plaistow engine shed on 6 April 1935. *Collection H. F. Wheeller, courtesy Roger Carpenter*

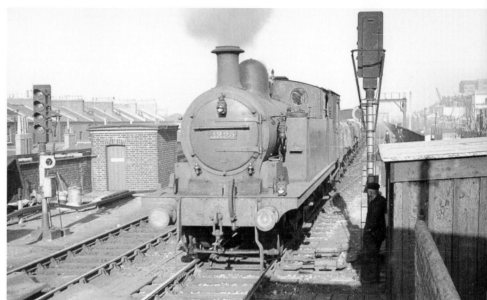

Taken on 20 October in 1935, this view of No 2225 on an Express freight train was photographed at Burdett Road. In the 1930 working timetable there was a 10.40am Express freight to Tilbury Docks, so it is probable that this was a similarly timed working that ran in 1935. *Collection H. F. Wheeller, 26/33 courtesy Roger Carpenter*

Plaistow Sidings

A number of down trains either terminated or originated at Plaistow. The details are given below.

MX	1.5 Arrival 11/30 freight from Acton GW
	1.5 Through freight to Tilbury Docks
	2.55 Stopping freight to Purfleet
	3.20 Stopping freight to Pitsea
	4.0 Mineral to Tilbury Docks
	5.20 Stopping freight to Upminster
	5.25 Stopping freight to Purfleet
	9.0 Mineral to Thames Haven
	10.39 Arrival 10.25 freight from Fairfield Road
SX	11.57 Mineral to Thames Haven
	11.59 Through freight to Tilbury
SX	12/9 Arrival 11.12 freight from St Pancras, worked by Western Division engines and men
	3/4 Mineral to Thames Haven
SO	4/5 Arrival 3/27, freight from St Pancras
SX	4/13 Mineral to Barking
SO	5/8 Mineral to Little Ilford Northern Sidings
SO	5/40 Arrival 4/15 freight from Acton GW
	8/32 Arrival 8/20 freight from Fairfield Road SO 8/0 from St Pancras
SX	8/43 Mineral to Tilbury
SO	11/11 Arrival 9/25 freight from Willesden

Little Ilford Sidings *Shunting engines*

MO	12.30 No 1 shunting engine. Arrives from Plaistow
MO	6.07 No 2 shunting engine. Arrives from Plaistow
MX	11.10 No 2 shunting engine. Arrives from Plaistow

Terminating or originating trains

	8.51 Mineral from Brent
	10.5 Mineral to Shoeburyness
SX	10.15 Mineral to Tilbury
	10.50 Stopping freight Little Ilford Northern Sidings to Dagenham Dock. Runs to Rainham on Saturday
	11.15 Arrival freight from East Ham
SO	3/0 Freight to Dagenham
	1/27 Arrival 12/15 mineral from Brent
SX	12/40 Freight to Dagenham
	12/30 Freight from Woodgrange Park
	3/3 1/55 Mineral from Brent
SO	3/20 Mineral to Shoeburyness
	3/50 Mineral to Tilbury
	5/45 Mineral to Tilbury (to Grays on Saturday only)
	6/40 Stopping freight to Pitsea
SO	7/0 Freight to Barking

The WTT shows some LNER goods trains as detailed below:

	4.30 Arrives at Little Ilford Northern Sidings
	11.30 Arrives at Little Ilford Northern Sidings
SO	7/35 Arrives at Little Ilford Northern Sidings

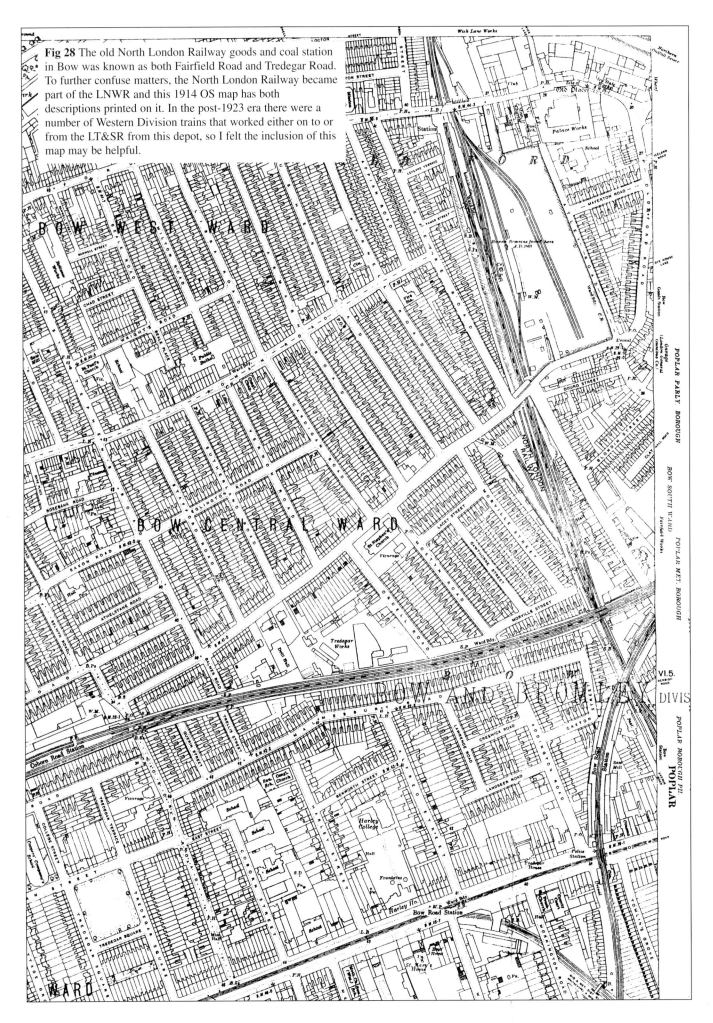

Fig 28 The old North London Railway goods and coal station in Bow was known as both Fairfield Road and Tredegar Road. To further confuse matters, the North London Railway became part of the LNWR and this 1914 OS map has both descriptions printed on it. In the post-1923 era there were a number of Western Division trains that worked either on to or from the LT&SR from this depot, so I felt the inclusion of this map may be helpful.

Engine and brake workings

E&B Q 2.20 From Plaistow to Tilbury to work 3.30 ex-Tilbury Docks to Commercial Road

E&B 4.40 Commercial Road to Plaistow Sidings

E&B 6.57 Commercial Road to East Ham

Light engine workings

MX 12.32 Plaistow Sidings to Barking

MX 2.12 Commercial Road to Plaistow Sidings

MX 4.0 Commercial Road to Plaistow Sidings

5.35 Romford to Upminster

10.30 Plaistow to Little Ilford Northern Sidings

SX 11.59 Plaistow Sidings to Little Ilford. Runs coupled in front of 11.59 from Plaistow Sidings

SX 3/10 Leigh to Shoeburyness

SO 1/50 Plaistow to Little Ilford Northern Sidings

SO 3/35 Leigh to Shoeburyness

3/14 Plaistow to Little Ilford Northern Sidings

WSX 3/31 Upminster to Tilbury

SO 4/12 Commercial Road to Plaistow

7/11 Devons Road to Plaistow

SX LNER engine 7/58 Arrives at Little Ilford Northern Sidings

9/10 Southend shunting engine arrives at Shoeburyness

SX 9/10 Arrives from Purfleet

SX 9/35 Arrives at Plaistow from Temple Mills, Western Division engine and men

10/10 Grays shunting engine arrives at Tilbury

SX 10/25 Arrives at Little Ilford from Plaistow

SO 10/28 Arrives at Barking from Plaistow

Upton Park

This was the ex-LNWR goods depot served by LMS Western Division engines and men.

11.13 Freight from Tredegar Road

8.53 Freight from Tredegar Road

Dagenham Services

SX 3/35 Freight to Hornchurch

Romford and Upminster Branch

SO 12/32 Freight Romford to Upminster.

SX 12/45 Freight Romford to Upminster

WSX 3/15 E&B Romford to Upminster

Before we review the up line freight trains we must consider those freight trains that do not appear above, but which ran on the T&FRJR, terminating their journeys before reaching the LT&S Section. Following the purchase of the LT&SR, the Midland Railway regarded the old joint line as being Midland and the LT&S Section as beginning at Woodgrange Park Junction. This continued until the complete integration of the LT&SR into the Midland Railway in 1920. To simplify matters I have used single-line descriptions for these trains.

MX 12.30 Stopping freight Upper Holloway to Leytonstone arrives at 12.55

10.35 Stopping freight West End to Queens Road arrives at 12.40. Starts at 10/20 on Saturdays

11/40 Stopping freight Upper Holloway to Leyton arrives at 12.18

SX 3/50 Stopping freight Upper Holloway to Queens Road arrives at 4/25

Sunday only 12.30 Stopping freight Upper Holloway to Leytonstone arrives at 12.55

Up Direction Trains

Shoeburyness and Southend originating trains

4.26 Mineral to Little Ilford Northern Sidings

1/55 Freight Southend East Sidings to Southend

4/30 Mineral to Brent

7/55 Stopping freight to Plaistow Sidings

Barking

11/10 Stopping freight to Plaistow Sidings

Dagenham

SX 5/19 Freight to Little Ilford Northern Sidings

SO 7/2 Freight to Little Ilford Northern Sidings

Grays

MX 1.0 Mineral to Commercial Road

8/40 Mineral to Plaistow Sidings (on Monday, Tuesday and Wednesday leaves at 8/30 and picks up at West Thurrock Sidings)

Hornchurch

SX 4/45 Freight to Dagenham.

SO 6/22 Freight to Dagenham.

Pitsea

9.15 Stopping freight to Little Ilford Northern Sidings

10/50 Stopping freight to Plaistow Sidings

Purfleet

6.15 Mineral to Little Ilford Northern Sidings

2/35 Freight arrives, 2/30 from West Thurrock Sidings

3/5 Mineral to Plaistow Sidings

7/55 Freight to Purfleet Rifle Range

10/5 Mineral to Plaistow Sidings

11/10 Mineral to Brent

Rainham

2/42 Stopping freight to Little Ilford Northern Sidings

Thames Haven

SX 12/10 Mineral to Plaistow Sidings

SO 1/10 Mineral to Plaistow Sidings

SX 2/50 Mineral to Little Ilford Northern Sidings

6/30 Mineral to Plaistow Sidings

7/0 Mineral to Brent

Tilbury

2.20 Express freight to Commercial Road

Q 3.30 Express freight to Commercial Road

5.15 Express Freight to Commercial Road

MO 6.40 MX 7.5 Stopping freight to Purfleet

9.57 Through freight to Commercial Road

SX 1/10 Express freight to Commercial Road

SO 1/15 Through freight to Commercial Road

SX 12/10 Mineral to Little Ilford Northern Sidings

2/5 Through freight to Commercial Road

3/20 Mineral to Brent

6/5 Through freight to Little Ilford Northern Sidings

6/15 Through freight to Plaistow Sidings

SX 6/40 Through freight to Commercial Road

SO 7/40 Freight to Grays

Tilbury continued...

SX	9/28 Freight to Plaistow Sidings
SX	11/0 Mineral to Grays

Little Ilford Northern Sidings

MX	1.0 Mineral to Brent
	5.52 Freight to Commercial Road
MX	9.48 Freight to Plaistow Sidings. This train was worked by Little Ilford No 2 Shunting engine
	9.55 Mineral to Cricklewood Junction
	10.40 Mineral to Cricklewood Junction
	11.30 Freight to Woodgrange Park
SX	12/30 Freight to Plaistow Sidings
	1/36 Mineral to Cricklewood Junction
	2/40 Mineral to Brent (suspended on Saturdays)
SX	4/55 Arrives, 4/50 Stopping freight from Barking
	6/15 Mineral to Brent
	7/2 Freight to Plaistow Sidings
	8/20 Stopping freight to Commercial Road

Upminster and Romford Branch

	5.5 Freight Upminster to Romford
	9.0 Stopping freight Ockendon to Romford
SX	1/28 Freight Upminster to Romford
SX	1/45 Mineral Upminster to Plaistow Sidings
SO	2/25 Mineral Upminster to Plaistow Sidings

Plaistow Sidings

MX	12.45 Mineral to Willesden, Western Division engines and men
	1.42 Mineral to Commercial Road
MX	2.5 Freight to St Pancras
	11.35 Freight to St Pancras, Western Division engine and men
	3/33 Freight to St Pancras, Western Division engine and men
SO	6/45 Freight to St Pancras, Western Division engine and men
	7/41 Freight to St Pancras, Western Division engine and men
	9/30 Freight to Acton GW, Western Division engine and men
	10/20 Freight, passes Bromley at 10/45, destination not given
SX	11/0 Through freight to Commercial Road
	11/59 Freight to St Pancras, Western Division engine and men

Upton Park LNWR Goods Depot, Worked by Western Division Engine and Men

MX	2.30 Freight to Willesden

Engine and brake workings

	6.57 Little Ilford to Black Horse Road then LE to Brent
	9.37 Tilbury to Tilbury Docks
	12/44 Tilbury to Tilbury Docks
	1/30 Upton Park to Plaistow Sidings, Western Division engine and men
SO	6/5 Plaistow to Devons Road, Western Division engine and men
QS	7/25 Tilbury Docks to Grays
	9/25 West Thurrock Sidings to Purfleet

Light engine workings

	4.26 Southend shunting engine, coupled to 4.26 Shoeburyness to Little Ilford
	7.45 Thames Haven to Thames Haven Junction
	9.54 Plaistow to Commercial Road
	11.30 Tilbury to Grays. Grays shunting engine
QS	12/30 Plaistow Sidings to Thames Wharf, Western Division engine and men
	12/45 Shoeburyness to Leigh. Shunts at Leigh
SO	1/10 Little Ilford to Plaistow Sidings
SX	2/0 Plaistow to Devons Road, Western Division engine and men
	2/45 Tilbury to Tilbury Docks
SO	4/45 Thames Haven to Tilbury
	5/35 Tilbury to Tilbury Docks. To work 6/5 to Little Ilford
WO	6/28 Tilbury Docks to Purfleet
WSX	6/25 Tilbury to Purfleet
TO	6/32 Grays to Purfleet
SO	7/36 Little Ilford to Plaistow
SX	10/30 Little Ilford to Plaistow
SX	11/5 Little Ilford to Plaistow

LNER trains

MX	1.40 Departs from Little Ilford Northern Sidings
	5.15 Departs from Little Ilford Northern Sidings
	12/55 Departs from Little Ilford Northern Sidings. Follows the 12/55 L&NE Barking to Liverpool Street (QSO)
SO	8/25 Departs from Little Ilford Sidings
SX	8/30 Departs from Little Ilford Northern Sidings

Finally there are the up direction trains that ran on the T&FGJR that do not appear on the main LT&S Section working timetable. As before, they are recorded in single-line descriptions:

MX	1.50 Stopping freight Leytonstone to Upper Holloway arrives 2.27
SX	11.42 Empties from Bow to Upper Holloway. LE to St Pancras
	1/58 Stopping freight from Leyton to Queens Road arrives 2/24
	2/5 Stopping freight to Upper Holloway arrives at 4/20
SX	4/55 Stopping freight Leyton to Upper Holloway arrives at 7/0
Sunday only	1.50 Stopping freight Leyton to Upper Holloway arrives at 2.27

Sunday Trains

There were very few trains that ran after midnight on Saturday; they were generally trains that had started their journeys on Saturday evening and arrived at their destination during the early hours of Sunday. There were some 'out-and-back' turns by LNER and Western Division engine and men that worked home and the light engine movements were required to return the engines to their home stations.

Above left:

I conclude this chapter with a reference to the staff employed by the LT&SR. Unlike those, including myself, who were familiar with national agreements and nationwide rates of pay, the pay structure for employees on the LT&SR was graded according to where they worked. The information given below is based upon the Conditions of Service agreed by the company effective from 20 January 1912 and remained in force until 1 July 1913.

Gangers in the permanent way department at their maximum rate were paid 33s per week if they worked between London and Barking, while the top rate for men working between Tilbury and Vange and on the Thames Haven branch was 29s. Sub gangers working at the same locations would receive 28s 6d and 23s 6d respectively, while the rate for platelayers was 26s and 22s. After seven years' service goods guards could earn 33s as a head guard or 27s as an under guard. Top pay for a police constable at Commercial Road was 28s after five years' service and porters and shunters earned between 22s and 23s after four years' service. The schedules run to many pages and make fascinating reading, but I will close with a note about the pay for drivers and firemen.

A fireman, when cleaning, was paid 3s 3d per day and when firing, 3s 9d. The top pay was 5s per day after five years' service. Firemen, when driving, were paid 5s 6d per day and drivers were paid 5s 9d per day in their first year, rising to 7s 9d per day in their 11th year of service in that grade.

Apart from pictures where the members of staff are in the background, finding illustrations of employees during both the LT&SR and Midland period has proved to be impossible. However, Audrey Field was kind enough to loan me two pictures, taken from the Field family album, which show her father, Claude William and grandfather, William Wood.

Driver William Wood was born in 1880 and joined the LT&SR when he was about 17 years of age. Unfortunately, the date that he became a driver is not known, but it would almost certainly have been during the period of Midland Railway ownership. This picture was taken towards the end of his service and shows him in the cab of an unidentified locomotive. The number 134x suggests it is No 1344, one of the ex-Midland Railway 0-4-4T engines stationed on the LT&S Section; however, reference to the middle picture on page 67 and the absence of an opening in the cab side sheet would make this unlikely. *Courtesy Audrey Field*

Above right:

Claude William Wood was the eldest son of William Wood and was born in 1905. He began work as a porter at East Ham and his railway service took him through the grades before becoming a signalling inspector at Euston. This picture of a young porter is believed to be at Bromley; the signals are, from left to right: to Bow NLR, to Whitechapel & Bow line, splitting distant Campbell Road Junction and on the right, from the electric line to Fenchurch Street. Fig 29 should make this clear. *Courtesy Audrey Field*

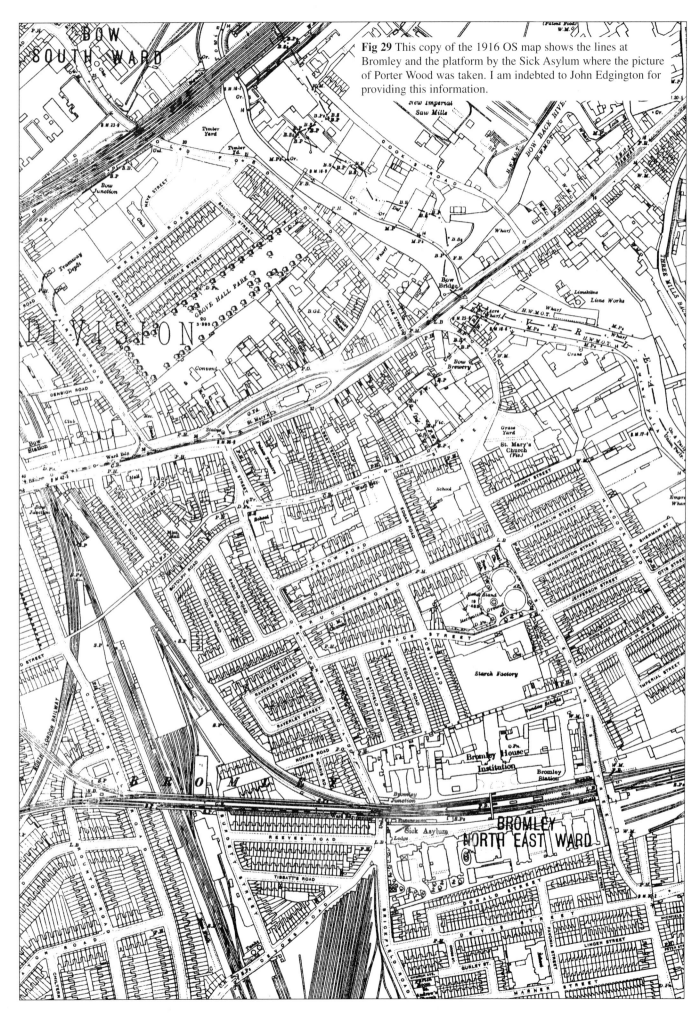

Fig 29 This copy of the 1916 OS map shows the lines at Bromley and the platform by the Sick Asylum where the picture of Porter Wood was taken. I am indebted to John Edgington for providing this information.

Part Two.
The Locomotives

4. A Review of LT&SR Locomotives: Their Development and Associated Livery Details

During the 50-year period between 1862, when the company became a separate legal entity, and 1912, when it was taken over by the Midland Railway, the LT&SR owned only 82 locomotives. All were constructed during the final 32 years of the company's lifetime. It is also worth noting that no locomotives owned by the LT&SR were scrapped until after the Midland Railway became part of the LMS. A further 12 tank engines, four more 0-6-2Ts and eight 4-6-4Ts to a new design were on order at the time the railway was purchased by the MR, but because they were not delivered until after the takeover in August 1912, they did not carry any LT&SR identity and entered traffic in Midland livery, carrying their allotted Midland Railway numbers.

Prior to 1880, the Eastern Counties Railway and then the Great Eastern Railway, as the ECR became, had supplied both the locomotives and rolling stock to work the line. Although the story of the locomotives used prior to 1880 is interesting, I consider it to be outside of the terms of reference that I have set for this work. For those interested in learning which GER locomotives were used between 1866 and 1880, or indeed from the ECR before the company became part of the Great Eastern, I can only suggest that the long-established Great Eastern Railway Society may be able to assist. Other possible sources are the books that I consulted, *Stepney's Own Railway*, and Peter Kay's Volume 1, details of which are given in the Bibliography. They both contain information about London & Blackwall Railway locomotives that could have seen some service on the LT&SR.

As far as the LT&SR's own locomotives were concerned, it began by purchasing a batch of 4-4-2Ts, ordered in time to enable them to commence work in 1880. Their construction, by the builders Sharp, Stewart, saw the start of a long relationship whereby that company began to provide the necessary motive power required to operate the railway, although they did not build all the locomotives that the railway owned. With but two exceptions, the LT&SR was to be a tank engine line with the majority of engines being to the 'Four Wheels Coupled Bogie & Pony Truck Tank Engine', or 4-4-2T wheel arrangement as it is called today. The LT&SR introduced this wheel arrangement into the UK. Collectively, these tank engines were amongst the most successful locomotives with this wheel arrangement to run in the British Isles. Such was their versatility that the first class of locomotives was to be referred to as 'Universal' in recognition of the simple fact that they worked all the traffic on the line. That they were a mixed traffic class is confirmed by the specification where, on the front page the words 'For Mixed Traffic' appear. At a time when most locomotives that were built by British railway companies were described as 'passenger, goods or mineral engines', with an implied specific use, I believe this may be one of the first, if not *the* first use of the term 'mixed traffic'.

Before we begin to consider the development of the various tank engines that were built during the company's lifetime and beyond, it is worth considering why a tank engine was chosen. When the class was ordered, the line to Southend was via Tilbury — the later direct line did not exist. Tilbury was about the midway point between the two ends of the railway and it was at the end of two short branches from the main line that formed a triangle; see Fig 3. Through trains between London and Southend that stopped at Tilbury travelled down one side of the triangle into Tilbury station, and departed along the other side of the triangle to rejoin the main line before continuing to Southend or London. A tender locomotive would enter Tilbury engine first and depart tender first. By using a single locomotive for the entire journey, half the distance run would be tender first. The alternative was to change engines at Tilbury to ensure engine-first running throughout or to use tank engines throughout. By adopting a tank engine as the universal engine for the railway the company achieved maximum availability.

The mainstream development of LT&SR locomotives was the 'Universal' or 'No 1' class 4-4-2Ts, enlarged and improved over the years, beyond indeed the 11-year period that the line was in Midland Railway ownership. In fact the Midland Railway solution to the LT&S Section operating requirements was to order more locomotives (albeit with detailed Midland design variations) of the final Tilbury design. However, the actual order was not placed until February 1923. I have described these locomotives in Chapter 10, although the locomotives in question did not enter traffic until the Midland Railway, together with the LT&S Section, had become part of the LMS. To those readers who are unfamiliar with the operating problems of the LT&S Section it may be surprising that further construction of the type was continued by the LMS. Nasmyth, Wilson built five more locomotives in 1925, with a further 10 being built at Derby in 1927. A final 10 were also constructed at Derby in 1930 — not a bad record for an updated 1909 design!

The arrival of Stanier as the CME of the LMS came after the nettle had been grasped by the LMS management and, in conjunction with the LNER, the changes required to allow more modern motive power to work into Fenchurch Street were set in motion. It was generally acknowledged that the LT&S was a difficult section to work and one author has suggested that, while the need for bigger engines was recognised, both the Midland and LMS adopted the policy of reducing train lengths in order to keep the loading within the capacity of the locomotives available. I believe this is an over-

PASSENGER TANK ENGINES.

We illustrate this week a tank engine, constructed from the designs and specification of Mr. Thomas Whitelegg

scale, and show, first, four-wheeled, then six-wheeled, and, lastly, double-bogie eight-wheeled coaches. We may add that the speeds have been considerably augmented, as well as the loads.

PROFILE OF THE LINE BETWEEN FENCHURCH-STREET STATION AND SHOEBURYNESS

for the London, Tilbury and Southend Railway last year, for dealing with the great increase which has taken place, and is still proceeding, in the demands made by growing

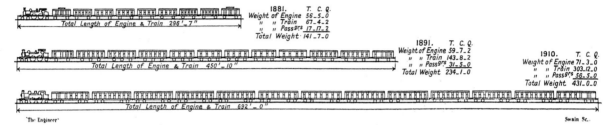

DIAGRAM SHOWING THE GROWTH OF TRAINS IN NINETEEN YEARS

traffic on the haulage power of the locomotives working that line. We give above a profile of the road. It will be seen that there are some heavy inclines, one of 1 in 110 at the 22nd mile, another of 1 in 100 at the 34th mile, followed by one of 1 in 80. Two ridges of hills have to be surmounted. Our second diagram shows graphically the growth in dimensions of the trains during nineteen years. In 1881 a 59-ton engine hauled a train of 85 tons. In 1891 the weight of the engine had increased by 3 tons only,

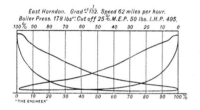

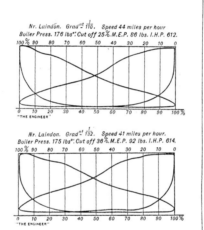

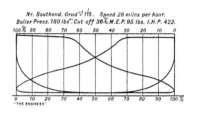

but that of the load hauled became 175 tons, or more than double. Last year the engine weighed 71 tons, while the load had risen to 360 tons—very suggestive facts in their bearing on the indefinite relations existing between the weights of locomotives and the loads they have to pull. The trains have been drawn to the same

The development of LT&SR tank engines from *The Engineer*, 1911.

---

simplification and the problem was really the bridges. Until the LNER bridge-strengthening programme was completed heavier locomotives were not permitted to travel over the section from Gas Factory Junction to Fenchurch Street.

Although I do not have any evidence to support the theory, I expect the LMS made a financial contribution to this programme which enabled it to get under way. Based upon official weight diagrams the comparisons were:

	Bogie	Leading Driving Wheels	Trailing Driving Wheels	Trailing Wheels	Total Weight Loaded
LT&SR 4-4-2T 'No 79' class	19 tons 19cwt	19 tons 11cwt	19 tons 12cwt	12 tons 1cwt	71 tons 3cwt

	Front Wheels	Leading Driving Wheels	Intermediate Driving Wheels	Trailing Driving Wheels	Rear Bogie	Total Weight Loaded
LMS Fowler 2-6-4T	12 tons	17 tons	18 tons 3cwt	16 tons 6cwt	22 tons 16cwt	86 tons 5cwt
LMS Stanier 2-cyl 2-6-4T	13 tons 14cwt	16 tons 19cwt	17 tons 14cwt	17 tons 1cwt	22 tons 19cwt	87 tons 17cwt
LMS Stanier 3-cyl 2-6-4T	12 tons 10cwt	18 tons 5cwt	19 tons 10cwt	19 tons 5cwt	22 tons 15cwt	92 tons 5cwt

Finally, it is worth noting the LT&SR 4-6-4T engines that were delivered after the LT&SR became part of the Midland Railway, which were:

	Front Bogie	Leading Driving Wheels	Intermediate Driving Wheels	Trailing Driving Wheels	Rear Bogie	Total Weight Loaded
'2100' class	18 tons 3cwt	17 tons 14cwt 1qtr	18 tons 1cwt 2qtr	17 tons 18cwt 3qtr	22 tons 15cwt	94 tons 12cwt 3qtr

Principal Dimensions of the LT&SR 4-4-2T Engines

Dimensions are generally as built

Class	'No 1'	'No 1'	'No 37'	'No 37 Rebuilt'	'No 51'	'No 79'
Engine Nos	1-30	31-36	37-48	37-48	51-68	79-82
Date of construction	1880-4	1892	1897-8	1905-11	1900-3	1909
Builder	Sharp, Stewart	Nasmyth, Wilson	Sharp, Stewart (43-8 Dübs)	Sharp, Stewart (43-8 Dübs)	Sharp, Stewart (63-8 N. British)	North British
Cylinders	17in x 26in	17in x 26in	18in x 26in	19in x 26in	18in x 26in	19in x 26in
Coupled wheel diameter	6ft 1in	6ft 1in	6ft 6in	6ft 6in	6ft 6in	6ft 6in
Boiler pressure	160psi	160psi	170psi	170psi	170psi	170psi
Maximum axle load[1] (tons)	16.025	16.1	17.75	19.0	17.5	19.8
Adhesion weight[1] (tons)	32.05	32.1	35.15[3]	38.0	35.0	39.5
Loco weight in working order[1] (tons)	56.1	56.4	63.15[4]	70.0	68.2	71.65
Boiler diameter inside	4ft 1in	4ft 1in	4ft $\frac{7}{8}$in	4ft 7$\frac{5}{8}$in	4ft 5in	4ft 7$\frac{5}{8}$in
Boiler pitch, centre line above rail level	7ft 0in	7ft 0in	7ft 6in	8ft 3in	7ft 9in	8ft 3in
Boiler length between tube plates	10ft 10$\frac{5}{16}$in	10ft 10$\frac{5}{16}$in	10ft 10$\frac{5}{16}$in	10ft 10$\frac{5}{16}$in	10ft 10$\frac{5}{16}$in	10ft 10$\frac{5}{16}$in
No of tubes and outside diameter	200 @ 1$\frac{5}{8}$in	189 @ 1$\frac{5}{8}$in	199 @ 1$\frac{5}{8}$in	217 @ 1$\frac{5}{8}$in	201 @ 1$\frac{5}{8}$in	217 @ 1$\frac{5}{8}$in
Evaporative surfaces						
tubes	924sq ft	873sq ft	919sq ft	1,002sq ft	929sq ft	1,002sq ft
firebox	97sq ft	97sq ft	107sq ft	119sq ft	117sq ft	119sq ft
total	1,021sq ft	970sq ft	1,026sq ft	1,121sq ft	1,046sq ft	1,121sq ft
Grate area	17.25sq ft	17.25sq ft	19.57sq ft	19.77sq ft	19.77sq ft	19.77sq ft
Coupled wheelbase	8ft 6in	8ft 6in	8ft 9in	8ft 9in	8ft 9in	8ft 9in
Locomotive wheelbase	29ft 4in	29ft 4in	30ft 9½in	30ft 9½in	30ft 9½in	30ft 9½in
Total length over buffers	36ft 9in	36ft 9in	39ft 0in	39ft 0in	39ft 0in	39ft 0in
Water capacity (Imp gal)	1,300	1,300	1,500	1,728	1,590[2]	1,926
Coal capacity (tons)	2	2	2¼	2¼	2¼	2¼

This table is based on information compiled by K. H. Leech and came from a number of sources. In certain instances it does not agree with other published information, including the author's own research, but it is a useful reference for the reader.

[1] According to K. H. Leech, most LT&SR weight diagrams are suspect. He considered they were made for the benefit of the Great Eastern Railways Engineer.
[2] Sharp, Stewart-built engines. Dübs engines were 1,632 gallons. [3] Sharp, Stewart-built engines. Dübs engines were 34.3 tons. [4] Sharp, Stewart-built engines. Dübs engines were 65.5 tons.

Cost of all Locomotives

Engine Nos	
1-12	£1,970 each
13-15	£2,395 ,,
16-18	£2,360 ,,
19-30	£2,590 ,,
31-36	£1,998 ,,
37-42	£2,500 ,,
43-48	£2,785 ,,
49-50	£3,008 5s 8d each
51-62	£2,995 each
63-74	£2,848 ,,
75-78	£3,350 ,,
79-82	£3,224 ,,
2190-2193	£3,100 ,,
2100	£4,092

No prices known for other engines. (Source: LT&SR Register held at Kew.)

This strengthening programme was to lead to the introduction of the 2-6-4T arrangement on the Tilbury line. The three-cylinder series, whose LMS numbers were 2500-2536, worked the heaviest passenger trains, probably exclusively until 1945 except for a few two-cylinder engines that were on loan c1935 whilst the three-cylinder locomotives were fitted with Hudd ATC equipment. The following chapters consider, in some detail, each class of LT&SR-built engines, but I begin with an overview and introduction. The conclusion of the chapter will be an examination of the painting styles that are commonly referred to as livery details, for the LT&SR, Midland and LMS Railway periods.

The first class of LT&SR-designed locomotives was the 'No 1' class 4-4-2T. It is clear from an article written by K. H. Leech, who commenced as an articled pupil in 1910 at Plaistow Works, that William Adams was largely responsible for the specification. At the time the locomotives were designed he was Superintendent of the Great Eastern Railway.

The class was to become 36 in number, built between 1880 and 1892. I believe that the first batch of 12 engines was originally fitted with steam and handbrakes only and that the Westinghouse brake, to be adopted as the standard brake for the line, was fitted later.

It seems clear that Adams, in conjunction with the builders, designed the class, while Stride, at that time General Manager, merely signed the order, but before the first engines were delivered Thomas Whitelegg was to be appointed as Chief Assistant in the locomotive department. Thomas Whitelegg was born in 1840 and was a pupil with Sharp, Stewart before seeking work elsewhere. He was employed at GER's Stratford Works and it seems likely that it was on William Adams's recommendation that he joined the LT&SR on 1 November 1879. He was appointed Locomotive, Carriage & Marine Superintendent in April 1881 and retired in 1910.

His son, Robert Harben Whitelegg, succeeded him. Robert entered the service of the LT&SR in 1888 becoming a draughtsman at Plaistow Works. He was promoted in 1898 becoming Assistant to the Locomotive Superintendent and then Assistant Locomotive Superintendent in 1909. He succeeded his father in 1910 and was responsible for the company's locomotives, passenger and freight rolling stock, together with the ferry boats. Following the Midland Railway takeover he left the company in 1913 and took a number of posts over the years including that of CME, as the position became known, of the Glasgow & South Western Railway from 1918 until 1923. It could be said that his second design of 4-6-4T for the Scottish company was no more successful than his design for the London, Tilbury & Southend Railway and that there was no really successful British design that employed this wheel arrangement.

The original specification for the 'No 1' class engines included a trailing pony truck but it has been suggested by others that it was Whitelegg who, at that time prior to his appointment to the LT&SR was a chargehand erector with Sharp, Stewart, suggested that an alternative arrangement should be employed. According to Thomas's son Robert, what happened was that his father advised Adams that a radial axlebox would produce a steadier riding locomotive when running bunker first and this idea was accepted. The question of the Adams modifications is covered in greater depth in the next chapter. Although equipped with short-travel flat slide valves with Stephenson motion, the class was free running. One engine is reported to have reached 68mph down the 3¾-mile Laindon Bank, so it may be just possible that the figure of 70mph was achieved by one of the locomotives of this class. The introduction of more modern classes, in particular from 1900 onwards, ensured the end of their regular employment on the principal fast London to Southend trains, and from then on they were to be found on less important work including the Romford branch, together with use on goods trains. I have included a side elevation only of the drawing (Fig. 30, page 108) that formed part of the original specification. The design was plain and symmetrical, with the centres of the bogie, cylinder exhaust pipes, smokebox and chimney all in line. One interesting external feature was the use of a mudguard over the bogie trailing wheels. One-inch-thick plates were used for the engine frames, and the design allowed the firebox to drop between the frames and to employ a flat firegate. The need to secure the compensating beam brackets restricted the size of the ashpan but in all the assembly permitted a low boiler centreline, some 7ft above rail level. Two Hancock injectors were fitted.

When the class was complete the 36 locomotives of the 'No 1' class handled all LT&SR trains for five years, but increasing traffic demanded more locomotives. This requirement was met by the construction of 12 more locomotives that entered traffic in two batches of six: the first batch in 1897, with the second in 1898. These engines were the 'No 37' class and in their rebuilt form marked the beginning of the final style of LT&SR 4-4-2T.

At this time a number of developments in railway technology were taking place and the 'No 37' class were to benefit accordingly. One change was the method of making the locomotive wheel centres. In keeping with the practice that applied when they were built, the 'No 1' class were made from wrought iron. This type of wheel can be identified by the flat face of the wheel spokes, but the new engines, whose driving wheels were increased in size by five inches compared with the 'No 1' class, were made from cast steel. This increase in wheel size was partly responsible for the boiler centreline becoming 7in 6in above rail level, but nevertheless, the relative location of frame, bogie and radial axlebox configuration of the 'No 1' class was retained. In addition, the driving wheel diameter and coupled wheelbase dimension then remained the same for all LT&S Section 4-4-2T engines built up to 1930. The measurement of 7in x 9in for the coupled axlebox journals of the 'No 1' class now became 8in x 9in on the 'No 37' class and this increased size was to remain unaltered for all future construction. Finally, it is worth noting that no further change was made to either the connecting rod length of 6ft 5½in, or the distance between the tubeplates, although boiler dimensions were to increase. The frame plate thickness was increased on the 'No 37' class to 1⅛in, although the use of iron in the 'Universal' engines now became rolled steel for the 'No 37' class. Water capacity for the '37s' was increased from 1,300 gallons of the 'Universals' to 1,500 gallons; further details are given in the class chapters.

The next new locomotives to enter service were in some respects rather unusual; they were the first and indeed only tender engines to be owned by the LT&SR. They were built for the Ottoman Railway in Turkey but were never delivered and their story is told in Chapter 7. It is worth recording that the arrival of No 50 was to prompt the directors and officers to commemorate this milestone in the company's history by holding a formal dinner at the Tilbury Hotel.

It was both the increasing weight of trains, together with the increase in traffic brought about in part by the 1902 developments with the District Railway, that meant more locomotives were required. This led to the introduction of the 'No 51' class, which was built in two batches: 12 in 1900 and six in 1903. Cylinder and wheel diameter dimensions remained unaltered from the 'No 37' class, but the boiler centreline was now pitched 7ft 9in above rail level with the boiler diameter measuring 4ft 5in. In addition to the increased boiler size, the class marked the first application of a steam reverser on the LT&SR and it seems appropriate to record the development of the apparatus at this point of the story since it is encountered on other LT&SR locomotives.

This gear, as described by Leech, consisted of a water cylinder (called the cataract cylinder) some 5in in diameter and designed to lock the reversing arm in position, and the operating steam cylinder, 7in in diameter, with a common stroke of 8in. It looked rather like a small Westinghouse air pump laid on its side. It was reasonably effective as a seat for the driver; the little detachable seats that were provided and hung from the bunker plate were quite useful when meals were to be taken, using the tank top as a table. When the driver was seated the regulator, brake and other boiler backplate controls were generally out of reach. The method of using the steam reverser was to point the handle on the steam cylinder rotary valve either to the front or rear of the engine depending on which direction the driver wished to travel. He then moved the gear to forward or reverse position and had to juggle the water valve handle to 'on' and 'off' so that the gear moved reasonably slowly in the desired direction. When notching up the aim was to move about half a notch (out of the eight from full to mid gear) nearer to mid gear than was necessary. Then, when reversing the steam valve the small amount of cushioning that was impossible to eliminate in the cataract cylinder let the gear down to the desired position. Occasionally the water cylinder leather cup packing would fail completely and the only sensible course then was to work the engine in full gear until it could be repaired. In these circumstances I suspect the driver failed the engine as quickly as possible.

At first the 'No 51' class was rarely called upon to haul more than 10 bogie coaches, although they could handle 11 or 12 on all but the fastest schedules. The c1906 Westcliff and Southend non-stop trains, made up to 13-14 bogies with a tare weight of about 330 tons, were beyond them and this probably led to the decision to rebuild the 'No 37' class locomotives. I have described the 'No 51' class in greater detail in Chapter 8, but we illustrate on page 111 an example of the class in its original condition. They were the most symmetrical of all the 4-4-2Ts to be owned by the company and from the enginemen's point of view, they were reputed to be better steamers, whose ride was superior to the later larger engines. In their final years, with extended smokeboxes and Midland fittings, they were to work off the parent system and as such they are also illustrated in this guise later in the class chapter.

Before we come to what is, to all intents and purposes, the start of the final part of the story, namely the rebuilding of the 'No 37' class into what became the prototype for all future LT&SR 4-4-2Ts, we must record the development of the freight tank engines of the 'No 69' class 0-6-2Ts. Six engines were ordered in 1903 at the same time as the order was placed for the second batch of 'No 51' class 4-4-2Ts. The 0-6-2Ts were to enter traffic in three batches; the second batch of four were built in 1908, with the final series of locomotives, also four in number, not arriving from the builders until after the LT&SR had become part of the Midland Railway. The final batch did not carry their allotted LT&SR running numbers, which would have been Nos 83-86, nor were they painted in LT&SR green livery. Unlike the other members of the class these four engines were to carry a plain black livery throughout their lifetime's service. Illustrated on page 111 is one of the original series with all variants covered in Chapter 9. The final four engines were built with steam sanding gear. This was the first time this equipment had been applied to any Tilbury locomotive, and in view of the fact that steam sanding was standard Midland practice, it seems likely that this modification was made before the locomotives left the builders. What is surprising is that although the Midland Railway made considerable use of steam sanding, the fitting on these engines proved to be unreliable in use and after a year or so it was removed. Thereafter these engines ran with dry sand gear. However, this was to prove to be a problem and I return to this subject when the question of de-sanding gear is examined. Their boilers were the same size as those fitted to the 'No 51' class, that were ordered at the same time, but the boilers were not interchangeable between the two classes.

The next development to be considered is the 'No 37' class

rebuilds. This was the direct result of the need to provide more powerful locomotives and two options were open to the company. The first was to introduce new, more powerful engines and thereby render some of the 'Universal' class surplus to requirements. At the time it was considered that these engines had many years of active life still in front of them so a second option was adopted. This was to rebuild (today we would probably call it an upgrade), a number of existing engines and the obvious locomotives were the 12 'No 37' class, which had been built in 1897/8 and were only seven to eight years old. The rebuilding programme commenced in 1905 and took seven years to complete. The class is described in Chapter 6; here I propose to outline briefly the actual rebuilding programme.

The Tilbury purchased all its locomotives from the 'Trade', but the rebuilding programme for the '37s' was undertaken at Plaistow Works, which probably explains why it was spread over several years. The first engine to be reconstructed was No 37, this being carried out in 1905 and no more were dealt with until 1907, so it is possible that the company wished to evaluate the potential before rebuilding additional engines. Therefore it seems reasonable that while the need for more powerful locomotives existed, it was not that pressing or perhaps it was a case of Plaistow Works being unable to cope with the work, but we will probably never know. The No 79 class, described in Chapter 10, was in service two years before the final engines of the 'No 37' class had been rebuilt, or reconstructed, as the LT&SR works plates described the changes which had taken place. The rebuilds are described in Chapter 6 although an example is illustrated on page 108. It is also worth mentioning that some were turned out in the short-lived lavender-blue colour with black borders and panels lined out in white, a style introduced in 1907. It would seem this livery did not wear very well in service and a return to Tilbury green was made. By 1909, the morning Southend to Fenchurch Street and evening return business train was made up to 13 bogies and one six-wheel coach, the maximum train length which could be accommodated at the longest platform at Fenchurch Street. This was a far cry from the early c1880 trains, which had a tare weight of about 105 tons. The 17 March 1911 issue of *The Engineer* contained an article about the new No 79 class and the trains they were called upon to work between Shoeburyness, Southend and Fenchurch Street. I have reproduced this information on page 102 because it illustrates both the nature of the line in terms of gradients and the way that the train weights increased between 1881 and 1910.

These rebuilds were at first allocated to Shoeburyness, and along with the No 79 class comprised the top link of locomotives for express passenger work. In many respects the 'No 37' class rebuilds and the No 79 class should be considered together. In operating terms they were the top link passenger engines and just that little bit more powerful than the 'No 51' class. However, as can be seen from the illustration on page 113 of one of the four engines built by Robert Stephenson, these exhibited both deeper side tanks and bunkers. In addition, the arrangement of the platform around the tanks was not identical. There is another illustration of the preserved example of the class, No 80 *Thundersley* on page 149, but here it is just necessary to record that two of this class of four, Nos 79 and 80, are believed to have been painted in lavender-blue when new, while Nos 81 and 82 were green from the outset. At this point in time some confusion exists about exactly which engine was in what colour, contemporary and other sources consulted being at variance.

The enlarged side tanks of the No 79 class contained 1,926 gallons of water and this was rather more than the 1,728 gallons for the 'No 37' class rebuilds. There is no doubt that this additional capacity would have been very welcome to the engine crews when working heavy trains. According to Kenneth Leech, Robert Whitelegg intended to fit extended smokeboxes to these engines as and when the smokebox became due for replacement, but this was never done. It was left to the Midland Railway to implement this change to the original engines and to the 35 locomotives of the No 79 class, which were to enter service during the LMS period of ownership.

One of the major problems on the LT&SR was the bad, chalky water found all over the system and this was the principal cause of priming which was a continued source of worry to all enginemen. As a result, it was necessary to wash out all boilers every week and from the third day to 'blow down' the boilers daily, sometimes twice a day on engines employed on top link working. This was done by placing the engine over a pit in the locomotive yard with a 'potful' (full boiler) of water and then opening the blowdown cock which was situated on the front of the firebox just above the foundation ring, by means of a big handle on the footplate in the cab. This action would cause a terrific roar of steam and water, with the engine disappearing from view for two or three minutes until the cock was shut again and the water gauge was showing empty. This action was calculated to cost about 200 gallons of water and the coal wasted was thought to be about 3-4lb per engine mile run. However, it did remove most of the build-up of sediment that was the principal cause of priming.

Other detail changes which the new owners made included Midland Railway boiler mountings, smokebox doors and the replacement of the bunker lids prior to fitting coal rails. No doubt this modification coincided with the change from the use of Scottish coal that the Tilbury had used prior to 1912. The Midland would have supplied the LT&S Section with coal purchased from collieries in Yorkshire where the company had most of its contracts for the supply of locomotive coal. Scottish coal came to the LT&SR by sea and because it was rather dusty it was probably felt that it would be better if it was totally enclosed, while the harder coal used by the Midland Railway was less likely to prove too troublesome when running bunker first. Another fitting that did not find favour with the Midland was the variable blastpipe, a device first used with 0-6-2Ts Nos 75-78, as detailed later. These were fitted at the same time as spark arresters, probably in an attempt to reduce claims for compensation from lineside fires caused by sparks being thrown from locomotives. However, they also reduced the locomotive's ability to produce steam.

This spark arrester took the form of a sort of skeleton drum about 2ft in diameter and 1ft in height, with ribs consisting of 16 gauge steel wire bent round to form a circle and kept at ½in centres, one above another by vertical spacers. The drum was located inside the smokebox, fitted snugly at the top to the flare of the chimney liner while at the bottom it was bolted by means of a circular flange to the base of the blastpipe cap. It had the effect of reducing the area for the flow of gases to the base of the chimney by about one third. The small amount of space available in the short smokebox did not make it easy to fit and it is possible that a better arrangement could have been achieved. The LT&SR was using soft Scottish coal but the hard Yorkshire coal as used by the parent system led to the Midland altering the tube diameters and method of fixing,

whereupon, according to K. H. Leech, matters deteriorated somewhat.

The only official instructions I have been able to find are two LMS era orders that were placed to fit spark arresters to Midland Division engines working the Thames Haven branch. The first, order number 7191, was dated 13 August 1928 and read: 'Please put your work in hand in connection with fitting 7 Midland Division engines Nos 1667, 1786, 2948, 3035, 3177 and 3407 with spark arresters and charge to o/n 7191.' Three days later a pencil note was added: (also engine No 3050.) 'Drawing No RS-912 will be marked and issued in due course. Engine No 3407, now in Derby Shops, should be fitted before leaving. The arresters are to be sent to Plaistow for fitting and when ready please advise me so that the necessary instructions may be issued.' The works superintendent at Derby signed the order. The second order was No 7429 dated 17 June 1929 and was similar, referring to the alterations to be made to Cricklewood engines Nos 3306 and 3772. I have not found anything else about the use of spark arresters on the LT&S Section.

I have perhaps digressed slightly from the story when expressed in chronological terms, but have almost reached the end of the strictly LT&SR period as far as the No 79 class is concerned. To represent the post-1912 developments there are illustrations of examples of locomotives built to an LT&SR design but ordered by the LMS on pages 149, 151 and 152.

Finally, in this review of LT&SR classes, we must examine the design which never saw service while the company was a separate legal entity and which, if truth be told, was something of a white elephant to the Midland Railway. One of these 4-6-4Ts is shown on page 151, just after delivery from its builders, Beyer Peacock. A model, built to the scale of 1in to 1ft, was produced at Plaistow Works and while the external finish does not follow the then current LT&SR livery practice, it is just possible that this is the way it would have developed but for the Midland takeover. The model suggested that LT&SR numbers would have been 87-94 and the model, No 94, was named *Arthur Lewis Stride*. Possibly, the other engines in the class would have carried other directors' names and would have been subject to the livery variations displayed by the model, which included the use of raised numbers on the engine tank sides. This model is now on display at the NRM, York. The story of these locomotives in Midland and LMS ownership is told in Chapter 11.

LT&SR Locomotive Details and MR and LMS Modifications

Generally, the story of locomotive details will be told in the class chapters but I shall cover screwjacks here. This was not a Midland Railway feature, and not surprisingly, the new owners removed this equipment following the purchase of the LT&SR. It would appear that it was originally LT&SR practice to carry them on the top of the side tanks. At about the turn of the century they began to be located at the front end of the locomotive platform or running plate and as such will be seen in various pictures. Fortunately, I have a Robert Stephenson drawing renumbered 13-9188 by the Midland Railway that shows the screwjack as supplied for the No 37, 51 and 79 class engines. It is reproduced at Fig **31** on page 109.

A second contractor's drawing that was renumbered by the Midland Railway is reproduced at Fig **33** on page 113 and illustrates the various tools supplied with each locomotive

Continued page 117

List of LT&SR Locomotive Stock by Class

'No 1' Class (MR Class 1; LMS post-1928 Class 1P)

No	LT&SR Name	Built By	Date Built	Boiler New Dates[1]: At 1912 MR Takeover	MR Last New Boiler	MR No	Date MR Renumber where known	LMS No and date	1929 No	Date Withdr'n From Service
								1923		
1	Southend	Sharp, Stewart	Apr 1880	1901	Dec 1922	2110	11.10.1912	2200	2077	11.30
2	Gravesend	,,	Jun 1880	1898	May 1920	2111		2201	2078	9.35
3	Tilbury	,,	May 1880	1910	Jan 1919	2112		2202	2079	9.35
4	Bromley	,,	May 1880	1897	Nov 1922	2113	18.4.1913	2203	2080	12.32
5	Plaistow	,,	May 1880	1899	Nov 1920	2114		2204	2081	8.30
6	Upton Park	,,	May 1880	1911	Oct 1916	2115		2205	2082	12.32
7	Barking	,,	Jun 1880	1898	Oct 1921	2116		2206	2083	9.35
8	Rainham	,,	Jul 1880	1898	Jun 1920	2117		2207	2084	12.32
9	Purfleet	,,	Jul 1880	1896	Jan 1923	2118		2208	2085	6.30
10	Grays	,,	Jul 1880	1897	Nov 1920	2119	26.4.1913	2209	2086	6.30
								1925		
11	Stanford	,,	Jul 1880	1899	Feb 1923	2120		2210	2087	11.30
12	Pitsea	,,	Aug 1880	1896	Nov 1923	2121		2211	2088	12.30
13	Benfleet	,,	Apr 1881	1899	Aug 1922	2122		2212	2089	11.32
14	Leigh	,,	May 1881	1896	Sep 1921	2123		2213	2090	9.35
15	East Ham	,,	May 1881	1898	No record	2124		2214	2091	12.32
								1927		
16	Low Street	,,	Dec 1881	1899	Apr 1918	2125		2190	2067	7.34
17	Thames Haven	,,	Dec 1881	1910	Jul 1921	2126		2191	2068	9.35
18	Shoeburyness	,,	Dec 1881	1896	May 1921	2127		2192	2069	8.30
19	Dagenham	,,	Dec 1884	1900	Aug 1924	2128		2193	2070	9.35
20	Hornchurch	,,	Dec 1884	1901	Jul 1914	2129	24.1.1913	2194	2071	11.32
21	Upminster	,,	Dec 1884	1900	Sep-Oct 1923	2130	25.9.1912	2195	2072	9.35
22	East Horndon	,,	Jan 1885	1900	May 1919	2131		2196	2073	10.35
23	Laindon	,,	Jan 1885	1896	Sep 1922	2132		2197	2074	12.30
24	Ockendon	,,	Jan 1885	1911	Nov 1924	2133		2198	2075	9.35
25	Stifford	,,	Jan 1885	1900	Feb 1921	2134		2199	2076	9.35
26	West Thurrock	,,	Jan 1885	1900	Nov 1924	2135			2056	12.32
27	Whitechapel	,,	Jan 1885	1901	Apr 1924	2136			2057	12.32
28	Romford	,,	Jan 1885	1900	Dec 1923	2137			2058	9.35
29	Stepney	,,	Jan 1885	1902	Jun-Jul 1923	2138			2059	9.32
30	Fenchurch	,,	Jan 1885	1900	Sep 1920	2139			2060	9.34
31	St Pancras	Nasmyth, Wilson	Jan 1892	1904	Feb 1923	2140			2061	12.32
32	Leyton	,,	Feb 1892	1904	Jul-Aug 1923	2141			2062	12.32
33	Wanstead	,,	Feb 1892	1905	Feb 1924	2142			2063	9.35
34	Tottenham	,,	Apr 1892	1905	Jan 1924	2143			2064	12.32
35	West Ham	,,	May 1892	1904	Mar 1922	2144			2065	12.32
36	Walthamstow	,,	Jul 1892	1903	Jul-Aug 1923	2145			2066	8.32

Renaming details are given on page 115.

[1]New boiler is a Midland Railway term that covered both a new or second-hand repaired boiler. The Boiler New dates at 1912 were taken from the LT&SR Register and with two exceptions agree with the MR Register that ceases to record details about 1932.

Dates, other than for withdrawal, have been taken from either the LT&SR or MR Railway Register, or are shown otherwise. The withdrawal dates are LMS four-weekly periods.

'No 1' class engine No 15 *East Ham* was built in 1881 and this picture illustrates the locomotive in original condition. *L&GRP 5617*

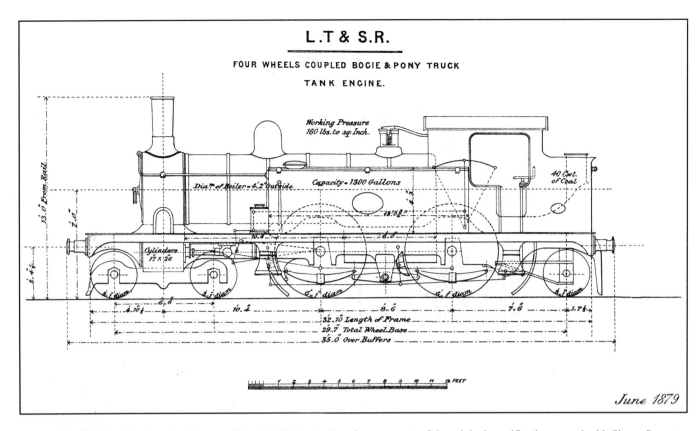

Fig 30. This side elevation diagram of the 'No 1' class tank engines was part of the original specification agreed with Sharp, Stewart. A general arrangement drawing of this class is illustrated in Chapter Five. *Collection R. J. Essery*

'No 37' Class (MR Class 3; LMS post-1928 Class 3P)

No	LT&SR Name	Built By	Date Built	Date Rebuilt	Boiler New Dates[1]: 1912[2]	Last New Boiler[4]	MR[3] No	Date MR Renumber	LMS No 1929	BR No	Date Withdrawn From Service
37	Woodgrange	Sharp, Stewart	Mar 1897	Nov 1905	1905	Jun 1925	2146	16.3.1913	2135	41953	8.51
38	Westcliff	,,	Apr 1897	Dec 1908	1908	Dec 1924	2147	3.12.1912	2136	41954	8.51
39	Forest Gate	,,	Apr 1897	Sep 1907	1907	Jul 1922	2148	7.12.1912	2137	41955	2.51
40	Black Horse Road	,,	Apr 1897	Dec 1910	1910	Mar 1924	2149		2138	41956	9.51
41	Leytonstone	,,	Apr 1897	Dec 1909	1909	Oct 1924	2150		2139	41957	9.51
42	Commercial Road	,,	Apr 1897	Jul 1910	1910	Apr 1924	2151		2140	41958	12.51
43	Great Ilford	Dübs	Dec 1898	Dec 1906	1906	Apr 1922	2152		2141	41959	9.51
44	Prittlewell	,,	Dec 1898	Feb 1911	1911	Dec 1924	2153		2142	41960	2.51
45	Burdett Road	,,	Dec 1898	Nov 1909	1909	Oct 1924	2154		2143	41961	10.51
46	Southchurch	,,	Dec 1898	Jul 1910	1910	Aug 1924	2155		2144	41962	2.51
47	Stratford	,,	Jan 1899	Apr 1908	1908	Dec 1923	2156		2145	41963	2.51
48	Little Ilford	,,	Jan 1899	Jan 1899	1911	May 1924	2157		2146	41964	2.51

[1]The Midland Railway Locomotive Register does not have a clear cut-off point, but generally ceases in 1932.
[2]At Midland Railway 1912 takeover.
[3]Also LMS 1923 No.
[4]Prior to 1932 when Register ceases.
Renaming details are given on page 115.
Dates, other than for withdrawal, have been taken from either the LT&SR or MR Railway Register, or are shown otherwise. The withdrawal dates are LMS four-weekly periods.

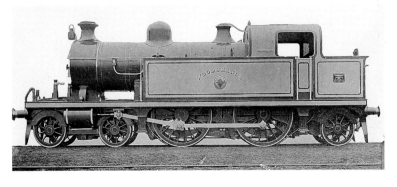

This picture of No 37 *Woodgrange* illustrates the engine in its 1905 rebuilt condition displaying the short-lived lavender-colour livery used between 1907 and 1910. According to George Dow in *Midland Style*, the usual arrangement of panelling was employed but the lining colour was black and white. An additional black line edged white was around the front and rear cab windows. Black and white lining was used on the buffer casings, Westinghouse cylinders, jacks and headlamps. The buffer beams and guard irons were in vermilion, while the cylinder covers were in grey planished steel, with polished steel end plates. *Locomotive Publishing Co*

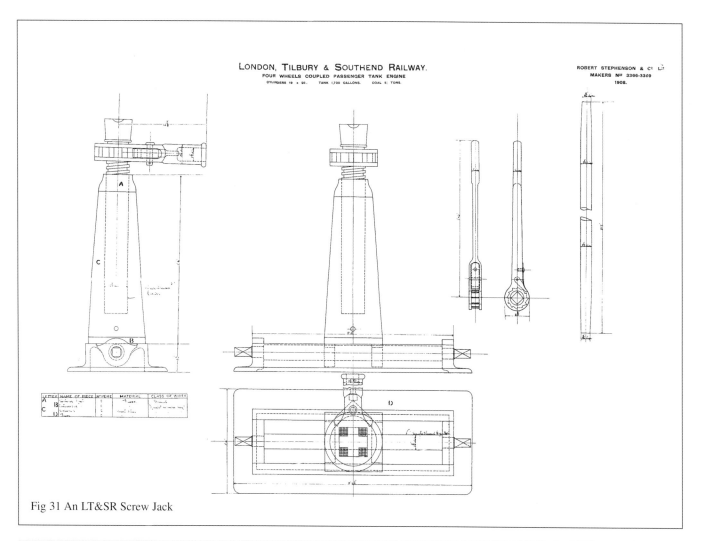

LONDON, TILBURY & SOUTHEND RAILWAY.
FOUR WHEELS COUPLED PASSENGER TANK ENGINE
CYLINDERS 19 x 26.   TANK 1,720 GALLONS.   COAL 2½ TONS.

ROBERT STEPHENSON & Cº Lᵗᵈ
MAKERS Nº 3366-3369
1908.

Fig 31 An LT&SR Screw Jack

This delightful view of No 46 *Southchurch* represents the 'No 37' Class. Built by Dübs in 1898, its painting and lining are shown to good effect. The two goods vehicles are worthy of some comment. The vehicle to the rear of the engine is a cattle wagon that has been partly sheeted over, while the vehicle to the front is a goods brake van. The LT&SR employed a most unusual design of goods brake van with an open verandah, which can clearly be seen in this picture. *Collection R. J. Essery*

'No 49' Class (MR Class 2; LMS post-1928 Class 2F)

No	LT&SR Name	Built By	Date To LT&SR	Boiler New Dates[1]: 1912[2]	Last New Boiler	MR[3] No	Date MR Renumber	LMS No	Date Withdrawn From Service
49	-	Sharp, Stewart	Jun 1899	1899	Oct 1922[4]	2898	23.12.1912		12.33
50	-	,,	Jun 1899	1899	Jun 1924[4]	2899	3.1913	22899 (1.35)	2.36

[1] The Midland Railway Locomotive Register does not have a clear cut-off point, but generally ceases in 1932.
[2] At Midland Railway 1912 takeover.
[3] Also LMS 1923 No.
[4] Fitted with a G5½ Altd boiler (ie a modified standard G5½ boiler)
Dates, other than for withdrawal, have been taken from either the LT&SR or MR Railway Register, or are shown otherwise. The withdrawal dates are LMS four-weekly periods.

This side elevation of 0-6-0 No 49 was probably taken at Plaistow. It shows the arrangement of lining on the tender side, cabside panel, boiler clothing bands, wheel centres and sandbox. NRM 522/68

'No 51' Class (MR Class 2; LMS post-1928 Class 2P)

No	LT&SR Name	Built By	Date Built	Boiler New Dates[1]: 1912[2]	Last New Boiler[4]	MR[3] No	Date MR Renumber	LMS No	BR No	Date Withdrawn From Service
51	Tilbury Docks	Sharp, Stewart	Sep 1900	1900	Feb 1922	2158		2092		9.48
52	Wennington	,,	Sep 1900	1900	Feb 1925	2159	3.2.1913	2093		3.53
53	Stepney Green	,,	Sep 1900	1906	Feb 1924	2160		2094		8.49
54	Mile End	,,	Oct 1900	1911	May 1923	2161		2095		6.49
55	Wellington Road	,,	Oct 1900	1910	Sep-Oct 1923	2162	12.11.1912	2096		5.50
56	Harringay	,,	Oct 1900	1900	Jun 1924	2163		2097		3.51
57	Crouch Hill	,,	Oct 1900	1900	Jan 1924	2164		2098		3.51
58	Hornsey Road	,,	Oct 1900	1900	Jun 1925	2165		2099		3.51
59	Holloway	,,	Oct 1900	1906	Jun 1925	2166		2100		12.49
60	Highgate Road	,,	Oct 1900	1913	Apr 1923	2167	11.3.1913	2101		3.51
61	Kentish Town	,,	Oct 1900	1912	May 1923	2168	11.1.1913	2102		6.49
62	Camden Road	,,	Oct 1900	1912	Apr 1925	2169		2103		3.51
63	Mansion House	North British	Jun 1903	1903	Jun 1925	2170		2104	41922	3.53
64	Charing Cross	,,	Jun 1903	1903	May 1925	2171		2105		11.47
65	Victoria	,,	Jun 1903	1903	Jan 1925	2172		2106	41923	12.49
66	Earls Court	,,	Jun 1903	1903	Dec 1924	2173	3.9.1912	2107		12.49
67	Westminster	,,	Jun 1903	1903	Jun-Jul 1923	2174		2108	41925	4.52
68	Mark Lane	,,	Jun 1903	1903	May 1924	2175		2109		3.51

[1] The Midland Railway Locomotive Register does not have a clear cut-off point, but generally ceases in 1932.
[2] At Midland Railway 1912 takeover.
[3] Also LMS 1923 No.
[4] Prior to 1932 when Register ceases.
Renaming details are given on page 115.
Dates, other than for withdrawal, have been taken from either the LT&SR or MR Railway Register, or are shown otherwise. The withdrawal dates are LMS four-weekly periods.

The 'No 51' class were delightful-looking engines and this picture of No 57 *Crouch Hill* displays their lines rather well. Built in 1900 by Sharp, Stewart, the engine was to become No 2164 when renumbered by the Midland Railway in 1912. The screwjack, clearly numbered 57, together with the fixing arrangement, can be seen in this picture.
Collection R. J. Essery

'No 69' Class (MR Class 2; LMS post-1928 Class 2F)

No	LT&SR Name	Built By	Date Built	Date Last New Boiler[1]	MR No	Date MR Renumber	LMS No 1923	LMS No 1939	LMS No 1947	BR No	Date Withdrawn From Service
69	*Corringham*	North British	Jun 1903	Feb 1920	2180	5.10.1912	2220	2180	1980	41980	5.58
70	*Basildon*	,,	Jun 1903	Aug-Sep 1923	2181		2221	2181	1981	41981	6.62
71	*Wakering*	,,	Jun 1903	Jul 1922	2182		2222	2182	1982	41982	2.59
72	*Hadleigh*	,,	Jun 1903	Oct 1920	2183		2223	2183	1983	41983	2.59
73	*Cranham*	,,	Jul 1903	Mar 1922	2184		2224	2184	1984	41984	2.59
74	*Orsett*	,,	Jul 1903	Apr 1921	2185		2225	2185	1985	41985	2.59
75	*Canvey Island*	,,	Aug 1908	May 1921	2186	1.12.1913	2226	2186	1986	41986	2.59
76	*Dunton*	,,	Aug 1908	May-Jun 1923	2187	30.11.1912	2227	2187	1987	41987	2.59
77	*Fobbing*	,,	Aug 1908	Jun 1922	2188		2228	2188	1988	41988	4.58
78	*Dagenham Dock*	,,	Sep 1908	Feb 1922	2189		2229	2189	1989	41989	4.58
(83)[2]		Beyer Peacock	Nov 1912	Jul-Aug 1923	2190		2230	2190	1990	41990	2.59
(84)[2]		,,	Nov 1912	Jun-Jul 1923	2191		2231	2191	1991	41991	2.59
(85)[2]		,,	Nov 1912	Nov 1922	2192		2232	2192	1992	41992	2.59
(86)[2]		,,	Nov 1912	Sep 1921	2193		2233	2193	1993	41993	2.59

[1] All 'No 69' class locomotives transferred to Midland Railway in 1912 takeover with their original boilers. The Midland Railway Locomotive Register does not have a clear cut-off point, but generally ceases in 1932. These are the last dates recorded.
[2] Nos 83-6 delivered after the LT&SR became part of the Midland Railway and did not carry allocated LT&SR numbers, being delivered with MR numbers.
Dates, other than for withdrawal, have been taken from either the LT&SR or MR Railway Register, or are shown otherwise.

'No 69' class engine No 73 *Cranham* was built by the North British Locomotive Company in 1903 and survived until February 1959 when withdrawn by British Railways as No 41984. In this undated picture there appears to be no lining other than on the buffer beam, buffer casing and Westinghouse cylinders.
Locomotive Publishing Co

Above and **Fig 32** *(Below):*
Livery details for the 'No 69' class 0-6-2T engines. This photograph of No 69 *Corringham* and the accompanying drawing by
P. E. Barnes show the full LT&SR painting style as applied to the first six locomotives, Nos 69-74. The next four carried the simpler
style of livery, similar to that used with the 'No 1' class, while the final four entered service in Midland Railway black goods engine
livery. *Collection R. J. Essery*

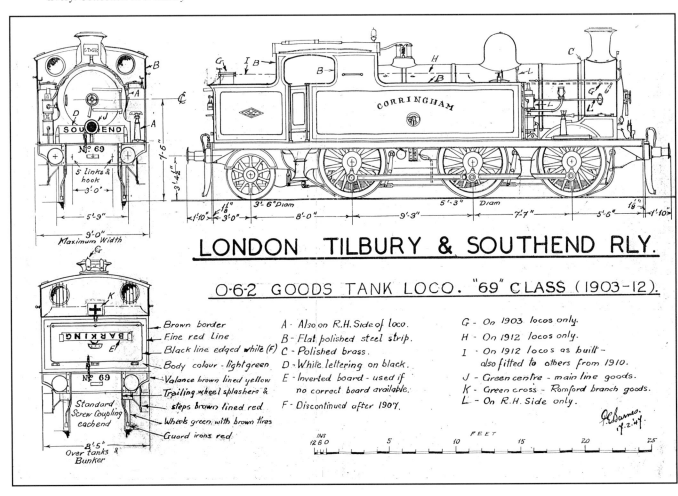

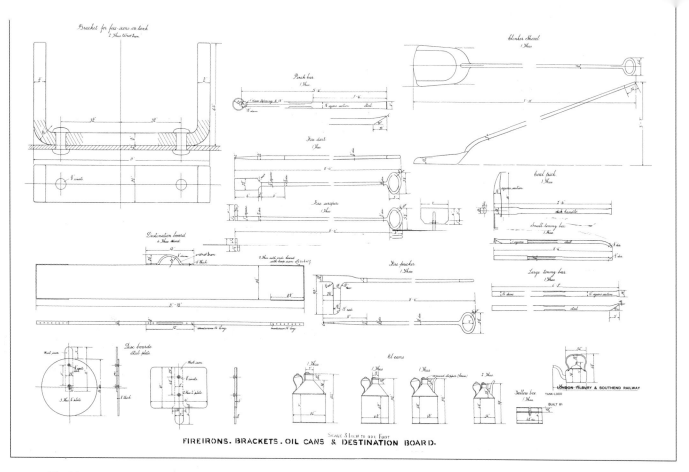

FIREIRONS. BRACKETS. OIL CANS & DESTINATION BOARD.

Fig 33 The North British Locomotive Co Ltd drawing reproduced here and renumbered 13-8908 by the Midland Railway shows the various tools etc, supplied with the batch of 'No 69' class engines. I would not expect to find that these tools were different from the other classes of locomotives, except the Baltic tank engines where longer-handled fire irons would probably be supplied.

'No 79' Class (MR Class 3; LMS post-1928 Class 3P)

No	LT&SR Name	Built By	Date Built	Date Last New Boiler[1]	MR No[2]	Date MR Renumber	1929 LMS No	BR No	Date Withdrawn From Service
79	*Rippleside*	Robert Stephenson	May 1909	Apr 1924	2176	4.12.1912	2147	41965	2.51
80	*Thundersley*	,,	May 1909	Jun 1924	2177		2148	41966	6.56[3]
81	*Aveley*	,,	May 1909	Mar 1924	2178	12.12.1912	2149	41967	11.52
82	*Crowstone*	,,	Jun 1909	Dec 1925	2179		2150	41968	2.51

[1] All 'No 79' class locomotives transferred to Midland Railway in 1912 takeover with their original boilers. The Midland Railway Locomotive Register does not have a clear cut-off point, but generally ceases in 1932. These are the last dates recorded.
[2] Also 1923 LMS No.
[3] Preserved as part of the National Collection.
Renaming details are given on page 115.
Dates, other than for withdrawal, have been taken from either the LT&SR or MR Railway Register, or are shown otherwise.

No 80 *Thundersley* was the only LT&SR engine to feature a polished brass safety valve cover, clearly visible in this picture. The locomotive was exhibited in the lavender-grey livery when new at White City in 1909 and carried the name *Southend-on-Sea*. The engine was awarded a gold medal. Upon entering service the allocated name was applied and in 1910 it received the green livery.
Collection R. J. Essery

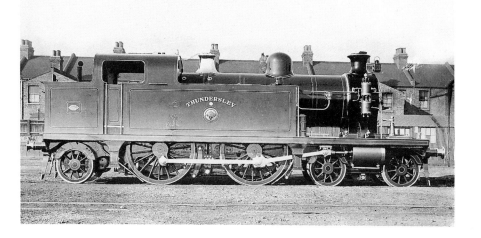

Ordered by the LT&SR but delivered after the company became part of the Midland Railway

MR No	Built By	Date Built[1]	1929 LMS No	Date Withdrawn From Service
2100	Beyer Peacock	Apr 1913		2.29
2101	,,	Apr 1913		12.29
2102	,,	Apr 1913		12.29
2103	,,	Apr 1913	2195	10.30
2104	,,	May 1913	2196	12.32
2105	,,	May 1913	2197	3.33
2106	,,	May 1913	2198	5.34
2107	,,	May 1913		9.29

Notes

[1] As shown in the Midland Railway Register.
Other than boiler Nos 89-96 no details are given. The locomotives retained their original boilers.
Dates, other than for withdrawal, have been taken from either the LT&SR or MR Railway Register, or are shown otherwise. The withdrawal dates are LMS four-weekly periods.

This side elevation picture of No 2101 emphasises the length of the 4-6-4T engines which measured 47ft 8in over the buffers, compared with the 4-4-2Ts which were 39ft overall. In the Midland Railway colour of crimson lake they would have presented a magnificent sight. *Collection R. J. Essery*

No 2118 was built at Derby in 1923, and the locomotive is seen here in crimson lake livery with the short-lived small 'LMS' applied to the bunker side prior to the introduction of the company's armorial device which was used with the pre-1928 LMS red livery.
Real Photographs W5009/NRM

'No 79' Class
As modified by the MR and LMS

LMS No	Order No	Built By	Date Built	LMS No 1947	BR No	Date Withdrawn From Service
2110	0/5871	LMS Derby	20 May 1923	1928	41928	2.59
2111	,,	,,	17 Jun 1923	1929	41929	9.51
2112	,,	,,	17 Jun 1923	1930	41930	9.52
2113	,,	,,	15 Jul 1923	1931	41931	3.51
2114	,,	,,	15 Jul 1923	1932	41932	9.51
2115	,,	,,	15 Jul 1923	1933	41933	9.51
2116	,,	,,	15 Jul 1923	1934	41934	9.51
2117	,,	,,	12 Aug 1923	1935	41935	10.51
2118	,,	,,	12 Aug 1923	1936	41936	9.58
2119	,,	,,	12 Aug 1923	1937	41937	3.52
2120	0/6377	Nasmyth, Wilson	9 Aug 1925	1938	41938	2.55
2121	,,	,,	9 Aug 1925	1939	41939	2.59
2122	,,	,,	9 Aug 1925	1940	41940	4.56
2123	,,	,,	9 Aug 1925	1941	41941	2.59
2124	,,	,,	9 Aug 1925	1942	41942	13.56
2125	0/6751	LMS Derby	22 May 1927	1943	41943	2.56
2126	,,	,,	19 Jun 1927	1944	41944	13.56
2127	,,	,,	19 Jun 1927	1945	41945	2.59
2128	,,	,,	19 Jun 1927	1946	41946	2.59
2129	,,	,,	19 Jun 1927	1947	41947	12.60
2130	,,	,,	17 Jul 1927	1948	41948	2.59
2131	,,	,,	17 Jul 1927	1949	41949	4.60
2132	,,	,,	17 Jul 1927	1950	41950	2.59
2133	,,	,,	17 Jul 1927	1951	41951	13.56
2134	,,	,,	14 Aug 1927	1952	41952	13.56
2151	0/7406	,,	Jan 1930	1969	41969	4.60
2152	,,	,,	Jan 1930	1970	41970	13.56
2153	,,	,,	Feb 1930	1971	41971	2.55
2154	,,	,,	Feb 1930	1972	41972	2.55
2155	,,	,,	Feb 1930	1973	41973	2.55
2156	,,	,,	Feb 1930	1974	41974	2.55
2157	,,	,,	Feb 1930	1975	41975	12.59
2158	,,	,,	Feb 1930	1976	41976	13.56
2159	,,	,,	Mar 1930	1977	41977	2.59
2160	,,	,,	Mar 1930	1978	41978	2.59

Notes
Other than the new boiler number, no details were recorded in the Midland Locomotive Register.
Dates, other than for withdrawal, have been taken from either the LT&SR or MR Railway Register, or are shown otherwise.

A number of LT&SR locomotives were involved in changes of name. Unless otherwise noted all the dates given have been taken from the LT&SR/MR register held at the Public Record Office, Kew.

No 9 *Purfleet* became *Tilbury Docks* on 27/11/1911.
No 13 *Benfleet* became *Black Horse Road* on 15/9/1911.
No 18 *Shoeburyness* became *Burdett Road* on 21/12/1911.
No 22 *East Horndon* became *Commercial Road* on 9/11/1911.
No 40 *Black Horse Road* became *Benfleet* on 30/12/1910.
No 42 *Commercial Road* became *East Horndon* on 16/6/1911.

No 45 *Burdett Road* became *Shoeburyness* on 16/6/1911.

No 51 *Tilbury Docks* became *Purfleet* on 3/7/1911.
No 55 *Wellington Road* became *Bow Road* in 1903. No further details are known.

No 58 *Hornsey Road* became *Hornsey* on 16/3/1911.
No 60 *Highgate Road* became *Highgate* on 16/6/1911.
No 62 *Camden Road* became *Camden*. No date recorded. Some sources give 1911 which seems likely.
No 80 *Southend-on-Sea* became *Thundersley* prior to entering service after being exhibited at the Imperial International Exhibition, May to October 1909. The locomotive was awarded a gold medal, a replica of which was mounted on the tankside, below the name and above the coat of arms. See Photo on page 148

The change of names was not tidy and in a number of cases two engines carried the same names for some while. Other authors have only recorded the year that the change of name took place and generally they agree with the details given here, but I cannot be sure if two locomotives ran in service with the same name. Possible explanations are that one engine was in the works for repair and another is that one engine was in store, returning to traffic with a new name.

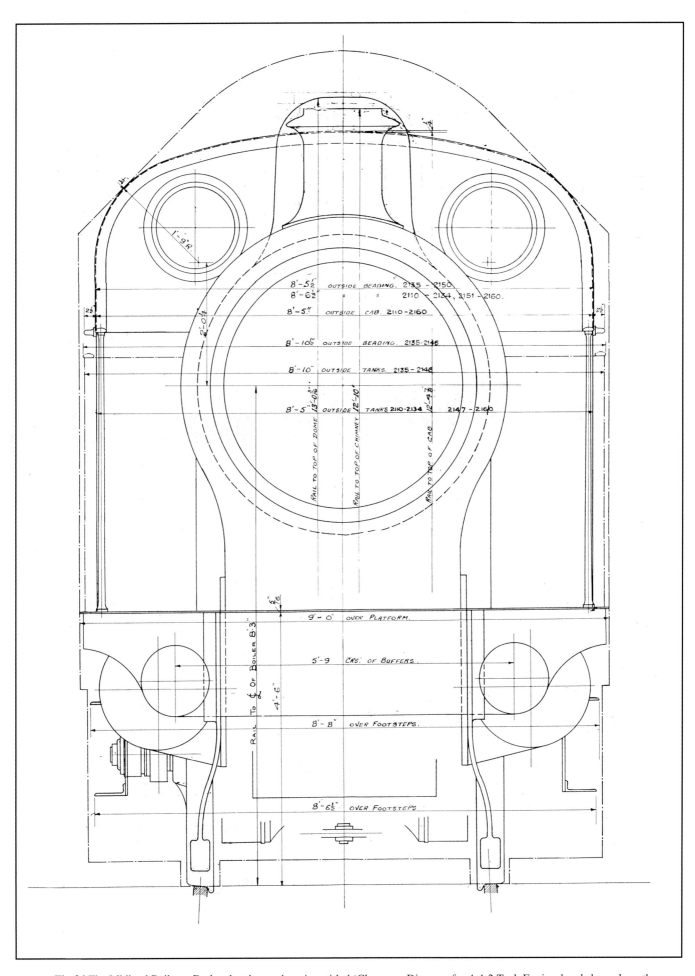

Fig 34 The Midland Railway Derby sketch seen here is entitled 'Clearance Diagram for 4-4-2 Tank Engines' and shows how the various classes were enlarged over the years.

purchased from the North British Locomotive Company in 1908. Judging by the original drawing number, 97-18504, I suspect this refers to the tool requirement for the 4-4-2Ts Nos 37-42 built in 1897 by Sharp, Stewart. In 1903, Sharp, Stewart, together with Dübs and Neilson amalgamated to form the North British Locomotive Company. The drawing is extremely valuable because it provides the dimensions of both the destination boards and the oval and rectangular discs used for train identification purposes. Enginemen who are familiar with modern-day firing tools will find some of the items that were standard equipment unfamiliar.

During my research into the subject I was able to examine the LT&SR drawing register now at the NRM, York. Amongst the references I found were drawing No 1303 dated 23 March 1905 for an automatic variable blastpipe for engine No 62 and drawing No 1447. This was dated 27 May 1907 and referred to ejector details, but no other information was given. From the Midland Railway drawing reproduced at Fig 35 it is clear that changes to fire doors were required. There was a reference to drawing 1689 dated 14 May 1910 to the effect that the drawing applied to all engines except Nos 49 and 50. The only other reference was of a general nature, drawing No 1775 dated 9 February 1911. The register recorded coal bunker additions for Nos 51-68, 69-81 and 37-48 (not 40 and 44). This suggests a proposal to increase the coal bunker capacity that the Midland Railway did by fitting coal rails or coal fenders, as some Derby orders describe them.

Sanding and De-sanding Gear

The LT&SR, with the exception of the final four 0-6-2T engines delivered after the Midland Railway purchase of the railway, used dry sanding for its locomotives. Derby drawing No 14-9091 was produced in February of 1914 and shows the firebox backplate of various classes of LT&S engines. The register also provides some information about the other items noted on the drawing. Drawing No 13-8864 is described as 'leading splashers and sandbox', drawing No 13-9126 is 'sandbox details', drawing No 14-9069 is 'front sand gear 'No 1' class', and drawing No 14-9068 is 'details of bracket carriers and tray for fire door'. Many enginemen would probably refer to this fitting as the drip tray, most often used for holding the tea can. The 1902 drawing No 02-5349 was for the Midland fire door as shown, and rather different from the two-flap door arrangement used on many Midland engines including those built as LMS Standard engines post-1923, Fig 35 below.

LT&SR locomotives were built with dry sanding gear, and although this would cause difficulties later with track circuits, this was to be an LMS problem. The Midland Railway conducted a trial with steam sanding and order No 4427 dated 12 March 1914 provides the details. 'Steam sanding for trial on LT&S Section engine. Please prepare flanges and carriers to drawing Nos 2046 for fitting one engine of the 2190-2193 class with Gresham & Craven steam sanding for trial. Four

Fig 35 This Midland Railway drawing, No 14-9091, shows the firebox backplate of four different classes of LT&S Section locomotives. The drawing was made to show the change of fire door, but it also provides other useful information.

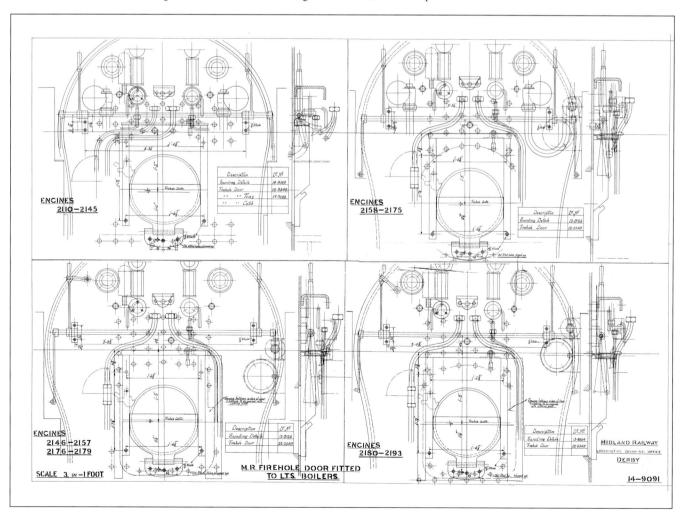

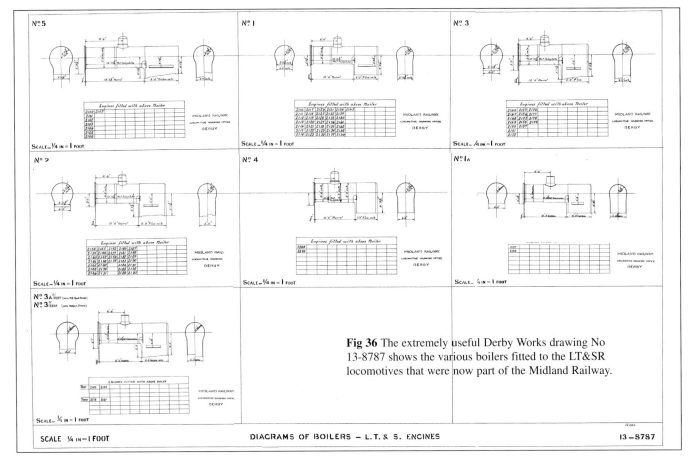

Fig 36 The extremely useful Derby Works drawing No 13-8787 shows the various boilers fitted to the LT&SR locomotives that were now part of the Midland Railway.

SCALE ¼ IN = 1 FOOT   DIAGRAMS OF BOILERS — L. T. & S. ENGINES   13—8787

sand traps to drawing No 04-5986 and four sand ejectors to drawing No S-1668 will be required.' I can find no other evidence of further trials and I presume there was no attempt to alter any other LT&S engines.

The retention of hand sanding on engines following the widespread introduction of track circuits during the 1930s led to problems that were resolved during the LMS period by the introduction of de-sanding gear to those engines not fitted with steam sanding apparatus. New Work Order (NWO) 3138 and Derby Works order No 8495 dated 31 January 1934 were issued to begin dealing with the problem by fitting de-sanding gear to those locomotives that were likely to still be in service at the end of 1935. Other orders were No 8672 dated 19 February 1934 for LT&S engines Nos 2058-2160 and order No 8673 also dated 19 February for LT&S engines Nos 2220-2233. Further orders were 8751 of 29 May 1934, 9672 of 7 July 1936 and 9969 of 21 January 1937, which completed the work required to fit the No 2 and 3 class passenger tank engines Nos 2092-2162. The final order that I can trace is No 1010 dated 3 March 1939. This was described as 'Job 5118, modifications to de-sanding nozzle supports on LT&S No 3 class passenger tank engines Nos 2092-2160 and No 3 class freight tank engines Nos 2220-2233.'

Other LT&SR Locomotive Features

Cab Doors: The first locomotives of the 'No 1' class were not equipped with cab doors but I believe that later this fitting was universally applied to all LT&SR tank engines. In LT&SR, Midland and pre-1928 periods they were generally lined out in the appropriate style for the period.

Cab Roof: The question of the cab roof is dealt with elsewhere. The arrangement for rainstrips varied: some engines did not have any; others had an angle iron along the edge of the roof. The hooded cab engines received rainstrips from the mid-1930s.

Engine Lamp Holders: The arrangement of this fitting varied considerably between the classes and individual engines in the same class. After the purchase of the company by the Midland Railway, lampholders to suit Midland lamps began to be fitted.

Safety Chains: Safety chains were fitted to all new passenger tank engines built by the company and the first goods tank engines of the 'No 69' class. The Midland Railway removed them after 1912.

Smokeboxes, Doors and Chimneys: From time to time smokeboxes were changed together with their fittings. The original Adams-pattern smokebox door, used on the 'No 1' class, with the dart and locking lever handle, gave way to the Whitelegg door. These were dished, had longer holding straps and were secured by a dart and locking wheel arrangement. The question of the chimneys is dealt with in the class chapters.

Many readers will be model-makers and my advice is to study as many pictures of the chosen prototype as possible. LT&SR engines display a considerable range of detail variations that provide traps for the unwary.

Midland Vacuum Brake Valves as Fitted to LT&SR Engines

K. H. Leech's recollections were that the large ejector was mounted by the side of the smokebox in order to keep its efficiency unimpaired by the back pressure of a long pipe from the cab to the smokebox. It was operated by a push-and-pull loop handle and was non-gradual. The small ejector was an ordinary steam cock on the firebox backplate, which was opened just enough to maintain the 20in of vacuum required.

The application valve consisted of a rotary valve for air admission operated by a handle, which was moved from right to left to apply the brake but would not stop in any intermediate position between full application and brake off. There was no 'lap' position in which the brake remained applied to any desired degree as in both the Westinghouse and other vacuum brakes. Therefore, according to Leech, the driver made an application, then the brake would be released quickly by the small ejector, then he made a further application, and so on. For some, Leech added, this was a most distracting method of handling a train, especially when stopping at a water column. If the driver had misjudged and applied the brake too heavily, it was necessary to grab the ring of the large ejector-operating rod in order to 'blow the brakes off' quickly.

The earliest evidence of changes to the existing LT&SR practice is provided by Midland Railway Derby Works order No 4291 dated 2 July 1913. This required the preparation of material for six engines to be fitted with the automatic vacuum brake. The material was to be sent to Plaistow Works. Other orders were 5546 dated 11 January 1921 for fitting 'No 1' class engines Nos 2141-2143, and No 3 class engines, Nos 2147/2149/2153/2155 and 2156. I will deal with the brake conversion to the 2100 class in Chapter 11; however, there were other orders. Two orders, dated 30 May 1923, were to fit the remaining four No 3 class passenger tank engines Nos 2147/2149/2177 and 2178 with vacuum brakes as they passed through Plaistow shops (No 5933). The second order, No 5934, was to fit 10 more 'No 1' class engines between Nos 2120 and 2145. Those unfamiliar with Midland Railway practice may be puzzled by the reference to No 3 class etc. The Midland Railway, even indeed into the LMS period, used to refer to locomotives by their power classification, so No 1 and No 3 class were the power classes of these locomotives. Even after 1928, when the company adopted P for passenger and F for freight, the works documents ignored this refinement.

LMS Derby Works order No 8754 dated 31 May 1934 stated: 'Please put your work in hand with the conversion of 70 LT&S Section engines from Westinghouse to vacuum brake, 5 No 2, 51 No 3 and 14 No 3 0-6-2T engines. Material to be prepared at Derby and fitted at Bow. On 20 September 1934 the order was amended: 'It has been decided to retain eight engines with dual brakes', and on 9 November the order was annotated: 'Nos 2153-60 dual fitted'. Records of locomotive fitted with dual brakes vary; it seems clear that the equipment was transferred from time to time. The final order, No 9312 dated 5 November 1935, provides an interesting insight into the financial control exercised by the LMS at this time. It read: 'Stripping Westinghouse fittings taken off 70 LT&S engines. Please note that all work in connection with the stripping of any details for sale sent here from Bow taken off 70 LT&S engines order number 8754 is to be charged to this order No 9312. Authority for this work is the M&EE Committee Minute No 490 and the Traffic Committee Minute 3870 of 25 April 1934 DWO 3407. No 9 shop will report completion of this order.' An order number was issued to remove the fittings that were to be stripped down and sold but the cost of the work undertaken at Derby was to be accounted for separately.

In recording K. H. Leech's experiences I can only compare my own when firing to drivers working westbound coal trains from Birmingham down the Lickey Incline with many wagon brakes pinned down. Such was the control that many drivers had, using the same brake, that many times a stop 'right for water' was made. I suppose it was a case of what engineman grew up with, but to the author the Midland brake was

excellent — he knew no other;

The final drawing reproduced here at Fig 36 (left) was made on 12 August 1913 and shows the arrangement of the LT&S boilers, other than on the Baltics, in service at that date. I have also provided some details about boilers in the accompanying tables. This is probably a good point at which to conclude the mechanical aspect and return to the question of liveries.

LT&SR Painting Styles

The obvious starting point for any examination of LT&SR locomotive livery styles must be the original specification, dated June 1879. This is set out in full:

'Before any paint is applied the ironwork must be well cleaned, and be free from scales and rust. The boiler to receive one coat of boiled oil when hot, and two coats of red oxide paint before being lagged. The outside of boiler, clothing plates, frames, cylinders, wheels, outside and inside of cab, side tanks and outside of coal box, to have one coat of lead colour, three coats of filling up, and stopped with hard stopping; then to be rubbed down, followed by two coats of lead colour, faced with pumice stone between, after which two coats of approved colour, picked out and lined to pattern. The smokebox, chimney, back of firebox, ashpan, footplate, inside of coal box, top of tank sides, brake-work and side springs, to have one coat of lead colour paint and two coats of Japan black. The inside of frames and cross stays to have two coats of red oxide paint. The inside of tanks to have two coats of good thick red lead. The front of buffer-planks, life guards, and buffer-casings to be painted vermilion. The axles to have two coats of white lead. All the painting on the outside of the engine to have three coats of best hard-drying body varnish.

'The number of the engine to be figured in gilt numbers on front and hind buffer-plates. A number or name plate to be put on each wing tank in the centre.'

Fortunately, the 1897 specification has survived and comparison between the two specifications reveals a few differences that can be summarised as follows:

The coal box is now described as a coalbunker. The two coats of lead colour have been increased to three. The approved colour has now become 'of colour equal to sample supplied'. The insides of the frames are specified as vermilion and the varnish had to be supplied by Noble & Hoare. Otherwise there is no change from the 1879 specification.

Painting Styles for Tank Engines

Set out below is the basic painting styles for LT&SR locomotives prior to 1912. Any variations to this will be described in the individual class chapters.

The basic LT&SR standard green was described by George Dow as being slightly cooler and darker than Great Northern green. The model of the 4-6-4T displayed at the NRM, York is probably as close to the original colour that we will ever get. However, the lining and décor are probably a reflection of what was planned if the LT&SR had not become part of the Midland Railway and not how LT&SR locomotives were finished.

Boiler and firebox: Green, all boiler lagging bands chocolate brown with vermilion black and white lines in that order to each side.

Cab side, front and rear: Green, with chocolate brown lining, fine-lined vermilion on the inner edge. This lining on the cabside was a continuation of the lining on the tank and bunker sides and varied depending upon the style of cab. On the hooded cab engines the lining was taken over the cab roof whereas on the non-hood cab engines the lining was continued along the cab side just below the roof join merging with the lining, which was employed around the cab opening. The livery drawing for the 'No 69' class should make this clear.

Cab interior: Chocolate brown. According to *The Railway Magazine*, 1900, the company painted the driver's name inside the cab.

Cab doors: Green with convex-cornered black panel, fine-lined white either side.

Cab roof: Non-hood cab engines — black. Hooded-cab engines — green with lining.

Spectacle plate window frames: 'No 1' class originally specified as wood frames, other classes brass.

Tank top: Black.

Tank sides and front: Green, with chocolate border, fine-lined vermilion on inner edge.

Bunker sides and rear: Green, with chocolate border, fine-lined vermilion on inner edge. 'No 1' class engines with their rounded corner bunkers were treated as a single area and the 'panel' was taken around the bunker rear with no vertical lines at the bunker end. Within this bordering, on the tank sides, bunker sides and rear there were convex-cornered panels of black, fine-lined white on each side.

Similar panels were painted on the tank fronts and above the sandboxes. When larger sandboxes were fitted the panels were transferred to them. In the centre of the tank side panels the engine name was displayed in 4½ in gold serif letters, shaded black to the right and at the bottom. The engine name was set on a curve with the company's armorial device below.

Framing, running plate sides, footsteps, bogie and pony wheel splashers: Chocolate brown lined vermilion and fine-lined yellow inside with black edges.

Buffer beams and guard irons: Vermilion, the buffer beam was given a black border, and fine-lined yellow on the inside. The serif letters 'No.' and numerals were in gold, shaded black to the right and below. The drawbar hook slot was bordered black and fine-lined yellow on the outside. Buffer casings were painted chocolate brown, edged black, vermilion and yellow.

Wheels: Chocolate brown with black axle ends. A fine white line edged the axle ends and the inner edge of the tyre. Some locomotives also appear to have the outer edge of the tyre fine-lined in white.

Cylinders: Green, with black convex-cornered panels fine-lined white on each side.

Jacks: Base and upright column chocolate brown.

Locomotive headlamps: Chocolate brown, black edges with fine yellow panelling inside, and the name of the District was displayed. In 1900 *The Railway Magazine* recorded that the company was engraving the driver's name on a brass plate attached to the engine lamps.

Midland and LMS and British Railways Painting Styles

Shortly after the Midland Railway took over the LT&SR the removal of the names, renumbering and repainting of the LT&SR locomotives began, and elsewhere I have given repainting dates where known. The two 0-6-0 tender goods engines and the 10 existing 0-6-2T engines were repainted in Midland Railway goods engine black. The buffer beams were painted vermilion and the initials MR were placed on the beams. The initials were probably at both the front and hind ends of the engines, but the lack of photographic evidence means this cannot be confirmed. A cast numberplate was affixed to the smokebox door.

There was little change until after 1923, when the Midland Railway became part of the LMS, and the captions to the pictures used in the class chapters detail the changes that took place. There is no evidence of the use of power classification numbers until after 1928.

The passenger tank engines were painted in Midland Railway Crimson Lake livery until 1928 when they began to be repainted in black with red lining. The buffer beams were vermilion and the cast smokebox door numberplate was retained. Power classification was indicated by the use of small transfers applied to the upper cabside panel. The principal difference between the décor of Midland passenger tank engines and the LT&S engines was that the footsteps and valences of the latter engines were lined out and fine-lined, the valence being fine-lined on both the top and bottom edges. The running number for both the goods and passenger engines was a transferred numeral, in gold leaf, shaded black that was either 18in or 14in high. After 1929 the shading was changed to a blended red and c1937 the colour became chrome yellow with vermilion shading.

The company identity was not always used and the photographs in the class chapters summarise what evidence is available. During the period pre-1923 the Midland Railway used the armorial device on tender engines; only the '2000' class of passenger tank engines carried this feature, although it was used with some LT&S engines. For a short time after 1923 small LMS initials were used but the new LMS emblem soon replaced these. After 1928, the locomotive running number, which had been placed on the tank side before then, was moved to the side of the coalbunker and the LMS initials were placed on the tank side.

During the British Railways period, most locomotives were painted in plain black with red buffer beams. The new British Railways number was displayed on the smokebox by use of a cast numberplate. In the chapters that follow I have included some pictures of LT&S locomotives in various British Railways liveries, plain black and black with lining.

The subject of livery is extremely complex and for those readers who require more detailed information I recommend that they study the books listed in the Bibliography, in particular those by David Jenkinson and myself.

Right:
The splendid picture of No 34 *Tottenham* shows one of the Nasmyth, Wilson batch, whose numbers were 31-36.
Locomotive Publishing Co

5. The 'No 1' Class

The specification for the 'No 1' class locomotives was dated June 1879 and the undertaking by Sharp, Stewart 'to build and deliver, carriage free to the London, Tilbury & Southend Railway, at their Plaistow Works, London' was dated 22 July 1879. The order was for 12 engines at £1,970, each with delivery to commence within five months from date of order and to continue at the rate of not less than four engines per month. The general description was for a 'Four wheels coupled engine, the front part to be carried by a bogie, the hind part by a two-wheeled pony truck, arranged so as to take sharp curves easily. To have outside cylinders horizontally fixed over the bogie. The driving wheels to be under the barrel of the boiler and the trailing wheels behind the firebox. To have wing tanks and a tank at the trailing end, coal over the tank at the trailing end, sand boxes to driving and trailing wheels and a cab over the footplate.'

I have used the precise wording on the specification which continued with some of the principal dimensions: diameter of cylinder 1ft 5in; stroke 2ft 2in; centres 6ft 3in; length of boiler barrel 10ft 6in; diameter inside 4ft 1in; length of firebox outside 6ft; width outside 3ft 10½in; inside diameter of steam dome 1ft 6in; number of tubes 200, outside diameter 1⅝in; height of boiler centre from rails 7ft. Length of engine frame 32ft; thickness 1in; distance between 4ft; diameter of driving wheels and trailing wheels on tread 6ft 1in; bogie and pony truck 3ft 1in; wheelbase, front to hind wheels, 29ft 7in; centres

of bogie wheels 3ft 1in; centre of bogie to centre of driving wheels 10ft 4in; driving wheels to centre of trailing wheels 8ft 6in; trailing wheels to centre of pony truck 7ft 6in; height of centre of buffers from rail 3ft 4½in. Capacity of tank 1,300 gallons; capacity of coal bunker 40cwt; capacity of sandboxes (four) each 1½ cu ft; working pressure 160psi; width outside tanks 8ft 5in; width over footplate 9ft.

In keeping with general railway practice the approved suppliers of material and parts were included within the specification. For example, the two injectors were No 8 Hancock inspirators to be placed vertically, one each side of the engine on top of the trailing ends of the tanks. The specification for the cab was that the sides front and back were to be of the best Staffordshire iron ³⁄₁₆in thick; the roof to be of wood, tongued and grooved and covered with prepared canvas, which was to be secured by hoop iron strips on top and wood beading on the edges. (Although not mentioned in the specification, cab roofs were fitted with a sliding hatch, as K. H. Leech refers to them.) The four cab windows were to have ¼in thick plate glass, in wood frames (later altered in the specification, to brass, swivelling), hinged on the top and provided with fastenings. The bogie was to be W. Adams Patent and made to the form and dimensions shown on the drawing.

The brake gear was to be 'A steam and hand brake combined to be fixed on the engine as shown and so arranged that either

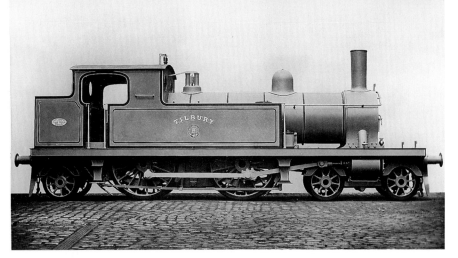

These are examples of the 'No 1' class locomotives. No 3 *Tilbury* was one of the original batch built by Sharp, Stewart in 1880 and this is the works grey photograph that was to be taken at the builder's expense, with 12 copies supplied to the LT&SR. The first engines were built with countersunk rivets, a slightly smaller dome and a rather severe stovepipe chimney.
Collection George Dow

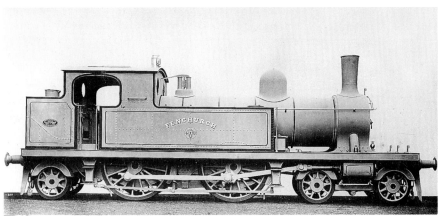

No 30 *Fenchurch* is in works grey for the photograph that was part of the contract. The series 13-30 was built with snap-head rivets that can be seen in this picture. The proportions of the dome and chimney are rather more pleasing.
Collection George Dow

No 20 *Hornchurch* with the train crew. Comparison of this picture with No 3 *Tilbury* above. will reveal lining variations. The sandbox of *Tottenham* is lined while that of *Hornchurch* is not, and the chimneys are not identical. *Collection R. J. Essery*

The picture of No 14 *Leigh* shows a locomotive with very little lining. Other than the footstep carrying brackets and the side valence of the running plate there does not appear to be any other lining on this engine. The picture shows the proportions of this class very well and, as a bonus, we can see examples of permanent way and part of a hand point lever. The object on the left of the picture is the flexible pipe of the water column. *K. H. Leech*

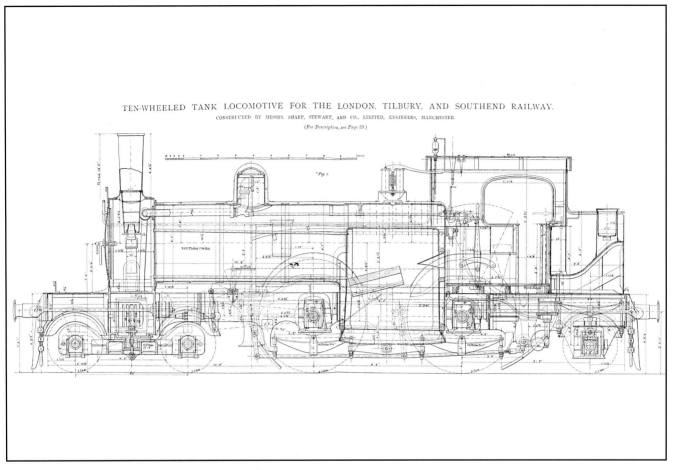

TEN-WHEELED TANK LOCOMOTIVE FOR THE LONDON, TILBURY, AND SOUTHEND RAILWAY.
CONSTRUCTED BY MESSRS. SHARP, STEWART, AND CO., LIMITED, ENGINEERS, MANCHESTER.
(For Description, see Page 39.)

Fig 37 The general arrangement drawing of the first batch of locomotives built for the LT&SR was published in the 14 January 1881 edition of *Engineering* and is for a locomotive equipped only with a handbrake.

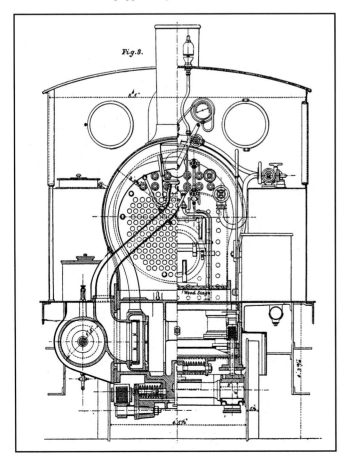

may be worked independently of the other. The driving and trailing wheels each to have one cast-iron brake block.' The boiler was to be tested to a pressure of 250psi with warm water and afterwards with steam to 170lb. The contractor was required to make complete general and detail drawings and to furnish copies of them to the engineer. In addition, the number of the engine was to be figured in gilt numbers on front and hind bufferplates and a number or name was to be put on each wing tank in the centre. One engine was to be photographed at the contractor's expense and 12 copies of the picture were to be supplied. This locomotive was to be finished, together with the rest of the order, in LT&SR green before being delivered to London. Finally, the engine had to run 1,000 miles consecutively without showing any signs of defect, either in materials or workmanship, when it would be taken over from the contractor. All royalties and patent rights were to be paid by the contractor.

The detail of locomotive specifications ran to several pages and the space available here does not permit more than the basic outline to be included.

I shall continue by considering some of the variations and developments that were to be seen between the batches as built and later during their lifetime, but first, some general comments about the design would not be out of place.

The close association between the Great Eastern and the London, Tilbury & Southend Railway and the circumstances whereby the LT&SR had to organise its own locomotive department led to the involvement of the GER's Locomotive Superintendent, William Adams, from an early stage. In the previous chapter I remarked that Adams exercised considerable influence over the design of this, the first class of LT&S locomotives. As K. H. Leech has pointed out, while it was not unknown for a locomotive superintendent of one

I do not have a date for this front view that illustrates No 32 *Leyton* together with the engine crew. Note that the screw jack is mounted on the top of the side tank. *L&GRP 22011*

Four locomotives were fitted with condensing gear in connection with the Whitechapel & Bow trains which they worked between Upminster and Whitechapel. This picture shows No 29 *Stepney* in the black livery with lining on the footstep carrying plate, mudguards over the front bogie and rear wheels and alongside the valence of the running plate. Note the shorter chimney that was fitted to these engines and the locomotive number on the side of the screwjack. *Collection R. J. Essery*

company to act as a 'consultant' in the design of a locomotive for another, it was a little unusual. What is of particular interest is that this original specification shows and indeed describes a pony truck and not the radial axlebox which was actually incorporated. What is not known is why or when this design change was made, although some ideas were speculated upon in Chapter 3.

Fortunately, the original specification has survived and it forms part of Rail 437 at the PRO, Kew. Attached to the specification are five pages of notes entitled 'Suggestions and enquiries by S. S. & Co. Ltd'. Written replies were received from Adams dated 13 August 1879, and verbal replies when at the works on the same date. Adams made another visit on 24 September when further questions were answered. In total, 44 queries were raised and while most were of a minor nature some are worth recording. The chimney base was originally to be 'Crewe type', Adams's reply was: 'Yes, will see it when drawn'. There is no further mention of this, so I presume the drawing was rejected.

The splashers in the tank were to be wrought iron instead of the specified cast iron. Wheel tyres were to be made to the drawing, 5in for the small wheels and 5½in for the large wheels. The drawing and written specification did not agree and this was one of several examples where the builder queried

these inconsistencies. The regulator was to be the S. S. & Co's but Adams was to send a tracing of the GER regulator to show the slides. The majority of the questions raised by Sharp, Stewart were in respect of detail and generally brought about improvements to the original design and specification. For example, the specification required an extinguisher tap in the ashpan. Sharp, Stewart suggested this be omitted on the grounds that the gauge glass drainpipe answered that purpose; Adams agreed. He also agreed to a modification that enabled the bogie springs to be removed without lifting the engine. It is clear that Adams took the contractor's advice and the answer to a number of questions was 'As S. S. think best'. This seems to suggest that he was prepared to listen to the advice of the builder; the company was very experienced in constructing steam locomotives for a variety of customers.

The design was plain and symmetrical. At the front end of the locomotive the centres of the bogie, cylinders, smokebox and chimney were all in line. The later series of engines were fitted with a more pleasing shape of dome casing, and this can be seen in the pictures reproduced here. This may have been the result of fitting a larger steam dome to help overcome problems due to priming. The earlier locomotives also received these domes. An interesting feature was the mudguards over both the bogie and trailing wheels.

Above:
The cabs of the condenser-fitted engines were altered to what was described as the 'hooded type' and this picture of No 7 *Barking* shows this style of cab. There appear to be traces of lining on the footstep carrying plate and there is lining on the side valence of the running plate on this otherwise black locomotive. *Locomotive Publishing Co*

Below:
The picture shown here is old No 6 as Midland Railway No 2115 in MR passenger livery. *F. Moore*

Above:
Old No 3, now Midland Railway No 2202, is seen here with the hooded cab that was fitted for work on the Whitechapel & Bow line. The condensing gear was removed in 1919, and this picture shows the locomotive as renumbered by the MR and in red passenger livery. *Real Photographs/NRM*

Below:
The first engine of the class, old No 1, carrying its 1923 LMS number, 2200, but without any evidence of company ownership. The 4T plate denotes a special train working, but I do not know the precise meaning (possibly Tottenham?). *Collection R. J. Essery*

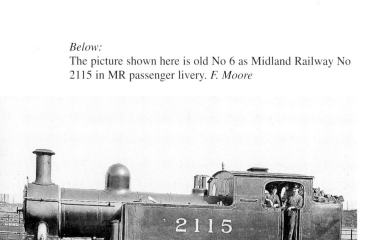

This shows old No 29 as Midland Railway No 2138 in red passenger livery at Plaistow engine shed. The hooded cab was retained until the locomotive was withdrawn from service in 1932. *W. L. Good, courtesy Richard Taylor*

Old No 27 as LMS No 2136 in pre-1928 passenger livery at Plaistow during the mid-1920s. In this picture, the opening cab roof hatch and side tank lid can be seen very clearly. *W. L. Good, courtesy Richard Taylor*

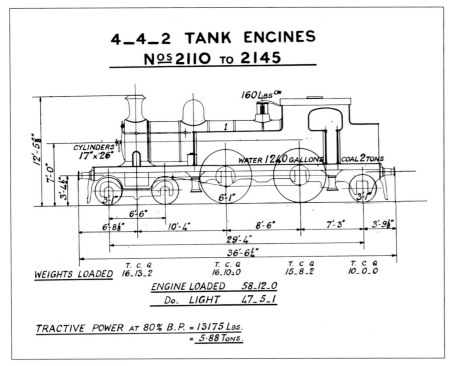

4_4_2 TANK ENGINES
Nos 2110 TO 2145

160 LBS □

12'-5⅝"
CYLINDERS
17" x 26"
WATER 1240 GALLONS   COAL 2 TONS
7'-0"
3'-4½"
3' 1"
6'-1"
3' 1"
6'-6"
6'-8½"   10'-4"   8'-6"   7'-3"   3'-9⅛"
29'-4"
36'-6¼"

WEIGHTS LOADED
T. C. Q   T. C. Q   T. C. Q   T. C. Q
16_13_2   16_10_0   15_8_2   10_0_0
ENGINE LOADED   58_12_0
Do. LIGHT   47_5_1

TRACTIVE POWER AT 80% B.P. = 13175 LBS.
= 5·88 TONS.

Fig 38 Engine diagrams are useful guides for dimensional details of locomotive classes and this is the first of several used in this and the chapters to follow. Drawn in 1921, it shows the typical arrangement of the 'No 1' class in Midland Railway ownership. I also have an undated diagram for this class which states all were fitted with the Westinghouse brake, that No 31 was also fitted with the vacuum brake and that 26 engines were equipped with steam heating apparatus.

The second and third Sharp, Stewart batches, engines Nos 13-30, differed from the first series in so far as they were built with snap-headed rivets on the sides and front of the wing tanks, sides or rear of the bunkers and cabs instead of the countersunk arrangement used on the first 12 engines. The final six Nasmyth, Wilson series, ordered in connection with the opening of the Romford to Grays line, employed countersunk rivets but differed in as much as their cylinder barrels were about ⅜ in shorter between the covers when compared with the Sharp, Stewart-built engines. In due course this caused problems because when the big end brasses were 'let together' this increased the effective length of the connecting rod and caused damage when the pistons struck the cylinder cover.

From 6 July 1898, the date of the drawing No 921, new cast-iron-lipped chimneys of a rather pleasing design began to replace the original Adams chimneys. In 1902, three engines, Nos 7, 23 and 29, were fitted with condensing apparatus and shorter chimneys for working over the Metropolitan District Line between Whitechapel and Upminster. In order to suit the restricted clearance in the tunnels the cabs were altered to rounded or hooded type on 18 March 1904, in accordance with drawing No 1204, and the reduced height of the chimney was achieved by cutting away a section of the chimney stem and refitting the chimney cap. A further engine, No 3, was also altered in a similar fashion in 1904. These locomotives were painted black, but the footplate edging, steps, etc were lined in a similar fashion to other engines. However, in 1905, following electrification of the line to Barking, the condensing gear was removed from engines Nos 23 and 29 and they reverted to the LT&S green livery. Engines Nos 3 and 7, later renumbered as Midland Railway Nos 2112 and 2116, retained the condensing gear until 1919 when it was removed from old No 7 (now No 2116) and this engine was repainted in MR Crimson Lake livery; No 2112 retained its condensing equipment until the end of its working life in 1935. For a number of years, one of these engines was always used on the Plaistow shunt where it was readily available as a replacement if there was a failure of electricity on the District Line.

The original rather severe stove pipe chimney, applied to engines Nos 1-12 differed slightly from the stovepipe chimney fitted to the later Sharp, Stewart and Nasmyth, Wilson engines. However, this is not the end of the chimney story, for during the 1890s engine No 35 was fitted with a hand-operated variable blast nozzle patented by George Macallan, then manager at Stratford Works of the GER. There is a reference in the drawing register to drawing No 929 dated July 1898 and this may have applied to this work. This device was also fitted to engines Nos 37-48 and 57-66, but it did not remain in service very long and the experiment ended when the gear was removed. It has been suggested that with two openings the fireman used only the smaller one, the sharper blast improved the steaming ability of the engine but not coal economy. The lining finish of the 'No 1' class was simplified from about 1907. The inner panel of a black band with a white line on each side was discontinued.

Brakes

The first 12 engines, Nos 1-12, were built with steam and handbrakes only (one source suggesting it was Nos 1-18) and some doubt exists if Nos 19-30 were fitted with Westinghouse brakes before arriving on the LT&SR. However, it is clear that from 1886 onwards Nos 1-30 were equipped with the Westinghouse airbrake that applied to the coupled driving wheels. From time to time, a number of engines were fitted with steam ejectors, driver's brake valves and vacuum brake train pipe for use with foreign stock that was only vacuum brake fitted but worked over the LT&SR. When the company became part of the Midland Railway, 18 engines were dual fitted and these included Nos 4, 8, 10 and 28. This equipment could be transferred from engine to engine but no records of which engines were so equipped appear to have survived. Photographic evidence is generally the only record available. Following the 1923 Grouping, equipping the class with vacuum brakes began; order No 5934 dated 30 May 1923 was to fit 10 engines of the class.

The original builder's plates were to be replaced by rebuilt plates between 1898 and 1907, probably when new boilers

I have referred to the Midland Railway practice of fitting dated rebuilt plates when locomotives were reboilered. I have no idea which engine was photographed with this particular plate but it has been included to illustrate the point. I have also included an enlargement of the Sharp, Stewart builder's plate that was carried by No 30 *Fenchurch. Collection R. J. Essery*

were fitted. The exception was old No 15, which retained its builder's plate throughout its period of LT&SR ownership. However, following the Midland Railway takeover in 1912, the Derby Works policy in respect of rebuilt plates began to apply, although it is recorded that No 14 retained its LT&SR rebuilt plate until it was withdrawn in 1935. This seems likely, as a photograph of the engine at Plaistow in June 1934 clearly shows the 'Rebuilt Plaistow' plate. An example of this type of works plate is depicted. Some engines ran without works plates during the later MR and LMS periods.

Extended Smokeboxes

A number of locomotives, at one time or another, were fitted with extended smokeboxes and it seems likely that some may have been transferred between locomotives when boilers were changed. Those of 'No 1' class known to have carried extended smokeboxes are set out below. The information was taken from photographs and therefore the list may not include every example of locomotives in this condition.

No 2 as 2078, No 5 as 2204, No 7 as 2083, No 10 as 2119/2209, No 14 as 2090, No 16 as 2067, No 21 as 2072, No 22 as 2073, No 25 as 2076, No 26 as 2056, No 27 as 2136, No 29 as 2138, No 30 as 2060, No 31 as 2140, No 33 as 2063, No 34 as 2143 and No 35 as 2144. In addition to my list, K. H. Leech recorded that during the Midland Railway period 15 engines were fitted with extended smokeboxes and listed the following engines, using the old LT&SR number: 1, 3, 12, 18, 22, 25-32, 34 and 35.

Coupling Rods

When built, a flat section rod was fitted, but due to some problems with bent coupling rods this was replaced by a fluted version and some extra balance weights were added to the driving wheels. There is no record known to the author of how many engines were so modified although K. H. Leech suggests that it was 12 in total. The principal cause of the problem appears to be that when they were being worked heavily in wet weather they 'lost their feet' and slipped badly.

All the class were fitted with lever reversing gear (nicknamed Armstrong for obvious reasons) and it seems that drivers used to carry ½bolts to drop across the second notch in the rack from mid gear to give '1½ notches' as a position for the reversing lever. It appears that the two-notch position was more than the

engines would take for a long period of time without overtaxing the boiler. Of course, this method was far from perfect and it was not unknown for the bolt to jolt out of the rack with the result that the engine would go into the full gear position. According to K. H. Leech, the drivers frequently steadied themselves against the gear lever and so, being thrown off balance towards the unlagged boiler front, or firebox backplate, to use the correct term, the language could be strong to say the least!

They were robustly built engines and would withstand full regulator working for a short period but they worked best if the regulator was pulled slightly back from the full open position. By the time of the Midland Railway takeover most of the class were on somewhat lighter duties, many being stationed at Tilbury or Upminster, where the work was less demanding than the jobs from Plaistow or Shoeburyness. They were used on workmen's trains made up with four-wheel coaches and many runs to Tilbury for summer trips on the Kent Coast steamers were handled by the 'No 1' class locomotives. Regular employment shunting at Commercial Road was also a feature of their work.

Although the class was maintained at Plaistow, following the Midland Railway takeover locomotives began to go to Derby Works for repairs. In due course, they started to receive Midland Railway fittings and some details of these changes have survived. The changes made included replacement Midland chimneys, boiler mountings and smokebox doors fitted. Pop safety valves replaced the Ramsbottom type and engines received coal rails to increase capacity. Derby Works orders that applied to this class included No 4326 dated 3 October 1923 for three spare boilers and 4955 dated 26 October 1916, for a new copper firebox for engine No 2124. This order took two years to complete, with completion recorded as 17 December 1918. Other orders for fireboxes followed and the first order for driving wheels was No 5271 dated 13 December 1918 for one pair of driving and one pair of trailing wheels. Order No 6328 dated 5 November 1924 was for handrails to be placed on the back of cabs of 'No 1' class engines Nos 2120-2145 and 2200-2209. The materials were to be prepared at Derby and fitted at Plaistow.

The final reference in the order book is something of a mystery. Order No 8293 dated 5 January reads: 'Fitting of LT&S engine No 2080 [old No 4, then MR 2113, LMS 2203 and finally 2080] with sleet brushes Barking-Upminster Electrification. Please put your work in hand in connection with preparation of material for the above and charge to

This three-quarters rear view of old No 28, now LMS No 2137, was taken at Plaistow c1925. The position of the LMS emblem varied: on this locomotive it is on the side of the coal bunker, on No 2136 (see page 125) it was placed on the tank side.
Real Photographs/NRM

Old No 25 as LMS No 2076 at Tilbury on 22 August 1931. Built as a Westinghouse-braked locomotive, the engine has now been dual fitted and the 'clutter' visible on the right-hand side of the boiler is the Westinghouse brake cylinder, the large ejector for the vacuum brake and the clack valve of the injector. The Midland locomotive register records the fitting of a second-hand boiler in 1921, but I am unsure if this was when the engine was dual fitted.
Collection R. J. Essery

Order No 8293.' The material was to be prepared at Derby and to be sent to Bow for fitting. The sleet brushes were to be specially ordered and drawings were to be issued; the numbers quoted, 12805-12807, were all new 1932 drawings. Although the Midland Railway Register that was kept up to date until about this time does not give a broken up or similar date, the withdrawal of this engine is considered to be December 1932. Unless another locomotive was substituted for No 2080, then it appears that the locomotive was employed for departmental use during the next few months.

A further order, No 8559 dated 14 November 1933, was for the removal of the gear from engine No 2079, shown in the records as being withdrawn in September 1935 and to refit it to a No 3 class LT&S engine. My guess is that No 2079 was substituted for No 2080 and fitted in accordance with the order, and not No 2080. It was not uncommon for engine numbers to be changed and the Derby Works order records held at Kew are not complete.

The LT&SR 4-4-2T engines had, during the pre-Midland Railway years, a reputation for smooth riding. The practice of fitting wedges to take up the wear in the driving axleboxes between the horns meant that axlebox knock was very rare

indeed. The connecting rod big ends were adjustable and this also helped to ensure that the ride was smooth. When working over the direct line from Fenchurch Street to Shoeburyness it was recorded that they needed to take water during the journey. This would depend upon where they were booked to stop, and one source has suggested it was Plaistow, Barking or Upminster. Many locomotives were double manned. The first set of men prepared the engine and worked a shift, with a second, or as K. H. Leech puts it, a backshift set of men concluding the day's working. The fireman on the second shift had to coal, water, and clean the fire which included raking off the tubeplate at the firebox end. During the summer months, when there was a shortage of firemen, it was not unusual for them to work four or five hours over their 10 hour day, with overtime rates being paid.

In their later days this class was frequently to be found upon freight train workings and in due course they were all withdrawn by the LMS between 1930 and 1935, having more than repaid their cost during their long period of service to three separate owning companies.

The first to be withdrawn were old Nos 9 and 10, as LMS 2085 and 2086 in June 1930, and the last to be withdrawn was old No 22, as LMS 2073 in October 1935.

6. The 'No 37' Class, Including Rebuilds

Five years were to elapse before more locomotives were required to handle the increasing traffic on the line and this led to the introduction of the 'No 37' class which was both a development and enlargement of the original 'No 1' class that had served the company well since 1880. Fortunately, the original specification for these 'Four-Wheels Coupled Bogie and Hind Radial Tank Engine for Mixed Traffic' engines has survived so it is possible to compare the original specifications for both classes of locomotives. The specification for the 'No 37' class was dated July 1897 and the copy held at the PRO, Kew, was not completed as far as price per engine or an agreed delivery date were concerned. Six engines built by Sharp, Stewart, Nos 37-42, entered traffic during 1897 and a further six were built by Dübs. This batch arrived on the LT&SR during 1897/98. The obvious visible differences when compared with the 'No 1' class were the higher pitched boiler, the shorter cast chimney and curved rain gutter on each side of the cab roof. From about 1902 the chimneys were shortened in a similar fashion to the 'No 1' class as already described.

The general description as given in the specification was similar to the 'No 1' class; however, the dimensions varied and those set in the written description were as below where I have used the same words that appeared in the document. Diameter of cylinders 1ft 6in; stroke 2ft 2in; centres 6ft 3in; length of boiler barrel 10ft 6in; diameter inside 4ft 0⅞in;

length of firebox, outside 6ft 9in; width of firebox outside 3ft 10⅝in. (This was altered to 3ft 10¾in in pencil on the specification.) Inside diameter of steam dome 1ft 9in; number of tubes 199; diameter of tubes, outside 1⅝in; height of centre of boiler from rails 7ft 6in; length of engine frame 35ft 2in, thickness 1⅛in; distance between frames 4ft. Diameter of driving and intermediate wheels on tread 6ft 6in; bogie and rear wheels 3ft 6in; wheelbase total from front to rear wheels 30ft 9½in; centres of bogie wheels 7ft; centre of bogie to centre of driving wheels 10ft 6½in; centre of driving to centre of intermediate wheels 8ft 9in; centre of intermediate wheels to centre of rear wheels 8ft; height of centres of buffer from rail 3ft 4½in. Capacity of tanks 1,500 gallons; capacity of coal bunker 45cwt; capacity of sandboxes (four) each 1½ cu ft. Working pressure 170psi; width outside tanks 8ft 5in; width outside footplate 9ft.

The layout and wording of the specification were very similar to the one issued in 1879. There was an interesting note about the drawings. The specification stated that the Locomotive Superintendent would supply the contractor with general and detail drawings on loan and allow him to make copies of them. At the conclusion of the contract the contractor was to supply a complete set of working tracings to the company. The specification was annotated: 'Note, tracings *must not* be coloured.'

When compared with the 'No 1' class, the 'No 37' class had

I believe this is the official Sharp, Stewart photograph of No 38 *Westcliff,* the supply of 12 copies being part of the contract. This suggests to me that at this time the LT&SR did not have an official photographer or even an arrangement with a photographer to undertake such work. *L&GRP 5616*

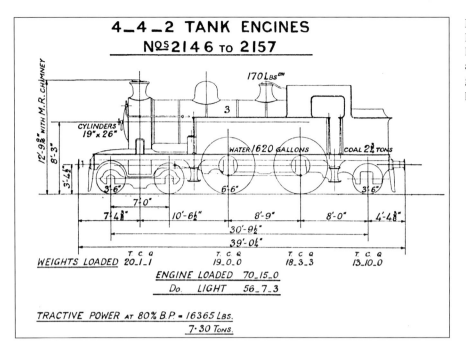

4 _ 4 _ 2 TANK ENGINES
Nos 2146 to 2157

170 LBS ᴰᴺ

12'-9⅝" WITH M.R. CHIMNEY
8'-3"
3'-4½"

CYLINDERS
19"x 26"

3
WATER 1620 GALLONS   COAL 2¾ TONS

3'-6"   6'-6"   3'-6"
7'-0"
7'-4⅞"   10'-6½"   8'-9"   8'-0"   4'-4⅞"
30'-9½"
39'-0⅛"

WEIGHTS LOADED
T. C. Q   T. C. Q   T. C. Q   T. C. Q
20_1_1   19_0_0   18_3_3   13_10_0

ENGINE LOADED   70_15_0
Do.   LIGHT   56_7_3

TRACTIVE POWER AT 80% B.P. = 16365 LBS.
7·30 TONS.

Fig 39 This illustrates the 1921 Midland Railway engine diagram for these locomotives in their rebuilt form. A later amendment was made to this diagram that gave the tractive effort at 80% boiler pressure as 16,365lb.

a higher boiler pitch and shorter chimney. In addition to the curved rain gutter fitted on each side of the cab roof, this was to be made of teak, tongued and grooved and covered with best canvas to sample supplied. A sliding door was to be fitted on the cab roof, and the cab was to be constructed within the LT&SR and MR's loading gauge. When built they were fitted only with Westinghouse brakes, supplied from one 13in cylinder and hand screw brake combined but at least one, No 37, was fitted with vacuum brakes before being rebuilt. Drawings Nos 956/957 dated 23 March 1899 refer to this conversion. One source suggests that all were fitted with automatic vacuum brakes prior to rebuilding but I cannot confirm this. The information given in Chapter 4 suggests that this is not correct. All were equipped with steam carriage warming equipment.

Apart from the dimensional differences, detailed here in the tables, other variations were the use of cast steel for the wheel centres instead of wrought iron used with the 'No 1' class. The size of the driving wheel increased from 6ft 1in to 6ft 6in and the bogie and trailing wheels from 3ft 1in to 3ft 6in. It can be seen in the illustrations that the frame shape forward of the smokebox was deepened to a curve and this feature was retained on all future LT&SR passenger tank locomotives although the final shape varied. Compared with engines Nos 1 to 30, one tube was replaced by a washout plug. K. H. Leech suggests that in their original condition, the engines were under-boilered for the 18in cylinders. Lubrication of the steam chest and cylinders was by a sight feed lubricator.

The adjustable brake pull rod, positioned outside of the driving wheels on the 'No 1' class, was moved to the centreline and led forward from the brake shaft to a compensating arm behind the rear beams with a second pull rod to the centre of the front cross beam. Again, this feature was retained upon subsequent 4-4-2T construction.

When built, they were fitted with long cast-iron chimneys with an ornamental lip, but c1900 these were cut down in height in a fashion similar to that employed with the 'No 1' class and the locomotives ran in this condition until they were rebuilt from 1905 onwards.

The increased speed and power potential of the 'No 37' class was, according to K. H. Leech, about 10% greater than the 'No 1' class and this was due to the increasing weight of the

Southend trains, which at peak times could amount to 16 to 18 six-wheel coaches with a tare weight of between 210 and 238 tons. The weight of these trains continued to increase and this lead to the introduction of the 'No 51' class, described in Chapter 8.

It may be wondered why it was necessary to rebuild what were in effect comparatively new engines, but the increasing weight of trains required more powerful locomotives. Therefore the LT&SR board had two options.

1) To build more powerful engines than the recently constructed 'No 51' class, and render surplus to requirements some of the existing but not time-expired locomotive stock of the 'No 1' class.

2) To rebuild, or as the company described it, reconstruct the 'No 37' class into more powerful units, and this was the course that was finally chosen.

The reconstruction was quite considerable and comprised a larger boiler, with 7in extra diameter that was pitched 9in higher. This enabled the engines to have a larger firebox-heating surface and a deeper fire (the foundation ring remained at the original level). New 19in diameter cylinders replaced the original 18in diameter cylinders. They were clothed with blue steel sheet and had polished steel bands and end covers in place of the painted and lined steel sheet clothing previously adopted. The larger boiler required the tanks to be wider apart and this led to further extensive alterations being made. One interesting feature was that the wheel splashers inside the tanks had to be moved to accommodate this change. The wider spacing of the tanks brought them out to the full width of the running plate and a recess that ran the entire length of the tank was formed just above platform level. This feature can be clearly seen in the various pictures of the rebuilt engines. It was probably useful because it provided a foothold and permitted enginemen and engine cleaners to move around the tank sides of the locomotives when they were stationary.

A new cab was fitted; the design was similar to the hood-style fitted to the four condensing engines of 'No 1' class. It has been suggested that these cabs were not as snug as the original design and rainwater dripped into the cab due to the lack of a rainwater strip on the cab roof and that the opening came into the curve of the roof. The fittings on the boiler backplate were new. Steam reversing gear, described in

No 45 *Burdett Road* in the standard green livery of the LT&SR.
Locomotive Publishing Co

Above left & right:
I don't know where these pictures were taken, but their inclusion is to show the lining details of the 'No 37' class engines. The first is No 40 *Black Horse Road*, while the other shows the rear three-quarters view of No 42 *Commercial Road*. *Collection R. J. Essery*

No 39 *Forest Gate* was rebuilt in 1907 and turned out in the short-lived lavender-grey livery. The overall finish is splendid, but I suspect that the wearing qualities left much to be desired. *Collection R. J. Essery*

Chapter 4, was originally fitted to the 'No 51' class, although it was also fitted to the 'No 69' class, both classes having been introduced before the 'No 37' class was rebuilt, and replaced the lever reversing gear. The shapely chimney had a narrow polished brass ring let into the outer edge of the lip; an expensive feature perhaps, but the LT&SR was not parsimonious concerning the livery and décor of its locomotives. The engines rebuilt before 1910 were turned out in the lavender-blue livery with black borders and panels, lined out in white, as previously mentioned. This was not a very suitable scheme for working steam locomotives, and in due course a return to the standard green livery was made. The first engines to be rebuilt did not have capuchons on the chimneys, but eventually all the rebuilds received them.

K. H. Leech records that the holding down nuts were countersunk, while the dome and safety valve casings were also edged with a narrow half-polished brass beading. It would seem that both these castings were handmade and, as a result, the valve castings varied slightly in shape from engine to engine. New connecting rods with a neater type of big end and later new H-section coupling rods were fitted. The injectors were on the tank tops but on the rebuilds their feed was delivered through external pipes to clack boxes on the front ring of the boiler.

A fascinating insight into Edwardian period management attitudes is offered by this delightful story told by K. H. Leech who asked Robert Whitelegg, then the company's Locomotive Superintendent, why he had fitted all the rebuilds with a capuchon on the chimneys. Logically it would have no value when the engine was running in reverse. Whitelegg's answer was simple: there was a distinct benefit when running engine first and no detrimental effect when running in reverse, but the most important factor was that 'he liked them' and felt they 'set the engines off'. I cannot think of a better reason; however, it cut little ice with the new owners, the Midland Railway, which removed them! The Midland also fitted extended smokeboxes, a feature that Whitelegg would have used if he had still been if charge when smokebox renewals were called for.

The early days of Midland Railway ownership saw a number of variations of Midland chimneys and smokeboxes. One interesting version was No 2153 (old No 44), which received a Midland boiler with an extended smokebox and flat-topped dome together with Midland-style safety valves. One feature of the Ramsbottom safety valve was that the valve lever came back into the cab on the LT&S engines whereas this was not the case with those on the Midland Railway.

One locomotive, No 40, was specially decorated for the celebration of Queen Victoria's Diamond Jubilee in 1897 (shortly after the engine was built). This took the form of a special flag display, a bust of the Queen at the chimney base, a special 'Jubilee' destination board and the letters 'VR' in large characters on the tank sides. Two other Tilbury engines were also to be decorated in a very ornate style to commemorate special events.

All the rebuilds were stationed at Shoeburyness and, together with No 79, they made up the top link of passenger tank engines. During the Midland period the rebuilt engines were classified as Class 3, and after 1928, in LMS ownership, they became Class 3P. A number of Derby Works orders referred to Class 3 passenger tank engines and to avoid duplication I have included all these details in Chapter 10 even though they would also apply to the 'No 37' class rebuilds. Most of the class were withdrawn during 1951, the last to go being No 41961 (old No 45) in October 1952.

No 43 *Great Ilford* was rebuilt in 1906 and this picture shows the immaculate finish that was the hallmark of the British railway companies in the years prior to the Great War. *Real Photographs/NRM*

Although contemporary writers decried the use of Midland Railway fittings on these engines, I think that this picture of No 2147, old No 38, with its Midland dome, chimney and extended smokebox, makes a handsome sight. The lining on the valence along the running plate and on the cab front, together with the lining on the wheel splashers and footstep carrying plate, is noteworthy.
Collection A. G. Ellis 21563

No 2148, old No 39, was repainted in Midland Railway crimson lake and returned to traffic on 7 December 1912; however, the extended smokebox came later. I believe this picture was taken c1923.
W. L. Good, courtesy Richard Taylor

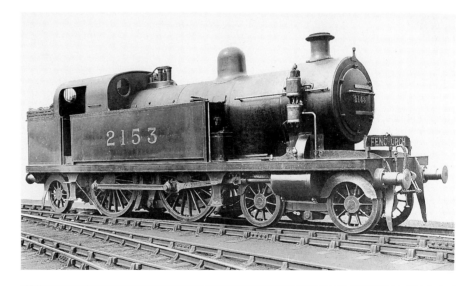

This picture shows old No 44 in Midland Railway red passenger livery as No 2153 and fitted with an extended smokebox, together with Midland boiler mountings.
Derby Collection NRM DY11386

This chapter on the rebuilt No 37 Class is concluded with this picture of old No 39 now in the service of British Railways as No 41955, but still carrying LMS on the tank sides. The photograph was taken at Pitsea on 26 September 1948. The engine had less than three years' service remaining, being withdrawn in February 1951.
Collection A. G. Ellis 22523

7. The 'No 49' Class 0-6-0 Tender Engines

With but two exceptions the LT&SR was a tank engine line and these two engines are described in this chapter. They were a pair of 0-6-0s purchased from Sharp, Stewart in 1899 that had been built the previous year for the Ottoman Railway in Turkey. For some reason, probably because the railway was unable to pay for them, they were not delivered and were purchased by the LT&SR. Not only were they the only tender engines to belong to the company but they were the only two engines not to be named. The LT&SR numbered them 49 and 50 and under Midland Railway ownership they became Nos 2898 and 2899. No 49 was repainted in MR black goods engine livery and returned to traffic on 23 December 1912 and No 50 in March 1913. No 2898 was withdrawn in December 1933, but No 2899 became LMS No 22899 in January 1935 and was withdrawn in February 1936.

For a number of years there was little goods traffic and it was not until Tilbury Docks opened in 1886 that this began to increase substantially. Prior to the arrival of Nos 49 and 50 the 'No 1' class handled whatever goods traffic was on offer but at the time the two 0-6-0s became available freight traffic was growing considerably, so it made good sense to acquire these engines for £3,008 each.

They came to the LT&SR without the weatherboard on the tender but this was fitted c1911 and, at the same time, the 'open tropical cab' was filled in by using an ordinary carriage window that slid up and down. This made a very snug cab, which was also fitted with small padded seats for both driver and fireman. They may have been rather hot in the heat of summer but on a cold winter's night it would have been somewhat better than a Johnson cab on a Midland goods engine!

Other changes in their appearance are dealt with in the photo captions but they were to receive the combined type of splasher and sandbox associated with the 0-6-2Ts described in Chapter 9. They were also fitted with new chimneys and buffers of both LT&S and Midland type. According to K. H. Leech, No 49 was to spend several years stationed at Tilbury working ballast or similar non-revenue-earning trains for the Engineers' Department, while No 50 was stationed at Plaistow, taking her turn in the goods link with the 0-6-2T engines of the 'No 69' class. Fuel consumption appeared to be heavy: on goods trains K. H. Leech suggests they burnt over 100lb per mile when working the Plaistow to Tilbury early morning freight trains.

The principal dimensions were: length over buffers 47ft 11½in; driving wheels 4ft 6½in; coupled wheelbase 7ft 5in + 7ft 11in; total 15ft 4in. Cylinders 18in x 24in, later reduced to 16½in diameter c1911 when both engines' cylinders were fitted with liners. Boiler described as telescopic, smallest outside diameter 4ft 4in; length 10ft, pitched 7ft from rail level; length inside firebox 4ft 9⅞in, width 3ft 4in; boiler pressure 150psi; grate area 16sq ft. The heating surface was 1,114sq ft, 96 for the firebox and 1,018 for the 216 steel tubes of 1¾in outside diameter. The tender ran on six wheels, 3ft 6½in diameter, and the tank held 2,640 gallons of water. (Note: some of these dimensions vary from those shown on the Midland Railway engine diagram, Fig 41.)

K. H. Leech records that the Westinghouse brake was used

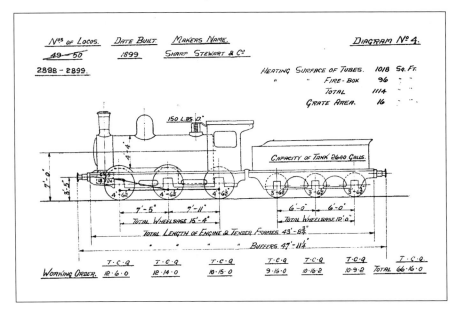

Fig 40 The LT&SR engine diagram for Nos 49 and 50 is included in order to show the original arrangement of the cab and the absence of the tender weatherboard. Note the water capacity is given as 2,640 gallons; the Midland diagram states 2,500 gallons.

when shunting, rather than the handbrake that was not good enough for this work. He goes on to say that some drivers funked using the airbrake for shunting for fear of breaking the couplings. In these circumstances the fireman would be continuously working the handbrake. He also said they were rather rough riding engines but even so, they had a long life when compared with some other small classes inherited by the LMS.

They were fitted with cut down chimneys similar to those on the 'No 1' class. The Midland Railway classified then as Class 2, 2F after 1928. Under LT&SR ownership they were painted in standard green with lining and carried the initials L.T.S.R. on the tender side. They were never given names. The number was on the cab side and later the crest was added. Under Midland Railway and LMS ownership they were painted in black.

They had a reasonable life in LMS ownership, bearing in mind that small classes of non-standard locomotives were generally scrapped rather quickly. No 2898 received a new Belpaire boiler, described in the register as G5½ Altd, in October 1922. This replaced the original boiler that had been numbered 13 by the Midland Railway. The boiler pressure remained at 150psi and the cylinders at 18in x 24in stroke. No 2899 was similarly treated in June 1924 and its old boiler, No 14, was replaced. The heating surface of the replacement boilers was 1,033.5sq ft. The only other alterations that I can trace as Derby Works orders are No 5735, dated 31 May 1922, to alter the safety valves of these two engines and a rather late in their life modification, to No 7604. This was dated 19 February 1930 and read: 'Fixing cast-iron blocks to hind end of the tanks of tenders of LT&SR engines Nos 2898/2899 to Drg S-4560 in order to increase the weight on the trailing wheels. The work is urgent, when complete the blocks are to be sent to Bow for fitting.' It would be interesting to know what was the reason for this change. Considering their origins, they served their owners well.

Right:
Fig 41 This is the 1921 Midland Railway engine diagram for the two engines that were originally the No '49' class of the LT&SR

Below:
The picture of No 49 reproduced here was taken before the sliding side cab window was fitted. I have not found any reference to these engines being equipped with the vacuum brake; however, I believe this picture shows No 49 as a dual-fitted locomotive. Note the end train pipe together with the Westinghouse pipe and the pipe running from the smokebox into the cab where presumably the ejector was fitted.
Locomotive Publishing Co

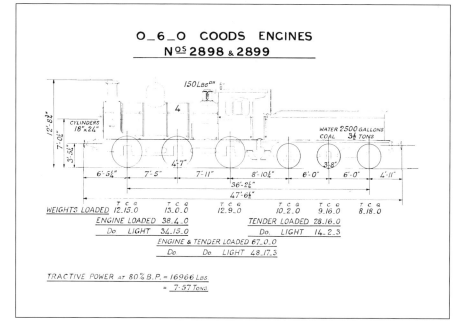

Compared with No 49, seen opposite in full livery, this picture of No 50 appears to show a locomotive in plain standard LT&SR green. Note also the addition of the ampersand between the T and the S on the tender side when compared with No 49. *Ken Nunn/LCGB*

Here we see old No 49 in Midland Railway ownership as No 2898 and painted in black freight engine livery. The locomotive is carrying the original LT&SR boiler, No 13, as shown on page 135, but the locomotive now has a tender weatherboard, Midland smokebox, combined front splashers and sandbox and Midland chimney. The pipe that ran from the smokebox to the cab has been removed and the engine does not have a front Westinghouse hose connection. *Derby Collection NRM DY11390*

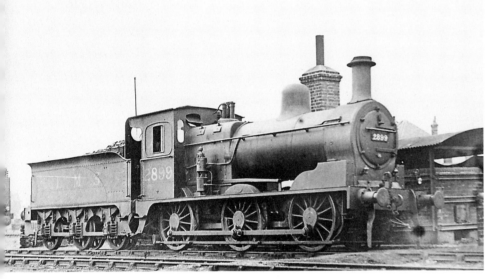

Left:
I conclude this chapter on the No '49' class with two pictures of No 2899, old No 50, in LMS ownership. This shows the engine with the G5½ Altd boiler No 5671 that was fitted in June 1924.

Below:
The locomotive has now been renumbered and is No 22899, a number it was to carry between January 1935 and February 1936 when it was withdrawn from service. Note the change of chimney, compared with the picture above, and no windguard. *Collection H. F. Wheeller, courtesy Roger Carpenter*

8. The 'No 51' Class

During the pre-1923 period the 18 locomotives of the 'No 51' class, built in two batches — 12 by Sharp, Stewart in 1900 and six by the North British Locomotive Company in 1903 — comprised the second most numerous class of LT&SR locomotives. The design was very similar to the 'No 37' class, unfortunately, unlike the '1' and '37' classes, I have not been able to find an official specification, so I have reproduced the details that were recorded by K. H. Leech.

The boiler, 4in larger in diameter, was pitched 3in higher; the wing tanks and coalbunker were also larger than the previous class. Some writers, including myself, consider they were the most symmetrical of all the LT&S locomotives. As far as I can see, both series were identical except that the chimney of the second series had a greater taper and was perhaps less pleasing. The principal dimensions were: length over buffers 39ft; driving wheels 6ft 6in; bogie and trailing wheels 3ft 6in; total wheelbase 7ft + 7ft ½ in + 8ft 9in + 8ft, total 30ft 9½ in. Cylinders 18in x 26in; boiler diameter 4ft 6in; length 10ft 6in; height of boiler centreline above rail level 7ft 9in; firebox length 6ft 9in; grate area 19.77sq ft; heating surface, tubes 929sq ft; firebox 117sq ft, total 1,046sq ft. Weight in working order 68 tons 2½ cwt of which 33 tons 17½ cwt was over the coupled wheels. Water capacity was shown as 1,565 gallons on the later Midland Railway engine diagram.

They were a modest enlargement of the 'No 37' class and were built to handle the ever-increasing traffic on the line. At the time of their construction this was the new work in conjunction with the Metropolitan District and the Whitechapel & Bow Railway and the widening between Campbell Road Junction and Barking. With the arrival of the 'No 79' class and the availability of the 'No 37' class rebuilds, the 'No 51' class were no longer the top link LT&SR passenger locomotives, but there was plenty of work for them to handle. In 1912, they were Tilbury's largest passenger engines with about three being stationed at that depot, the remainder, with one exception, being divided between Plaistow and Shoeburyness. The exception was the appropriately named *Kentish Town*, which was stationed at the Midland Railway engine shed of the same name.

This locomotive was to receive an ornate livery to commemorate the Coronation of King Edward VII in 1902, including a copper-rimmed chimney which it retained for many years. There were cast busts of the King and Queen on the platform behind the front buffer beam and oak shields with the Royal Arms on the tank tops and rear. In keeping with their work over the T&HJR into St Pancras, all of the class was dual brake fitted. No 61 was regularly employed on the St Pancras to Southend through service. The Westinghouse driver's brake valve was on the centre of the firebox backplate so that it could be applied from either side of the cab while the driver could see out of all windows, forward and to the rear. The vacuum ejector was on top of the right-hand tank within the cab area.

The first order, engines Nos 51-62, was placed with Sharp, Stewart and they were built at Atlas Works in Glasgow. The order for the second batch, engines Nos 63-68, was placed with Dübs & Co in December 1902, at the same time as the first six 0-6-2Ts of the 'No 69' class. By the time that the six 4-4-2T engines and the six 0-6-2T engines were delivered in

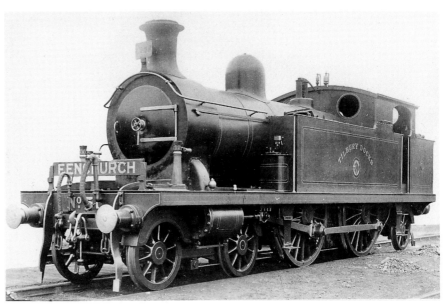

No 51 was the pioneer engine and at first was named *Tilbury Docks*. It was renamed *Purfleet* on 3 July 1911. This picture shows the locomotive in standard LT&SR green livery. *Collection T. J. Edgington*

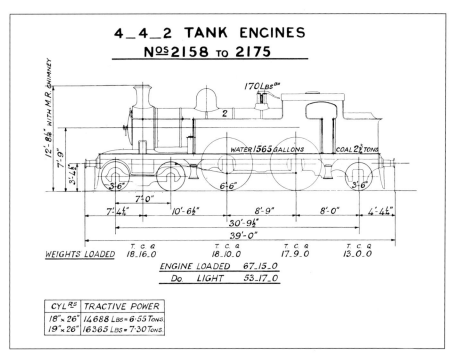

4_4_2 TANK ENGINES
Nos 2158 to 2175

170 LBS^{ᴼᴺ}

12'-8½" WITH M.R. CHIMNEY

7'-9"

3'-4½"

WATER 1565 GALLONS   COAL 2¾ TONS

3'-6"   6'-6"   3'-6"

7'-0"

7'-4½"   10'-6½"   8'-9"   8'-0"   4'-4½"

30'-9½"

39'-0"

WEIGHTS LOADED
	T. C. Q	T. C. Q	T. C. Q	T. C. Q
	18_16_0	18_10_0	17_9_0	13_0_0

ENGINE LOADED   67_15_0

Do.   LIGHT   53_17_0

CYL^{RS}	TRACTIVE POWER
18"×26"	14,688 LBS = 6·55 TONS
19"×26"	16,365 LBS = 7·30 TONS

Fig 42 The Midland Railway engine diagram dated 2 May 1921 gave the usual tractive power details at 80% boiler pressure and a later edition stated the 85% figures as 15,606lb for the 18in x 26in cylinder engines and 17,388lb for those fitted with 19in x 26in cylinders. The Midland Railway locomotive register used for compiling this information gives dates for altering the cylinders for all engines except old No 59. The first engine to receive the larger cylinders was old No 53 in January 1913, the last, other than old No 59 that was still running with 18in x 26in cylinders in 1925, was old No 54. This engine was fitted with larger cylinders on 31 October 1929.

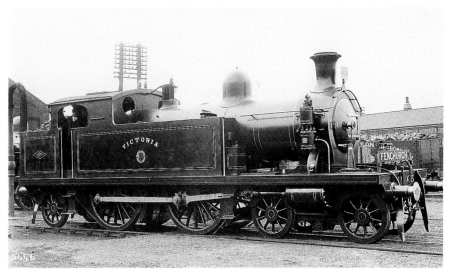

No 65 *Victoria* is seen here at Plaistow in pristine condition. There was to be little change in this class until after 1912 when the Midland Railway began to fit extended smokeboxes, Midland chimneys, domes, etc. *F. Moore*

June 1903 the North British Locomotive Co had been formed and both Sharp, Stewart and Dübs were part of the new company. These were amongst the first engines to carry the distinctive North British diamond-shape builder's plate. North British used differently shaped works plates for each factory, those from the old Dübs works at Queen's Park retained that company's diamond shape, while the engines built at the former Neilson Reid Hyde Park Works at Springburn were circular, and those at Sharp, Stewart Atlas Works were oval. Although the first application of steam reversing gear came to the LT&SR with the 'No 51' class, this subject has already been dealt with in Chapter 4.

During the years prior to becoming Midland Railway locomotives little change took place, the most noticeable being the fitting of covers over the coal bunkers. Under Midland Railway ownership a number of changes occurred, including the removal of the coalbunker covers and their replacement by coal rails. Other changes were the fitting of extended smokeboxes (continued after 1923), Midland chimneys, new cylinders of 19in diameter, and replacement safety valves. There is a reference to a number of drawings in the LT&SR locomotive drawing register beginning with No 1030. This is also shown as Midland drawing No 14-9266, vacuum brake for

'51' class. LT&SR drawing No 1040 did not have a Midland number and was made at Plaistow; it referred to reversing steam arms, '51' class. The final reference in the LT&SR register was for Midland Railway drawings Nos 13-9159 and 13-9164 in respect of steam arm gear.

Old No 68, now LMS No 2109, was given a top feed with what looked like a second dome as the cover. The traditional LT&S wooden cab roof was replaced by one made of iron with a smaller roof ventilator. It was recorded by K. H. Leech that this Derby modification was not well received by the ex-LT&S enginemen.

No 66 was recorded as being the first LT&SR engine to be repainted in crimson lake livery, becoming MR No 2173, and my own research supports that view. K. H. Leech also states that No 63 was still painted in standard Tilbury green when renumbered as MR 2170, but I understand that this was not the only example of a green-painted Midland Railway locomotive in the 20th century.

As more powerful locomotives became available during the LMS and early BR period, many engines of this class were transferred elsewhere to other depots on the Midland Division and, perhaps understandably, they were not popular with the engine crews who had to work with them. Many spent long

This picture of No 61 *Kentish Town* shows the ornate finish applied to this engine for the Coronation of King Edward VII in 1902. Although the busts, decorations, etc were soon removed, the locomotive ran with the copper-rimmed chimney for a number of years. The external finish of the locomotive is rather splendid. Note the finish on the metalwork, for example the buffer bases, screw link coupling, hooks on the end of the safety chains, wheel tyres, etc. For the engine cleaners to have achieved this degree of finish they would have had to have spent many hours of work on it. *Collection R. J. Essery.*

periods in store out of service. One locomotive, LMS No 2105, old No 64, was withdrawn in November 1947, the others becoming part of the stock of British Railways, but only three carried their allotted British Railways numbers. With the withdrawal of old No 63, as British Railways No 41922 in March 1953, the class became extinct.

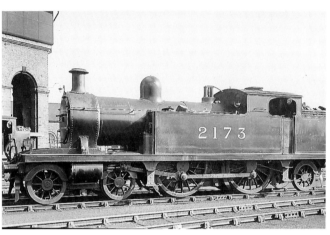

Compared with the previous picture, this view of No 66 *Earls Court* shows a locomotive in service and, although lacking the exhibition finish of No 61, it is more believable. *Collection R. J. Essery*

Old No 66, shown above, is seen here at Plaistow in Midland Railway red passenger engine livery and carrying its MR number, 2173. It was the first LT&SR locomotive to be renumbered by the new owners, the official date being 3 September 1912. I suspect this picture was taken at a later date, as coal rails have been fitted. *Collection Richard Taylor*

The alterations that took place to the 'No 51' class did not improve their looks as this picture of No 2171, old No 64 shows very clearly. No doubt the extended smokebox and the use of other standard Midland Railway fittings made commercial sense, but the well-proportioned appearance was lost. *Derby Collection NRM DY11572*

Taken at Tilbury on 22 August 1931, this picture shows old No 60, No 2167 in 1912, which was renumbered 2101 in 1929, as seen here. The engine is black with red lining — the painting finish used for all ex-LT&SR passenger tank engines. The engine was withdrawn in March 1951.
H. C. Casserley

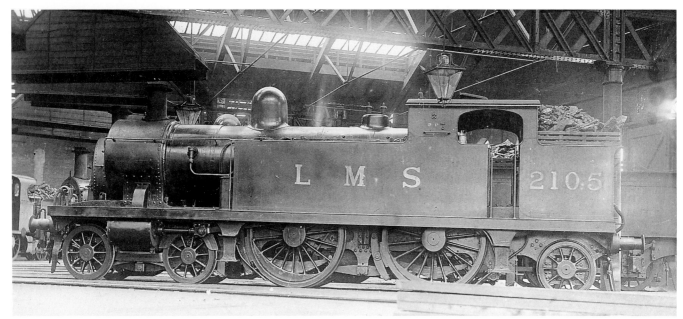

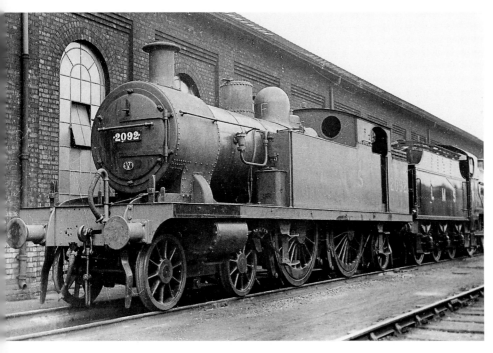

Many of the old 'No 51' class were displaced from the LT&S Section by the arrival of the Stanier three-cylinder 2-6-4T engines. This picture shows old No 64, now running as LMS No 2105, the number given in 1929, one of the locomotives that were transferred to other sheds on the Midland Division. In this c1938 view we can see the locomotive inside a roundhouse, possibly Bournville. *Real Photographs W8271/NRM*

Another engine to be transferred to the Midlands was old No 51, seen here at Derby as LMS No 2092 carrying a Derby 17A shed plate, with the dome casing removed, on 11 October 1936. This locomotive has had the Westinghouse brake end train pipe removed but it is not possible to say if the cylinders have also been taken off the locomotive.
L. Hanson

Old No 68, now running as LMS No 2109, was rather unusual: the boiler carried was fitted with a top feed and the leading dome was in fact the cover. When photographed on 6 July 1935 the locomotive was stationed at Bournville where the picture was taken. *L. W. Perkins*

On 25 May 1935 old No 61 was photographed at Nottingham as LMS No 2102, after working a three-coach passenger train from Derby. When transferred to the Midland Division these engines were employed on light work when compared with their duties on the LT&SR during their prime. *Collection Roger Carpenter*

Overhead views of these engines are extremely rare so I thought that I would conclude this chapter with these two views of old No 56, as LMS No 2097, when the engine was in store at Devons Road, prior to being withdrawn in March 1951. *Collection R. J. Essery*

9. The 'No 69' Class

Apart from the pair of 0-6-0s described in Chapter 7, these 0-6-2Ts were the only other freight engines owned by the LT&SR. Like most British goods and mineral engines built before Nationalisation, they were to last for many years. They were also to be involved in a remarkable series of renumbering programmes that saw them regain their Midland Railway numbers first allocated in 1912. I have summarised these changes below.

The original LT&SR numbers allotted to the North British Locomotive engines built in 1903 were 69-74. Their Midland numbers were 2180-2185 but the 1923 LMS numbers were 2220-2225 and in 1939 they were renumbered 2180-2185; in 1947 they became 1980-1985 and British Railways added 40,000 to these numbers so that they were Nos 41980-41985.

The second batch of four engines was built by the North British Locomotive Company in 1908 and numbered 75-78 by the LT&SR. The Midland Railway numbered them 2186-2189, in 1923 the LMS renumbered them 2226-2229 and then back to 2186-2189 in 1939. They became Nos 1986-1989 in 1947 and British Railways renumbered them 41986-41989.

The final batch of four was on order from Beyer Peacock but these engines were not delivered until after the LT&SR had become part of the Midland Railway in 1912, so they never carried their allotted LT&SR numbers which would probably have been 83-86. They became MR Nos 2190-2193, then LMS 2230-2233 in 1923, 2190-2193 again in 1939 and Nos 1990-1993 in 1947. British Railways renumbered them 41990-41993. The advantage of these various renumbering schemes is that it does assist with dating photographs. The first locomotive to be withdrawn was old No 69, as British Railways No 41980, in May 1958 and the last to be withdrawn was old No 70, as British Railways No 41981, in June 1962.

The first six locomotives of this class were part of the same order placed with the builders which included the final six engines of the 'No 51' class and they shared the same boiler. The locations of the clack box, on the front boiler ring on the goods tanks and on the firebox backplate on the passenger tank engines, meant that boilers could not be interchanged. The goods tanks did not have a steam cock for the vacuum ejector, but the passenger engines did. Other differences were the smokebox attachment to the frames, and the position of the steam pipe for the Westinghouse air pump. The final series from Beyer Peacock were not identical to the North British-built engines: chimneys were not quite the same shape and the locomotives were fitted with steam sanding gear which did not prove to be too successful. Within a year or so it was replaced by gravity sanding worked by hand linkage control gear. A further change was the injectors. The LT&SR normally used injectors made by Gresham & Craven but these four locomotives were fitted with 'hot water injectors' made by Holden & Brooke. My understanding is that these injectors returned the hot waste water from the injectors into the tanks but, in practice, they were not quite so easy to use, a factor which no doubt made them less popular than those by Gresham & Craven.

The 1908 batch were the first LT&SR engines to be fitted with Whitelegg's automatic variable blastpipe. Later it was to be fitted to all the other tank engine classes except the 'No 1' class locomotives, but the Midland Railway would have nothing to do with this item and it was to be removed from all ex-LT&SR locomotives after 1912. The device consisted of a cone, raised or lowered in the centre of the blastpipe to alter the effective area of the pipe. Its movement was controlled by the position of the reversing lever through an arm and a

The only official works picture that I have of the 0-6-2Ts is for No 75, the first of the 1908 batch of four engines that were built by the North British Locomotive Company in 1908. The words "Queen's Park Works' are inscribed on the photograph just below the rear end guard irons. The painting is in works grey and does not represent the LT&SR lining. *Collection R. J. Essery*

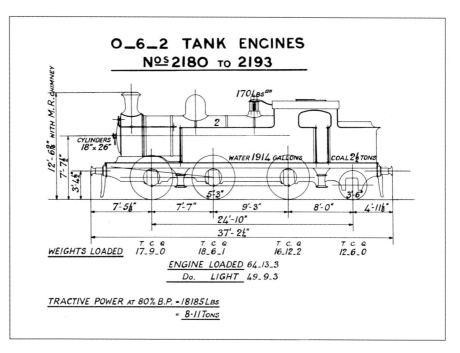

Fig 43 The Midland Railway engine diagram dated 2 May 1921 shown here gives the tractive power based upon 80% boiler pressure; a later diagram quotes the figures of 19,322lb for 85% boiler pressure.

O_6_2 TANK ENGINES
NOS 2180 TO 2193

CYLINDERS 18" x 26"

170 LBS 2

WATER 1914 GALLONS   COAL 2½ TONS

12'-6½" WITH M.R. CHIMNEY
7'-7½"
3'-4¼"

5'-3"   3'-6"

7'-5⅝"   7'-7"   9'-3"   8'-0"   4'-11⅛"
24'-10"
37'-2¼"

	T. C. Q	T. C. Q	T. C. Q	T. C. Q
WEIGHTS LOADED	17_9_0	18_6_1	16_12_2	12_6_0

ENGINE LOADED 64_13_3
Do. LIGHT 49_9_3

TRACTIVE POWER AT 80% B.P. = 18185 LBS
= 8·11 TONS

straight link, so that from mid gear to full gear the area of the pipe increased, at first very slowly and towards the end very rapidly. The coalbunkers were fitted with lids, a feature of all LT&SR tank engines ('No 1' class excluded). The problem was that for longer, heavier runs the bunkers needed to be really full of coal so the lids could not always be closed. In due course these lids were removed and coal rails were fitted.

The final four also had a long box fitted on the top of the side tanks. This was to hold the fire irons that were normally held in place by a U-shaped arrangement and a short upright bar at the cab end of the tank. The 4-6-4Ts were similar and this feature can be seen in the pictures reproduced in Chapter 11. The last engine to be built, No 2193, was fitted with a No 9 Westinghouse straight airbrake valve as well as the more usual No 4 automatic brake valve. This arrangement provided a very easily graduated straight air application and release of the engine brake cylinder only, and greatly assisted the driver when working goods trains or in shunting. They were fitted with a steam reverser, a labour-saving arrangement which no doubt was appreciated by train crews when shunting was taking place.

The last LT&S engines to be built with a wooden cab roof were Nos 73-78. K. H. Leech's description of the LT&SR wooden cab roof is not quite the same as that given in the specification reproduced previously, so I have quoted what he had to say on the subject. The original Tilbury style was to varnish the roof internally and cover the external roof with sheet zinc. The advantage these wooden roofs had over the curved steel or hood-type roof found upon the 'No 37' class rebuilds and the No 79 class was that they tended to be cooler in summer and warmer in winter; in addition, they did not sweat. The Midland Railway did not like wooden roofs so in due course steel roofs to the same profile replaced them. In my view, when these engines came to Derby Locomotive Works for repair it was more convenient to use the type of roof in regular use and the wooden roofs were replaced.

During the period of LT&SR ownership, none of the 'No 69' class was fitted with vacuum brake pipes, but later some, maybe all, were to be dual fitted. At first no steam heating cocks were fitted to these engines which meant that in normal conditions their use upon passenger work was somewhat limited and they were not suitable for such work during the steam heating season. The 1903 batch came to the Tilbury with a rather elaborate livery, while the 1908 batch and subsequent repaints of the 1903 batch carried a simpler livery style. K. H. Leech states that in LT&SR ownership the webs of the coupling rods were painted, but photographic evidence does not entirely confirm this statement. The Beyer Peacock

No 72 *Hadleigh* was built in 1903 by the North British Locomotive Company and carries the passenger livery that was given only to the first batch of locomotives. When these engines were repainted they were turned out in the style shown in the next photo.
Locomotive Publishing Co

No 76 *Dunton* was built by the North British Locomotive Co in 1908 and this picture is one of the few that confirms the webs of the coupling rods were painted in a chocolate colour. The external finish between No 72 opposite and this picture should be compared. Note the axle ends have been lined on No 76 but not on No 72, while the latter carries the fine-lining whereas No 76 only has the brown border. See also P. E. Barnes's drawing at Fig 32 (page 112).
Locomotive Publishing Co

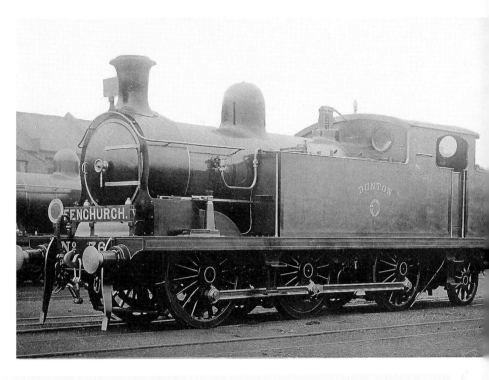

In Midland Railway ownership these engines were equipped with coal rails to increase the capacity of the bunker. This undated but Midland period picture of No 2193, the last engine of the class to be built and which never carried an LT&SR number, shows the locomotive at Tilbury with the coal rails in place. Note the fire iron retaining box on top of the side tank, which was fitted only to the final four engines built by Beyer Peacock.
Collection Richard Taylor

engines were delivered in Midland Railway goods engine black, a colour they were to retain, albeit with varying insignia, until they were withdrawn. During their service as Midland, LMS and British Railways locomotives further changes took place, the most noticeable being replacement chimneys, Midland Railway smokebox doors and the replacement of the Ramsbottom safety valve by a Ross pop safety valve. The changes were to suit Midland parts; for example, the existing design of MR blower cap was to be used but it was to be made 8in lower and the order called for 13 blastpipes 2ft 3in long. At the time the order was placed, No 2185 had already been fitted but the work was urgent; engines Nos 2182/8 were in Plaistow shops waiting for the replacement parts. This work was covered by order No 5737 dated 8 June 1922.

Some writers have suggested these engines were not fitted with carriage warming, but I do not believe this is correct. Order No 5768, dated 26 July 1922, was to fit the 0-6-2T engines with J&B, (Johnson & Bain) carriage warming to drawing No 22-9656, a new drawing made for this work. The material was to be prepared at Derby and to be sent to Plaistow for fitting. Continuous blowdown was fitted to these engines in 1938.

The '69s' were regarded as robust workmanlike engines and reasonable steamers but not free runners, and enginemen had to be careful when filling the tanks. If the water overflowed it was likely to find its way down into the driving axleboxes and wash away the oil. Unless dealt with this could lead to a hot box.

144

No 2222 was originally No 71 and became Midland Railway No 2182. The locomotive was one of the 1903 batch built by the North British Locomotive Co and is seen here as LMS No 2222 at Tilbury. The picture was taken from a similar angle to the previous plate, showing that other than the fire iron retaining box and perhaps the size of the cab roof hatch, they were identical. *Collection Richard Taylor*

No 2231 was photographed at Plaistow c1923 and illustrates the opposite side of one of the final batch of this class which did not enter service until after the LT&SR had become part of the Midland Railway. The fire iron retaining box on the top of the tank was on both sides of the locomotive, this picture being the opposite side of the engine to that of 2193 opposite. *Collection Richard Taylor*

As freight engines their colour was black in Midland, LMS and British Railways ownership. This picture of old No 70, here running as LMS No 2221, was taken during the mid-1930s and illustrates a locomotive that has probably just returned from a general overhaul and a repaint at a main works. *Collection R. J. Essery*

The old 'No 69' class was to be involved in a series of renumbering changes. This engine began life as LT&SR No 78 *Dagenham Dock*, the Midland Railway renumbered it 2189 in 1912 and the LMS changed it to 2229 in 1923. The number was changed again to 2189 in 1939, and then to 1989 in 1947. British Railways added 40,000 to the number and as No 41989 the locomotive was withdrawn from service in April 1958. *Collection R. J. Essery*

In 1948, the majority of the British Railways locomotive stock was renumbered, but in the first few months some non-standard styles were to be seen. This picture of old No 2193, the last engine of the class to be built and one that did not carry an LT&SR number, shows the engine with its final number, 41993. 'British Railways', written in full across the tank side, was applied to a number of engines during the first months of Nationalisation. *Collection R. J. Essery*

This undated picture of No 41990, taken during the 1950s, shows the engine at Plaistow. The locomotive displays the correct British Railways insignia; the tank side emblem is just visible beneath the grime and dirt. This locomotive was withdrawn from service in February 1959, together with several other members of this class that became extinct in June 1962. *Photomatic/NRM*

10. The 'No 79' Class, Including Midland and LMS-built Examples

When account is taken of the additional engines ordered by the Midland Railway and the subsequent batches built by the LMS, then the final design of LT&SR 4-4-2T engine was to be the most numerous class of locomotive to run on the London, Tilbury & Southend Railway. The constructional sequence is set out below.

Built by Robert Stephenson & Co 1909

LT&S No	LT&S Name	MR & First LMS No	LMS 1929 No	LMS 1947 No	BR No	Date Withdrawn
79	Rippleside	2176	2147	1965	41965	2/51
80	Thundersley	2177	2148	1966	41966	6/56
81	Aveley	2178	2149	1967	41967	12/52
82	Crowstone	2179	2150	1968	41968	2/51

No 80 was originally named *Southend-on-Sea* when exhibited at the 1909 Franco-British Exhibition at the White City, where the engine was awarded a gold medal. A replica of the medal was fixed to the tank side, being positioned below the name and above the crest. The temporary name was removed and the locomotive was given the allotted name of *Thundersley* prior to entering traffic.

The LMS-built locomotives were:

Builder	Date Built	First LMS Nos	Second LMS Nos	BR Nos	Dates Withdrawn
LMS Derby	1923	2110-2119	1928-1937	41928-41937	1952-8

Built to order No 5871 dated 5 February 1923.

Builder	Date Built	First LMS Nos	Second LMS Nos	BR Nos	Dates Withdrawn
Nasmyth, Wilson	1925	2120-2124	1938-1942	41938-41942	1955-6

Built to order No 6377 dated 27 January 1925.

Builder	Date Built	First LMS Nos	Second LMS Nos	BR Nos	Dates Withdrawn
LMS Derby	1927	2125-2134	1943-1952	41943-41952	1956-60

Built to order No 6751 dated 4 November 1926. The order read: 'These engines, with the exception of one or two minor details, will be similar to O/N 5871'. On 14 April 1927 a note was made, 'Engines to be numbered 2125-2134. Existing engines to be renumbered.'

Builder	Date Built	First LMS Nos	Second LMS Nos	BR Nos	Dates Withdrawn
LMS Derby	1930	2151-2160	1969-1978	41969-41978	1955-60

Built to order No 7406 dated 13 May 1929. The boilers were built to order No 7407 and numbered D8045-D8054.

First to be withdrawn were Nos 41965, old No 79, and 41968, old No 82, in February 1951. The last engine to be withdrawn was No 41947, old No 2129, in November 1960.

The four original engines, together with the 'No 37' class rebuilds, were to remain the LT&SR principal passenger tank engines for many years, and it was not until 1923 that the order for additional 4-4-2T engines of this class was issued. Dated 5 February 1923 (although the decision was probably made during 1922), Derby Works order No 5871 reads: 'Rebuilding 10 'No 1' class LT&SR engines, similar to No 3 class (between 2110 and 2119)'. The order continues and provides details of the work to be undertaken and the dates for completion. The boilers were to be made to Derby Works drawing No 20-9303 and were to be numbered 5526-5535. One month later, on 5 March, there was an instruction to

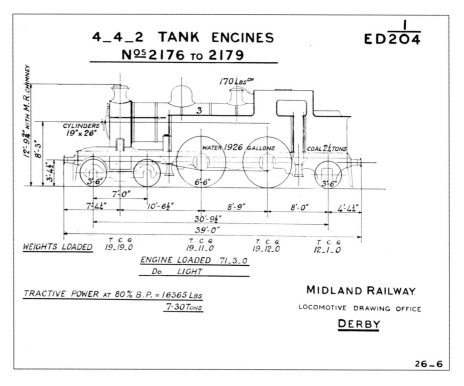

Fig 44 The Midland Railway engine diagram for these engines was ED 204 and, in accordance with the company's practice, recorded the tractive power at 80% of the boiler pressure. A later diagram revised the figure to give the tractive power at 85% of the boiler pressure and the figure was 17,388lb.

renumber engine Nos 2110-2119 to 2200-2209; the work was to be carried out at Plaistow. Finally, on 19 April, the order for the new construction was annotated 'engine Nos 2110-2119'.

The wording of the order is unusual and suggests that the new engines were to be the result of rebuilding 10 engines of the 'No 1' class. Clearly this did not happen; the first engines of this class were not withdrawn until 1930. However, it does confirm the date of the order to renumber the old engines of the 'No 1' class.

Returning to the LT&S-built engines, the No 79 class were very similar to the 'No 37' class rebuilds; the height of the bunker and side tanks on the '79s' was increased slightly and the chimneys were not the same, there being a short parallel section instead of the continuous curve of the rebuilt engines. The shape of the safety valve casing was also different, although for a time 'No 37' class rebuild No 42 carried a casing that was rather similar to those fitted to the No 79 class. While on the subject of safety valve casing shape, that of No 80 differed the other three locomotives in the No 79 class as it was made of polished brass and was not painted. There were

also considerable variations of painting styles, but first, the other detail variations.

Originally, the four engines were built with flat-section coupling rods but this was changed to an H-section rod c1911. The No 79 class were the first new LT&SR engines to be fitted with 19in cylinders, although the 'No 37' class rebuilds were also fitted with cylinders of this diameter. The No 79 class, including the LMS-built engines, together with the 'No 37' class rebuilds, handled the principal services until the Stanier three-cylinder 2-6-4T engines entered service in 1934. Robert Whitelegg's patent automatic variable blastpipe was fitted to the original four engines.

The No 79 class, being based upon the 'No 37' class rebuilds, used the same cylinders, boiler, motion and frame arrangements. The tanks were somewhat different and with this class it was possible to provide a 2½in ledge to the platform at the base of the side tanks and to dispense with the recess that was a feature of the 'No 37' class rebuilds. The cab roof of the No 79 class retained the hooded style first seen with the 'No 1' class condenser rebuilds, but with a smaller side

No 79 *Rippleside*, together with No 80, entered traffic in the lavender-grey livery as seen here. This picture shows the lining detail when engines were painted this way. Generally, British steam locomotives were painted in a serviceable colour, although from time to time there were exceptions and I feel that this was one of them. Contemporary reports suggest that it was retained for only three years at the most. *Locomotive Publishing Co.*

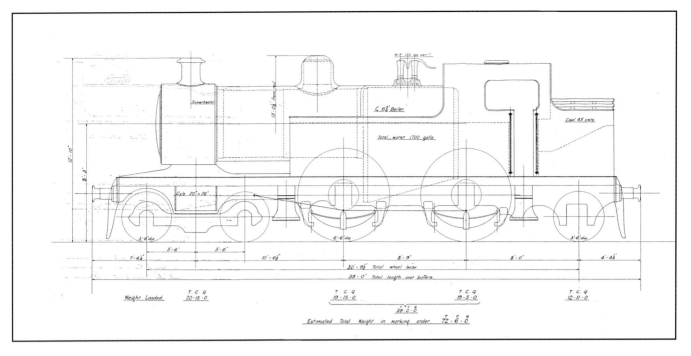

Fig 45 Dated 30 November 1922, this outline weight diagram or sketch was a Derby drawing office proposal for a 4-4-2T engine for the LT&S Section that was not proceeded with. The proposal shows larger cylinders, 20in x 26in, compared with 19in x 26in used with the 'No 79' class, a 5lb increase in boiler pressure, an altered weight distribution and a slightly greater total weight. The reduction in the water tank capacity would not have been helpful to the engine crews working heavy trains in adverse weather conditions. An extended smokebox was to be expected, but the G6¾ would have been a new class of boiler.

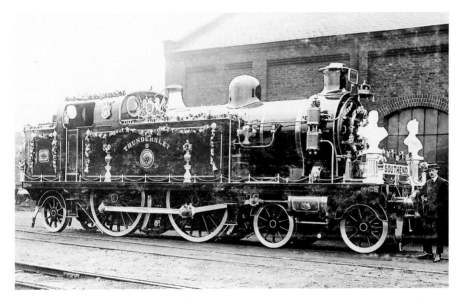

No 80 *Thundersley* with the highly ornate decorative treatment that was given to the engine to commemorate the Coronation of King George V. Clearly visible on the front corners of the engine platform are the white busts of the King and Queen Mary, while there was a similar bust of the Queen dowager, Queen Alexandra, at the rear of the bunker. It would be interesting to know what orders were given to the enginemen who worked the locomotive while it was decorated in this fashion.
Collection R. J. Essery

opening than fitted to 'No 37' class rebuilds. The bunkers and side tanks were higher and lids to the coalbunker were fitted.

The leading dimensions for these engines were: driving wheels 6ft 6in; bogie and trailing wheels 3ft 6in; wheelbase, 7ft + 7ft½in + 8ft 9in + 8ft, total 30ft 9½in. Length of frames 35ft 2in; height from rail to top of chimney 13ft 1³⁄₁₆in; boiler centreline from rail level 8ft 3in; from rail level to centre of buffers 3ft 4½in. Cylinders 19in x 26in; cylinder centres 6ft 4in apart; width over tank sides 8ft 5in; width over running plate 9ft. The heating surface was 1,122sq ft, tubes 1,003 and the firebox 119sq ft respectively; grate area was 19.77sq ft. There were 217 steel tubes, outside diameter 1⅝in increased to 1¾in for 12in at the smokebox end. The distance between the tubeplates was 10ft 10⁵⁄₁₆in; the boiler barrel was 10ft 6in long and 4ft 7⅞in inside diameter. Tank capacity was 1,926 gallons, the bunker held 2 tons 5cwt of coal. The working boiler pressure was 170psi.

The later LMS-built engines were about two tons heavier and the heating surface was increased to 1,205sq ft. Various weights have been published for these locomotives and the different 'official' figures may be in connection with the bridge problems on the approach to Fenchurch Street and the attitude of the Great Eastern Railway's engineer. I have included the 1924 Midland Railway diagram, but in view of the problems that existed cannot guarantee the accuracy of the information given.

The Nasmyth, Wilson engines had, according to K. H. Leech, the line of the cab altered and the old Tilbury polished beadings front and rear disappeared and in their place the cab roof plates were lengthened to overlap the front and rear spectacle plates. With the exception of the final batch, all the LMS-built engines were turned out in red passenger livery and thereafter were painted black with red lining.

I have briefly mentioned the special livery afforded to No 80 and I return to this engine again in order to describe fully the

At the beginning of the book, I showed a head-on view of No 80, taken in 1956 prior to becoming part of the National Collection. This picture was taken at the same time and shows the splendid livery carried by this engine. *Collection R. J. Essery*

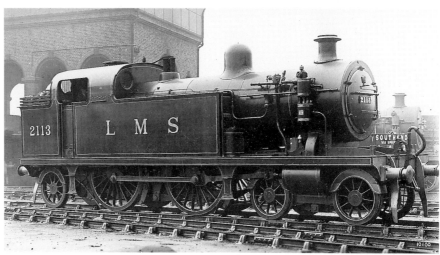

No 2113 was built at Derby and the date new in the register is given as 15 July 1923. This undated picture, taken at Plaistow, shows the engine in red passenger livery but with the post-1928 position for the locomotive number and letters LMS. This was one of the few LMS engines to enter traffic in red after the 1928 livery changes took place, which saw this class allocated the livery style of black with red lining. *F. Moore*

extravagant finish that was applied to this locomotive, in keeping with the company's policy of having engines specially decorated to commemorate royal occasions. The engine was first subject to a special finish for the exhibition at the White City, where it was awarded a gold medal. This engine, together with No 79 *Rippleside*, was painted in the lavender-blue colour, at times also described as lavender-grey, originally introduced in 1907 and retained on some engines for about three years. The footplate angle of No 80, together with the tank border, was painted in genuine Crimson Lake which, according to K. H. Leech, cost about twice as much as the variety of Crimson Lake used by the Midland Railway.

In view of the special finish applied for the White City exhibition it was not surprising that No 80 was the locomotive selected by the LT&SR for a special decorative treatment to commemorate the Coronation of King George V. A budget of £600 (quite a sizeable sum considering that the first cost of the engines was £3,224) was allowed for 'a special finish'. The highly ornate style was based upon decorations used for the Coronation of King Edward VII and the principal features were large white busts of both the King and Queen Mary that were carried on the front corners of the platform. A bust of the Queen dowager, Queen Alexandra, was carried at the rear of the bunker. A new chimney with a nickel-plated cap was fitted and the safety valve casing, together with the whistle, was also nickel plated. It is also possible that the smokebox door hand wheel received similar treatment, while both the lagging bands of the air pump cylinders and locomotive cylinders were fitted with polished-steel panels in which the Royal Arms were mounted.

Gold leaf replaced the black and white lining of the panels of the side tanks and bunker together with cobalt blue lining with somewhat elaborate transfer corners. In addition, the boiler clothing bands were of polished brass attached to a wider band of polished steel which projected by ½in each side of the brass centre strip. To this was added an edging of Crimson Lake with a red line on each side of the boiler band to complete the very ornate effect. Small gilt chains edged the footplate and festoons of decoration rosettes were draped along the tops of the tanks and bunker, while the smokebox and buffers were edged with polished steel bands.

The coupling rod valves were painted cream with a design rendered by a gold transfer, and finally a small ornamental fountain was placed on the footplate between the frames, immediately in front of the smokebox, the idea being that when the cock that connected it to the side tanks was opened, the fountain actually worked. It was perhaps rather too much, but probably in keeping with the sentiments of the Edwardian era. One source suggests that the engine worked three trains, the 12.15pm from Fenchurch Street to Shoeburyness and the 3.45pm return on the day of the Coronation and an Orient Line boat special from St Pancras to Tilbury on the day following; the decorations were then removed from the locomotive. I doubt if the Midland Railway would have permitted such measures if it had owned the railway at this time.

During the years that followed the acquisition of the LT&SR by the Midland Railway these four locomotives were repainted in Midland passenger engine livery and fitted with new chimneys, safety valves, extended smokeboxes and coal rails to replace the coalbunker lids. Nevertheless, the essential

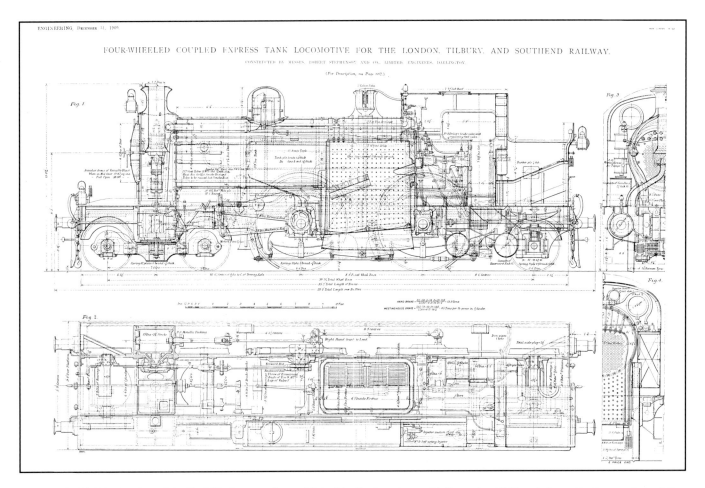

FOUR-WHEELED COUPLED EXPRESS TANK LOCOMOTIVE FOR THE LONDON, TILBURY, AND SOUTHEND RAILWAY.

CONSTRUCTED BY MESSRS. ROBERT STEPHENSON AND CO., LIMITED, ENGINEERS, DARLINGTON.

(For Description, see Page 882.)

Fig 46 This drawing of the No '79' class was first published in *Engineering* on 31 December 1909 and shows the four engines of the class as built by Robert Stephenson & Co for the LT&SR. In March, *The Engineer* also published a similar drawing and gave some brief details: the cylinders were 19in x 26in and the working pressure was 170lb. The leading bogie did not traverse, but the trailing wheels had a side play of 2¼in. The total heating surface was given as 1,130sq ft.

LT&S features were retained in the LMS-built engines which entered service from 1923 onwards. Before deciding to build further examples of the No 79 class the Midland Railway tried out some of the '2000' class Deeley 0-6-4T engines, fitted with Westinghouse brakes, but it was considered that they were not suitable and in due course they were returned to the parent system. At this point in time it is quite impossible to know if the reported failure of the '2000' class was because they were not up to the work required, or if the LT&S enginemen did not like them or know how to work them. I suspect the latter has much to do with their return to the Midland Railway. The only evidence that is available about the 0-6-4T in traffic appeared in *Midland Record No 11*.

Therefore, it was felt that the special requirements of this section could not be answered by existing or even new Midland Railway designs (see Fig 45) which helps to explain why an order for 10 was placed at the beginning of 1923, with eight of them entering service in Midland Railway livery. A report was written by Follows, a Vice-President of the LMS and Byrom, Chief General Superintendent, of the newly formed company. 'Service of the old LT&SR in many ways is special owing to the class of train and restrictions imposed by the LNER on locomotives working into Fenchurch Street, and the constantly increasing service. There are three classes of these tank engines, but the main service is worked by the most powerful or No 3 class. The boilers of a number of the smaller or 'No 1' class are at the end of their lives and the locomotives are not equal to the present work. We desire to replace 10 of

these with 10 of the No 3 class.' This request led to the construction of the new 4-4-2T engines Nos 2125-2134 with additional engines in 1925 (five), 1927 (10) and finally 10 in 1930. All were built with extended smokeboxes, Midland fittings and were dual brake fitted but, in due course, the Westinghouse equipment was removed.

The order for the 1923 engines refers to rebuilding and in keeping with Midland Railway practice that classified a new boiler as a rebuild, these engines carried 'Rebuilt Derby 1923' plates. A more accurate description would have been replacement, even though the engines they replaced were to run for a number of years more, albeit on lighter duties.

A number of orders were raised at Derby for work to be undertaken and details of some of these are set out here. Order No 5997, dated 3 September 1923, was to fit the Class 3 tank engines with mechanical lubricators. Order No 6051, dated 9 November 1923, was to alter the spring coil arm on engines Nos 2146-2179. Order No 8354, dated 3 March 1933, was to fit driver's leg guards on the new engines Nos 2153-2160 (except No 2155 already fitted). The work was completed by 21 June 1933. A further order, No 9354 dated 17 February 1936, was to fit the remaining LT&SR 4-4-2T Class 3 'shunting engines' with leg guards. Note the clerical error describing them as shunting engines.

During the 1930s, much LMS boiler work was transferred to Crewe and order No 8592 refers to LT&SR boilers built to the 1933 renewal programme. Order No 8715 dated 12 April 1934 was in respect of a modification to the radial axleboxes on

Top right:
No 2111, photographed at Plaistow, was one of the engines built at Derby in 1923 that entered traffic with Midland Railway insignia. The Midland locomotive register gives the date of construction as 17 June 1923, and confirms that locomotives were entering traffic at this time still carrying the MR coat of arms. Some sources suggest that Nos 2110-2117 entered traffic in this condition and the last two of Derby order No 5871 carried the LMS emblem. If this is correct, that is surprising as the Derby locomotive register records the date new for the last three engines as 12 August

1923. The locomotive was renumbered 1929 in 1947 and was withdrawn from service as No 41929 in September 1951. *F. Moore*

Right:
This picture of No 2122, taken at Plaistow, illustrates one of the five Nasmyth, Wilson engines built in 1925. The locomotive is in the red passenger livery and the picture was taken shortly after the engine entered service.
Collection A. G. Ellis 29174

In 1948, before the new British Railways insignia began to be applied, a number of engines ran with their new BR number but still carrying the initials LMS. One example was No 41967, seen here at Pitsea on 26 September 1948.
Collection A. G. Ellis

No 41945 began life as LMS No 2127 and was built at Derby in 1927. Seen here at Upminster, this locomotive was to remain in service until withdrawn in February 1959.
Collection R. J. Essery

LT&SR 4-4-2 tank engines. Sixty-nine No 2 and 3 class engines were to be fitted with modified radial axleboxes in accordance with two new drawings. The lubrication was to be with Tecalemit grease nipples. The engines were to be dealt with as they went through the shops and it was expected to take two years to alter all the engines involved. The material was to be prepared at Derby and fitted at Bow; this particular order was for the first 20 engines. It was normal Derby Works practice to control a major project by issuing orders for so many engines at a time. Order No 8859 for 20 engines and No 9342 for 29 engines completed the work. A further lubrication improvement was authorised by order No 9285 dated 16 October 1935, with the material to be prepared at Derby and the fitting to be undertaken at Bow. The final order that I can trace is No 9464 dated 17 February 1936, to alter the oiling arrangements of the connecting rod little ends.

The Class 3P engines were to continue to provide the mainstay for this section until the arrival of the Stanier 2-6-4Ts in 1934. By all accounts they were remarkable locomotives. Withdrawal took place during the 1950s, old No 2129 being the last withdrawn as British Railways No 41947 in December 1960. Fortunately, old No 80 *Thundersley*, has been preserved in the National Collection and is currently on display at Bressingham, Norfolk.

No 2154 was one of the batch built at Derby in 1930 and is seen here in the post-1928 livery of black with red lining, clearly visible on this clean engine. Photographed at Plaistow on 22 August 1937, the engine is carrying a 13D Shoeburyness shed plate.
L. Hanson

11. The 'No 2100' Class Baltics

The LT&SR introduced the 4-4-2T wheel arrangement into the UK and the railway's Locomotive Superintendent, Robert Whitelegg, also produced the first 4-6-4T engines in Great Britain. He was additionally to be responsible for the Baltic tank engines built by the Glasgow & South Western Railway. They also proved to be short-lived locomotives. Although the LT&SR locomotives were extremely handsome engines, the question has to be raised about the wisdom of building such a large locomotive without the design being approved by the engineer of the railway over whose lines it was to run if it was to be properly utilised by the owning company. The LT&SR enjoyed perpetual running powers over the final 2½ miles from Gas Factory Junction into Fenchurch Street, but which engines were allowed to run over this length of railway was not a decision that could be made by an officer of the LT&SR.

Design work began in 1911 and LT&SR records show the numbers of the general arrangement drawing as 1859/60 together with the date of 26 August 1911.

K. H. Leech recorded that Robert Whitelegg submitted his proposals to his Chairman and Managing Director, A. L. Stride, and at the same time pointed out that there may be problems with the Great Eastern people who might consider that the weight of these new locomotives would be too great for their section of the line, much of it laid on brick arches. Stride was a civil engineer, so he must have understood the implications of what Whitelegg had told him. According to the already published account, Stride told Whitelegg to submit the design and estimated weights to the GER and, in the absence of a 'no', to proceed. In many respects this was not a very businesslike way of conducting the company's affairs. It is possible that if the Midland Railway had not purchased the LT&SR then some acceptable compromise would have been reached with the GER's engineers. At this point in time it is difficult, if not impossible, to say how much effect the Midland Railway's ownership of the LT&SR had on the decision of the GER's engineer not to allow these engines into Fenchurch Street.

Human nature being what it is, I suspect that any possibility of a compromise was excluded by the turn of events. The root of the problem lay with the fact that Stride had failed to secure approval from the GER and the responsibility was his and his alone. Failing health probably was the real reason for his actions, although it could also be that he knew this would not be his problem once the Midland Railway assumed control of the railway.

Set out below are details of this class of locomotives which was ordered before the Midland Railway purchased the London, Tilbury & Southend Railway but were not delivered until after the company had become the LT&S Section of the Midland Railway.

Built by Beyer Peacock 1912; taken into stock by the Midland Railway in April 1913, (Nos 2100-2103) and May (Nos 2104-2107).

No 2101 shortly after delivery from the builders Beyer Peacock. The long fire iron retaining box on the tank top and the original smokebox door are prominent features of this locomotive in its original condition. *Collection Richard Taylor*

MR No	LMS 1929 No	Withdrawn	Notes
2100		2/29	Altered to saturated condition 4/14 and to superheated condition 5/22
2101	2193	12/29	
2102	2194	12/29	
2103	2195	10/30	
2104	2196	12/32	
2105	2197	3/33	
2106	2198	5/34	
2107		9/29	

No LT&SR engines had been superheated; these would have been the first but for the change of company ownership.

The principal dimensions were: driving wheels 6ft 3in; bogie wheels 3ft 1in; wheelbase 6ft 6ins + 5ft 6½in + 6ft 11in + 6ft 11in + 6ft 6ins + 6ft 6in, total 38ft 10½in; length of frame 43ft 9¾in; length over buffers 47ft 8in; length of firebox 8ft 6in; length of boiler barrel 14ft 6½in; diameter 5ft; cylinders 20in x 26in; heating surface was 1,446sq ft, including 141sq ft for the firebox. The grate area was 25sq ft and the working boiler pressure was 160psi. A Schmidt superheater was fitted. The tank capacity was 2,200 gallons and the coalbunker held 3 tons.

The original Schmidt superheater was fitted to the class, but these were later replaced with a Derby superheater and, at the same time the eight-feed Detroit displacement lubricator was changed for a Wakefield mechanical lubricator driven from the valve gear. The original copper-capped LT&SR-design chimney was replaced by one of Midland design although it is recorded that No 2100 retained the original chimney until at least 1921.

The Midland Railway had no real use for these engines and tried to sell them. One was loaned to the SE&CR, which was considering a 4-6-4T wheel arrangement at the time, but in due course it was returned to the parent system. Although some, notably No 2107, were always at Plaistow, most of their work was on the Midland Railway or the Midland Division of the LMS, as it became after 1923. During the Great War they were used as pilots for coal trains on the main line between Cricklewood and Wellingborough, while later, in 1921, they

were to be seen working on the St Pancras to Luton passenger trains.

Unlike the 4-4-2T engines that were often turned to ensure they ran engine first on the most important jobs, the Baltic tank engines were not turned as there was nothing to choose between the ride when running either engine or bunker first. Although they only had short travel valves of about 4¼in they were reputed to be quite fast. It was said that one engine was recorded as being timed at 94mph, although it was reported that the locomotive was rocking and lurching badly. Nevertheless, this was rather faster than the 65-70mph required for the normal services they worked.

A number of order details about the class have survived, the first being order No 4410 dated 31 January 1914. This read: 'LT&S Section engines 2100-2107. Please put in hand your portion of the work in connection with the provision of Schmidt piston valves, spindles, liners and mechanical lubricator driving gear and back stop valves for these engines.' Order No 4483 dated 15 May 1914 was to fit the engines with cylinder relief valves. This was followed shortly afterwards by order No 4490 dated 18 June to fit a new smokebox tubeplate, a new half copper tubeplate and a new set of tubes. The engine number was given as 2100 and coincides with the date that the locomotive was altered to a saturated condition. The drawing number quoted, 14-9267, and the Derby Works Locomotive Drawing Office register entry reads: 'Smokebox arrangement engs, 2100-2107 without ?' The final word, or rather initials, could mean superheater. However, the order also gives another engine number, 2102; the date on this entry is 17 November 1914. It is unclear if this engine ever ran in saturated condition.

Engine No 2104 was the subject of order No 4921 dated 3 August 1916. This order required the removal of the large superheater tube and refitting with copper ends, mechanical lubricator instead of sight feeds, and Midland standard steam sanding instead of the existing Holden & Brooke's type. New piston valves and liners were to be fitted (if not already fitted) and the bunker lids were to be removed. The release valves on the cylinders were to be repaired and the smokebox dampers were to be removed. The work was undertaken at Derby and completed on 19 December 1916. Further orders for the same work were placed: order No 4935, on 7 August for engine No 2105, completed on 17 December, and order Nos 4943 and

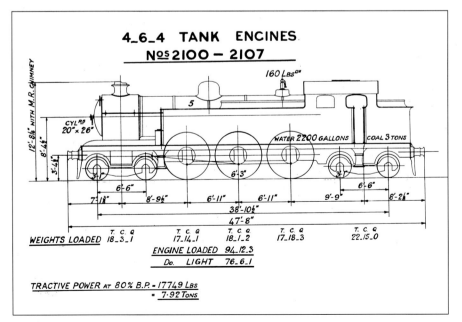

Fig 47 The Midland Railway engine diagram, dated 2 May 1921, shows the original smokebox door as fitted when they were built, but these had been replaced by a Midland smokebox door by the time this drawing was made. The fire iron retaining box had also been removed by this time. Engine diagrams can be a useful guide to the main dimensions but the information given needs to be interpreted and not taken for granted.

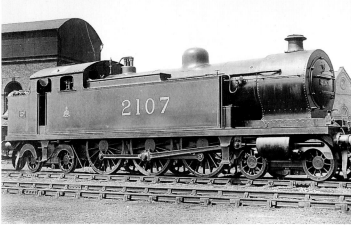

No 2101 at work on the Midland Railway with a four-coach train of Clayton carriages at Radlett. This picture is an opposite side view of the locomotive in the same condition to that shown on page 153. *Real Photographs/NRM*

The Baltics were soon to receive Midland features. This undated picture, taken at Plaistow, shows No 2107 with a Midland smokebox, chimney and safety valves. *Photomatic/NRM*

4944, both on 2 October for engines Nos 2106 and 2107. They were also completed on 17 December 1916.

Order No 5009 dated 25 January 1917, was to remove the blow-off cocks from engine No 2102 and to fit injector overflow pipes. The lamp irons were to be changed to MR pattern. Order 5022 dated 20 February was as order No 5009 but included the driver's brake valve to be moved to the side. The engine was No 2102. Order No 5042 dated 8 June was also the same as 5009, the engine being No 2100. The other orders in the file were generally marked as 'general repairs'.

These locomotives were dual fitted, the Westinghouse brake pump being situated in a metal cupboard inside the cab. However, I cannot trace any specific orders to remove the Westinghouse brake. Pictorial evidence shows that two

engines, Nos 2103/4, the latter later 2196, ran with the Westinghouse brake removed; there may have been others.

Liveries

These locomotives entered service in Midland Railway crimson lake with gold shaded black numbers, the Midland crest below the cab side windows. No 2103 was to be the first engine to display evidence of LMS ownership, being lettered LMS in place of the MR crest. The rest of the class carried the normal LMS pre-1928 passenger engine livery, ie all except the last three survivors, Nos 2196/7/8, which were scrapped in this condition. These three were to receive the intermediate passenger livery of black with red lining.

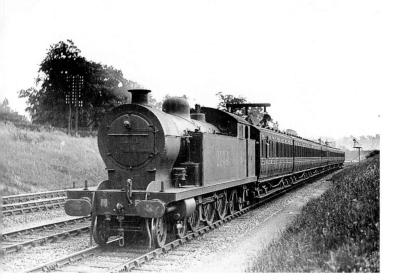

The picture of No 2104 seen here was taken near St Albans and shows the engine at work with an eight-coach train of Clayton carriages. The chimney is without a windguard, or capuchon as it is more commonly called. The Westinghouse brake and fire iron retaining box have been removed. The former was not required for engines working on the Midland Railway, but I have not found any explanation for the removal of the fire-iron retaining box. The only possible drawback was that it was probably easier to handle the fire irons if they were on the top of the tank and their removal may have been the result of enginemen's complaints. *Collection Richard Taylor*

Whatever their problems from an operating standpoint, the Baltics were handsome-looking engines as confirmed by this striking front view of No 2105. *Collection R. J. Essery*

The picture of No 2100 shows the condition of the class during the early LMS period: Midland smokebox, chimney and safety valves. This engine is dual fitted but the fire-iron retaining box has been removed. The locomotive is in red passenger livery with the LMS emblem on the side of the bunker. *Collection R. J. Essery*

It seems only appropriate to conclude this chapter with a picture of No 2198, old number 2106, the last engine of the class to remain in service. Taken at Derby Works in 1931, the engine was undergoing repairs. Withdrawal came in May 1934, and I suspect one reason for the seemingly early withdrawal of the class was that the boilers were non-standard and the family of 2-6-4Ts then in service were more efficient engines. *Collection J. A. G. H. Coltas*

Appendices

Appendix I. Engine Workings, June 1915
ENGINE WORKING,
Week Days, June, 1915, until further notice.

No. 1 PLAISTOW.

3.50 a.m.	(Light)	Plaistow	to Barking
4.22		Barking	to Fenchurch St.
5.45		Fenchurch St.	to Tilbury
8.45		Tilbury	to Shoeburyness
10. 5		Shoeburyness	to Tilbury
12.21 p.m.		Tilbury	to Fenchurch St.
2. 6		Fenchurch St.	to Shoeburyness
5.20		Shoeburyness	to Fenchurch St.
7. 4		Fenchurch St.	to Barking
7.48	(Light)	Barking	to Plaistow

On Saturdays after.

12.21 p.m.		Tilbury	to Fenchurch St.
1.48		Fenchurch St.	to Shoeburyness
6. 5	(Light)	Shoeburyness	to Southend
6.35		Southend	to Fenchurch Street
8.28	(Carrs.)	Fenchurch St.	to Barking
9. 0	(Light)	Barking	to Plaistow

No. 2 PLAISTOW.

4. 3 a.m.	(Light)	Plaistow	to Barking
4.38	(Carrs.)	Barking	to Dagenham
4.58		Dagenham	to Fenchurch St.
6.18		Fenchurch St.	to Dagenham Dock
7.10		Dagenham Dock	to Fenchurch St.
7.58	(Carrs.)	Fenchurch St.	to Plaistow

No. 3 PLAISTOW.

4.35 a.m.	(Light)	Plaistow	to Little Ilford S. Sidings
4.55	(Carrs.)	Little Ilford S. Sidings	to Barking
5.37		Barking	to Fenchurch St.
6.52		Fenchurch St.	to Tilbury
8.44		Tilbury	to Fenchurch Street
9.45	(Carrs.)	Fenchurch St.	to Plaistow
6.55 p.m.	(Carrs.)	Plaistow	to Fenchurch St.
7.33		Fenchurch St.	to Upminster
8.45	(Light)	Upminster	to Plaistow

On Saturdays after.

9.45 a.m.	(Carrs.)	Fenchurch St.	to Plaistow
11.52		Plaistow	to Pitsea
12.53 p.m.		Pitsea	to Plaistow (attached to 12.16 p.m. ex Shoeburyness)
3.27		Plaistow	to Shoeburyness
6.16		Shoeburyness	to Barking
7.12	(Light)	Barking	to Plaistow

No. 4 PLAISTOW.

4.28 a.m.	(Light)	Plaistow	to Fenchurch St.
5. 5		Fenchurch St.	to Shoeburyness
8.27		Shoeburyness	to Fenchurch St.
9.58	(Carrs.)	Fenchurch St.	to Plaistow
4.25 p.m.	(Light)	Plaistow	to Little Ilford S. Sidings
5.45	(Carrs.)	Little Ilford S. Sidings	to Fenchurch St.
6.26		Fenchurch St.	to Shoeburyness
9. 5		Shoeburyness	to Fenchurch St.
11.25		Fenchurch St.	to Barking
11.58	(Light)	Barking	to Plaistow

On Saturdays after.

9.58 a.m.	(Carrs.)	Fenchurch St.	to Plaistow
4.19 p.m.	(Carrs.)	Plaistow	to Fenchurch St.
5.16		Fenchurch St.	to Shoeburyness
10.15		Shoeburyness	to Fenchurch St.
12.18 a.m.	(Light)	Fenchurch St.	to Plaistow

No. 5 PLAISTOW.

6.50 a.m.	(Light)	Plaistow	to Barking
7.27		Barking	to Upminster
7.51	(Carrs.)	Upminster	to Romford
8. 6		Romford	to Upminster
9.14		Upminster	to Barking
9.50	(Light)	Barking	to Ilford N. Sidings—For Shunting and Goods Working.

No. 6 PLAISTOW.

6.45 a.m.	(Light)	Plaistow	to Upminster
7.55		Upminster	to Barking

Then Shunting and Goods Working.

No. 7 PLAISTOW,

7. 0 a.m.	(Light)	Plaistow	to Little Ilford S. Sidings
7.25	(Carrs.)	Little Ilford S. Sidings	to East Ham
7.33		East Ham	to Fenchurch St.
8.11		Fenchurch St.	to Tilbury
10.10		Tilbury	to Shoeburyness
12.16 p.m.		Shoeburyness	to Fenchurch Street
2.40		Fenchurch St.	to Tilbury
5.24		Tilbury	to Fenchurch Street
6.53		Fenchurch St.	to Shoeburyness
10.15		Shoeburyness	to Fenchurch St.
12.13 night	(Light)	Fenchurch St.	to Plaistow

On Saturdays after.

12.16 p.m.		Shoeburyness	to Fenchurch St.
2.30		Fenchurch St.	to Shoeburyness
9. 5		Shoeburyness	to Fenchurch Street
11.25		Fenchurch St.	to Barking
11.58	(Light)	Barking	to Plaistow

No. 8 PLAISTOW.

7.33 a.m.		Plaistow	to Fenchurch St
8. 2	(Carrs.)	Fenchurch St.	to Little Ilford S. Sidings
9. 3	(Light)	Little Ilford S. Sidings	to Plaistow
5.28 p.m.	(Light)	Plaistow	to Little Ilford S. Sidings
6.11	(Carrs.)	Ilford S. Sidings	to Barking
6.15		Barking	to Pitsea
7.25	(Light)	Pitsea to Tilbury Dks. N. Junc. (for 8.25 p.m. Up Goods)

Not Sats.

No. 9 PLAISTOW.

5.50 a.m.		Plaistow	to Tilbury
7. 5		Tilbury	to Barking
7.50	(Carrs.)	Barking	to Ilford S. Sidings
8. 8	(Light)	Ilford Sidings	to Plaistow
8. 6	(Light)	Barking	to Plaistow—Sats. only.

Not Sats.

No. 10 PLAISTOW.

Saturdays only.

6.55 p.m.	(Carrs.)	Plaistow	to Fenchurch Street
7.33		Fenchurch Street	to Upminster
8.45	(Light)	Upminster	to Plaistow

ENGINE WORKING,

Week Days, June, 1915, until further Notice.

No. 1 UPMINSTER.

6.27 a.m.		Upminster	to Fenchurch St.
7.32		Fenchurch St.	to Tilbury
9. 5		Tilbury	to Barking
10.26	(Light)	Barking to Plaistow (10.48 Weds.)	
1.22 p.m.	(Goods)	Plaistow to Commercial Rd.	Not
2.15	(Goods)	Commercial Rd. to Tilbury Docks N. Junc.	Sats.
10.26 a.m.	(Carrs)	Barking to Plaistow	Sats.
2. 5 p.m.	(Carrs)	Plaistow to Fenchurch St.	only
2.40		Fenchurch St. to Tilbury	
5.45	(Light)	Tilbury to Tilbury Docks N. Junc.	
6. 5	(Goods)	Tilbury Docks N. Junc. to Little Ilford N. Sidings	
	(Light)	Ilford N. Sdgs. to Barking	
8.50	(Goods)	Barking to Little Ilford N. Sidings Shunting	
11.50	(Light)	Little Ilford N. Sidings to Barking	
12. 0 midt.	(Light)	Barking to Little Ilford S. Sidings	
12.25 a.m.	(Carrs.)	Little Ilford S. Sidings to Barking	
12.30		Barking to Upminster—Pitsea on Sats.	
1.20	(Light)	Pitsea to Upminster—Sats. only	

No. 2 UPMINSTER.

6. 0 a.m.		Upminster	to Romford
6.15		Romford	to Upminster
6.30		Upminster	to Romford
6.50		Romford	to Upminster
7.16	(Carrs.)	Upminster	to Emerson Park
7.27		Emerson Park	to Upminster
8.18		Upminster	to Barking
8.55	(Light)	Barking	to Upminster
10.55		Upminster	to Romford
11. 8		Romford	to Grays
11.48		Grays	to Barking
12.49 p.m.		Barking	to Upminster
3.16		Upminster	to Romford
3.35		Romford	to Upminster
3.49		Upminster	to Emerson Park
4. 0		Emerson Park	to Upminster
5. 1		Upminster	to Emerson Park
5.12		Emerson Park	to Upminster
5.20		Upminster	to Romford
5.45		Romford	to Upminster
6.23		Upminster	to Emerson Park and Locals until
12. 7 a.m.	(Carrs.)	Emerson Park	to Upminster
12.50		Upminster	to Emerson Park	Thurs.
1. 0	(Carrs.)	Emerson Park	to Upminster	only.

On Saturdays after.

8.55 a.m.	(Light)	Barking	to Upminster
1 35 p.m.		Upminster	to Emerson Park
1.46	(Carrs.)	Emerson Park	to Upminster
1.56		Upminster	to Grays
2.25		Grays	to Romford
3.26		Romford	to Upminster
3.41		Upminster	to Emerson Park
4. 3		Emerson Park	to Upminster
5. 8		Upminster	to Emerson Park
5.24		Emerson Park	to Upminster
5.34		Upminster	to Romford
5.51		Romford	to Upminster
6.50		Upminster	to Romford and Locals until
9.43 p.m.		Romford	to Upminster
10. 2		Upminster	to Barking
10.19	(Carrs.)	Barking	to Little Ilford S. Sidings
10.45	(Light)	Little Ilford S. Sidings to Barking	
11.48		Barking	to Upminster

No. 3 UPMINSTER.

7. 9 a.m.		Upminster	to Romford
7.40		Romford	to Upminster
8.15	(Carrs.)	Upminster	to Emerson Park
8.26		Emerson Park	to Upminster
8.39	(Carrs.)	Upminster	to Emerson Park
8.49		Emerson Park	to Upminster
9.17		Upminster	to Romford
9.34		Romford	to Upminster
9.48		Upminster	to Romford
10. 1		Romford	to Grays
10.58		Grays	to Romford
11.56		Romford	to Grays
12.32 p.m.		Grays	to Romford	
1.15		Romford	to Upminster	Sats. only
2.57		Upminster	to Grays	
12.44		Grays	to Romford	
1.22		Romford	to Grays	Not
2. 8	(Light)	Grays	to Tilbury	Sats.
3.35	(Light)	Tilbury	to Grays	
3.52		Grays	to Romford	
4.36		Romford	to Grays	
5.41		Grays	to Romford	
6.40		Romford	to Tilbury (6.30 on Sats.)	
7.32		Tilbury	to Romford (7.21 on Sats.)	
8.18		Romford	to Grays	
9.30		Grays	to Upminster	
10. 2		Upminster	to Barking	Not
10.19	(Carrs.)	Barking to Little Ilford S. Sdgs.	Sats.
10.45	(Light)	Little Ilford S. Sdgs. to Upminster	
9.30		Grays	to Romford	
10.46		Romford	to Upminster	
11. 0		Upminster	to Emerson Park	
11.11		Emerson Park	to Upminster	Sats.
11.55		Upminster	to Emerson Park	only.
12. 7 a.m.	(Carrs.)	Emerson Park	to Upminster	
12.50		Upminster	to Emerson Park	
1. 0	(Carrs.)	Emerson Park	to Upminster	

No. 1 TILBURY.

5.30 a.m.		Tilbury	to Fenchurch St.
7 20		Fenchurch St.	to Shoeburyness
9.53		Shoeburyness	to Barking
11.13	(Carrs.)	Barking	to Ilford S. Sdgs	Not
	(Light)	Ilford Sidings to Barking Shunting	Sats.
2.35 p.m.		Barking	to Upminster	
3.50		Upminster	to Barking	Weds.
5.37		Barking	to Upminster	only.
6.10		Upminster	to Tilbury	
6.14 p.m.	(Light)	Barking	to Ilford Southern Sidings	
6.43	(Carrs)	Ilford Sidings	to Barking	Not
6.50		Barking	to Pitsea	Weds.
7.55	(Light)	Pitsea	to Tilbury	& Sats.
2.32 p.m.		Barking	to Upminster	
2.58		Upminster	to Pitsea	
4. 5	(Carrs.)	Pitsea	to Tilbury	
6.20		Tilbury	to Fenchurch St.	Sats.
8.18		Fenchurch St.	to Tilbury	only.
10.50		Tilbury	to Fenchurch St.	
12. 0 midt.		Fenchurch St.	to Tilbury	

ENGINE WORKING,

Week Days, June, 1915, until further Notice.

No. 2 TILBURY.

5.15 a.m.	(Light)	Tilbury	to Pitsea
6.0		Pitsea	to Tilbury
6.52		Tilbury	to Shoeburyness
9.29		Shoeburyness	to Tilbury
5.10 p.m.		Tilbury	to Purfleet Rifle Range
5.39		Purfleet Rifle Range	to Tilbury
6.25	(Light)	Tilbury	to Upminster
7.27		Upminster	to Tilbury

On Saturdays after.

9.29 a.m.	Shoeburyness	to Tilbury
11. 8	Tilbury	to Shoeburyness
3. 6 p.m.	Shoeburyness	to Tilbury
5.24	Tilbury	to Fenchurch St.
6.53	Fenchurch St.	to Tilbury
9.14	Tilbury	to Fenchurch St.
10.45	Fenchurch St.	to Tilbury

No. 3 TILBURY.

5.45 a.m.	(Carrs.)	Tilbury	to Grays
6. 0		Grays	to Tilbury
6.50		Tilbury	to Grays
7.21		Grays	to Tilbury
8. 0		Tilbury	to Fenchurch St.
9.12	(Carrs.)	Fenchurch St.	to Little Ilford S. Sidings
10. 7	(Light)	Little Ilford S. Sidings	to Plaistow

Then Goods as required.

8. 5 p.m.		Tilbury	to Grays	} Not
9.45		Grays	to Tilbury	} Sats.
12.48	(Carrs.)	Plaistow	to Fenchurch St.	} Sats
1.15		Fenchurch St.	to Tilbury	} only

No. 4 TILBURY.

5.45 a.m.	(Light)	Tilbury	to Pitsea
6.50		Pitsea	to Plaistow
11.45		Plaistow	to Pitsea
1.15 p.m.	(Light)	Pitsea	to Tilbury
3. 0		Tilbury	to Southend
4.35		Southend	to Tilbury
6.20		Tilbury	to Fenchurch St.
7.41		Fenchurch St.	to Tilbury
9.24		Tilbury	to Pitsea
10.10	(Carrs.)	Pitsea	to Tilbury
11.48		Tilbury	to Pitsea
12.20 a.m.	(Light)	Pitsea	to Tilbury

On Saturdays after.

6.50 a.m.		Pitsea	to Plaistow
12.15 p.m.	(Light)	Plaistow	to Little Ilford S. Sidings
12.50	(Carrs)	Little Ilford S. Sidings	to Fenchurch St.
1.35		Fenchurch St.	to Tilbury
4.50	(Light)	Tilbury	to East Ham
5.45		East Ham	to Tilbury

No. 5 TILBURY.

6.26 a.m.		Tilbury	to Fenchurch St.
7.42	(Carrs.)	Fenchurch St.	to Plaistow
8.55	(Light)	Plaistow	to Tilbury
10.25		Tilbury	to Fenchurch St.
12.15 p.m.		Fenchurch St.	to Shoeburyness
2.25		Shoeburyness	to Fenchurch St.
4.16		Fenchurch St.	to Tilbury
6.55		Tilbury	to Fenchurch St.
8.13		Fenchurch St.	to Tilbury

On Saturdays after.

12.15 p.m.		Fenchurch St.	to Shoeburyness
4.35		Shoeburyness	to Fenchurch St.
6.38		Fenchurch St.	to Tilbury
11.48		Tilbury	to Pitsea
12.20 a.m.	(Light)	Pitsea	to Tilbury

No. 6 TILBURY.

6.12 a.m.	(Carrs)	Tilbury	to Grays
6.25		Grays	to Tilbury
7.24		Tilbury	to Fenchurch St.
8.38	(Carrs.)	Fenchurch St.	to Little Ilford S. Sidings
10. 7	(Light)	Little Ilford S. Sidings	to Plaistow
4.25 p.m.	(Light)	Plaistow	to Little Ilford S. Sidings
5. 5	(Carrs.)	Little Ilford S. Sidings	to Fenchurch St.
5.46		Fenchurch St.	to Tilbury
7.45		Tilbury	to Pitsea
8.25	(Light)	Pitsea	to Tilbury
9.14		Tilbury	to Fenchurch Street
10.45		Fenchurch St.	to Tilbury

On Saturdays after.

10. 7 a.m.	(Light)	Little Ilford S. Sidings	to Plaistow
12.40 p.m.	(Carrs.)	Plaistow	to Fenchurch St.
1.11		Fenchurch St.	to Pitsea
2.50	(Carrs.)	Pitsea	to Tilbury

No. 7 TILBURY.

7.15 a.m.	(Light)	Tilbury	to Pitsea
8. 7		Pitsea	to Romford
9. 0		Romford	to Upminster
10.14		Upminster	to Romford
10.39		Romford	to Upminster

Goods Shunting at Upminster and Crauham Sidings until

1.41 p.m.		Upminster	to Romford	
1.55		Romford	to Upminster	
2.10		Upminster	to Barking	} Not
2.35		Barking	to Upminster	} Weds
3.50		Upminster	to Barking	
5.37		Barking	to Upminster	
6.10		Upminster	to Tilbury	}
2. 8 p.m.	(Goods)	Upminster	to Romford	}
5.30	(Goods)	Romford	to Upminster	}
6.15	(Light)	Upminster	to Little Ilford S. Sdgs.	} Weds.
6.43	(Carrs.)	Ilford S. Sidings	to Barking	} only
6.50		Barking	to Pitsea	}
7.55	(Light)	Pitsea	to Tilbury	}

On Saturdays after.

10.39 a.m.		Romford	to Upminster
10.55		Upminster	to Romford
11. 8		Romford	to Grays
11.48		Grays	to Barking
12.47 p.m.		Barking	to Grays
1.35		Grays	to Romford
2. 9		Romford	to Upminster
2.21		Upminster	to Romford
2.34		Romford	to Upminster
4.15		Upminster	to Barking
6.15		Barking	to Upminster
6.45		Upminster	to Tilbury
9.24		Tilbury	to Pitsea
10. 5	(Light)	Pitsea	to Shoeburyness
10.52		Shoeburyness	to Tilbury

No. 8 TILBURY.

5.45 a.m.	(Light)	Tilbury	to Pitsea
6.30		Pitsea	to Upminster
7. 6		Upminster	to Barking
7.37		Barking	to Fenchurch St.
8.20		Fenchurch St.	to Shoeburyness
11.18		Shoeburyness	to Tilbury
1.45 p.m.	(Light)	Tilbury	to Grays
2. 5		Grays	to Romford
2.40		Romford	to Grays
3.15	(Light)	Grays	to Tilbury
4.20		Tilbury	to Southend
5.25	(Light)	Southend	to Shoeburyness
6.55		Shoeburyness	to Fenchurch St.
9.25		Fenchurch St.	to Tilbury

On Saturdays after.

11.18 a.m.		Shoeburyness	to Tilbury
3.13 p.m.		Tilbury	to Pitsea
4. 0	(Light)	Pitsea	to Shoeburyness
6.55		Shoeburyness	to Fenchurch St.
9.25		Fenchurch St.	to Tilbury

ENGINE WORKING.

Week Days June, 1915, until further notice.

No. 9 TILBURY.

Goods Working; then

7.26 a.m.	(Light)	Plaistow	to Upminster
8.21		Upminster	to Tilbury
12.53 p.m.		Tilbury	to Southend
2.12		Southend	to Tilbury
5.27		Tilbury	to Shoeburyness
7. 5		Shoeburyness	to Tilbury

Sats. only.

No. 10 TILBURY.

6.10 a.m.	(Carrs.)	Tilbury	to Pitsea
6.58		Pitsea	to Tilbury
9.45		Tilbury	to Fenchurch St.
11.45		Fenchurch St.	to Tilbury (11.18 Weds.)
1.50 p.m.		Tilbury	to Fenchurch St.
3.25		Fenchurch St.	to Tilbury
5.27		Tilbury	to Shoeburyness
7. 5		Shoeburyness	to Tilbury
1050		Tilbury	to Fenchurch St.
2. 0 Midt.		Fenchurch St.	to Tilbury

Not Sats

No. 1 SHOEBURYNESS.

4.45 a.m.	(Light)	Shoeburyness	to Southend (Carrs on Mons.
5. 5		Southend	to Barking
6.40		Barking	to Grays
8. 4		Grays	to Upminster
8.35	(Light)	Upminster	to Shoeburyness
10.17		Shoeburyness	to Fenchurch St.
12.25 p.m.		Fenchurch St.	to Tilbury
5. 5		Tilbury	to Fenchurch St.
6.17		Fenchurch St.	to Shoeburyness

On Saturdays after.

12.25 p.m.		Fenchurch St.	to Tilbury
2.12		Tilbury	to Southend
6.20		Southend	to Tilbury
8.11		Tilbury	to Fenchurch St.
9.44	(Carrs.)	Fenchurch St.	to Barking
10.40		Barking	to Shoeburyness

No. 2 SHOEBURYNESS.

6.50 a.m.		Shoeburyness	to Tilbury
7.58		Tilbury	to Shoeburyness
11.10		Shoeburyness	to Fenchurch St.
1.48 p.m.		Fenchurch St.	to Tilbury
5.52		Tilbury	to Fenchurch St.
7.20		Fenchurch St.	to Shoeburyness

On Saturdays after.

7.58 a.m.		Tilbury	to Shoeburyness
11.10		Shoeburyness	to Barking
2. 7 p.m.	(Carrs.)	Barking	to Fenchurch St.
3. 8		Fenchurch St.	to Shoeburyness
7.50	(Carrs.)	Shoeburyness	to Southend
8.30		Southend	to Fenchurch St.
10.25		Fenchurch St.	to Barking
11.40		Barking	to Shoeburyness

No. 3 SHOEBURYNESS.

6.10 a.m.		Shoeburyness	to Fenchurch St.
7.53	(Carrs.)	Fenchurch St.	to Little Ilford S. Sidings
9. 3	(Light)	Little Ilford S. Sidings	to Plaistow
4.52 p.m.	(Carrs.)	Plaistow	to Fenchurch St.
5.25		Fenchurch St.	to Tilbury
6.47		Tilbury	to Southend
7.50	(Light)	Southend	to Shoeburyness
9.15		Shoeburyness	to Tilbury
10.30		Tilbury	to Shoeburyness

On Saturdays after.

5.25 p.m.	Fenchurch St.	to Tilbury
7.13	Tilbury	to Fenchurch St.
8.41	Fenchurch St.	to Shoeburyness

No. 4 SHOEBURYNESS.

6.30 a.m.	(Light)	Shoeburyness	to Southend
7. 0		Southend	to Tilbury
8. 5		Tilbury	to Fenchurch St.
9.26		Fenchurch St.	to Shoeburyness
12.40 p.m.		Shoeburyness	to Fenchurch St.
2.25		Fenchurch St.	to Shoeburyness
5.50	(Light)	Shoeburyness	to Southend
6.20		Southend	to Tilbury
8.11		Tilbury	to Fenchurch St.
9.44	(Carrs.)	Fenchurch St.	to Barking
10.40		Barking	to Shoeburyness

On Saturdays after.

12.40 p.m.	Shoeburyness	to Fenchurch St.
2.15	Fenchurch St.	to Tilbury
4.20	Tilbury	to Shoeburyness
7. 5	Shoeburyness	to Tilbury
10.17	Tilbury	to Fenchurch St.
12.10 a.m.	Fenchurch St.	to Shoeburyness

No. 5 SHOEBURYNESS.

6.54 a.m.		Shoeburyness	to Southend
7.20		Southend	to Barking
10.38		Barking	to Shoeburyness
1.50 p.m.		Shoeburyness	to Barking
4.49		Barking	to Pitsea
6. 0	(Light)	Pitsea	to Dagenham
7.48		Dagenham	to Shoeburyness

On Saturdays after.

10.38 a.m.	Barking	to Shoeburyness
1.56 p.m.	Shoeburyness	to Tilbury
4.10	Tilbury	to Fenchurch St.
6.26	Fenchurch St.	to Shoeburyness

ENGINE WORKING.

Week Days, June, 1915, until further notice.

No. 6 SHOEBURYNESS.

6.45 a.m.	(Light)	Shoeburyness	to Southend—To assist 7.30, 7.56, 8.18, & 9.27 ex Shoeburyness
9.19		Southend	to Upminster
11.25		Upminster	to Shoeburyness
1.56 p.m.	(Carrs.)	Shoeburyness	to Southend } Not
2.25	(Light)	Southend	to Shoeburyness } Sats.
4.48		Shoeburyness	to Plaistow
8.18		Plaistow	to Barking
9. 8		Barking	to Shoeburyness

No. 7 SHOEBURYNESS.

6.54 a.m.		Shoeburyness	to Fenchurch St.	
8.29		Fenchurch St.	to Tilbury	
11. 8		Tilbury	to Shoeburyness	
1. 0 p.m.	(Light)	Shoeburyness	to Southend	
1.30		Southend	to Barking	
3.55		Barking	to Fenchurch St.	Weds.
4.46		Fenchurch St.	to Tilbury	only
6.11		Tilbury	to Southend	
7.12	(Light)	Southend	to Shoeburyness	
12.34	(Light)	Shoeburyness	to Tilbury	
1.40		Tilbury	to Fenchurch St.	
3. 8		Fenchurch St.	to Shoeburyness	
6. 5	(Light)	Shoeburyness	to Southend	Not
6.35		Southend	to Fenchurch St.	Weds.
8.25	(Carrs.)	Fenchurch St.	to Barking	
9.41		Barking	to Southend	
10.40	(Light)	Southend	to Shoeburyness	

On Saturdays after.

8.29 a.m.		Fenchurch St.	to Tilbury
10.55	(Carrs.)	Tilbury	to Little Ilford S. Sidings
12.45 p.m.	(Carrs.)	Little Ilford S. Sidings	to Fenchurch St.
1.25		Fenchurch St.	to Southend
2.40	(Light)	Southend	to Shoeburyness
4.20		Shoeburyness	to Tilbury
5.55	(Light)	Tilbury	to Barking
6.51		Barking	to Shoeburyness

No. 8 SHOEBURYNESS.

7.10 a.m.	(Light)	Shoeburyness	to Southend
8. 4		Southend	to Fenchurch St.
9.18	(Carrs.)	Fenchurch St.	to Plaistow
4.19 p.m.	(Carrs.)	Plaistow	to Fenchurch St.
4.57		Fenchurch St.	to Southend
6.10	(Light)	Southend	to Tilbury
7.13		Tilbury	to Fenchurch St.
8.41		Fenchurch St.	to Shoeburyness

On Saturdays after.

9.18 a.m.	(Carrs.)	Fenchurch St.	to Plaistow
12. 6 p.m.		Plaistow	to Shoeburyness
2.25		Shoeburyness	to Fenchurch St.
4.16		Fenchurch St.	to Tilbury
6.11		Tilbury	to Southend
7.12	(Light)	Southend	to Shoeburyness
9.15		Shoeburyness	to Tilbury
10.30		Tilbury	to Shoeburyness

No. 9 SHOEBURYNESS.

7.56 a.m.		Shoeburyness	to Fenchurch St.
9.34	(Carrs.)	Fenchurch St.	to Plaistow
6. 0 p.m.	(Carrs.)	Plaistow	to Fenchurch St.
6.38		Fenchurch St.	to Tilbury
10.17		Tilbury	to Fenchurch St.
12.10 a.m.		Fenchurch St.	to Shoeburyness

On Saturdays after.

9.34 a.m.	(Carrs)	Fenchurch St.	to Plaistow
12.10 p.m.	(Carrs.)	Plaistow	to Fenchurch St.
1. 0		Fenchurch St.	to Shoeburyness

No. 10 SHOEBURYNESS.

7.30 a.m.		Shoeburyness	to Fenchurch St.	
9. 5		Fenchurch St.	to Tilbury	
11.14		Tilbury	to Fenchurch St	
12.55 p.m.		Fenchurch St.	to Southend	Sats.
2.25	(Light)	Southend	to Shoeburyness	only
1. 0		Fenchurch St.	to Shoeburyness	
4.10		Shoeburyness	to Fenchurch St.	
6. 7		Fenchurch St.	to Barking	
7. 7		Barking	to Fenchurch St.	Not Sats.
8. 0		Fenchurch St.	to Shoeburyness	
10. 0	(Carrs.)	Shoeburyness	to Southend	
10.24	(Light)	Southend	to Shoeburyness	

No. 11 SHOEBURYNESS.

7.40 a.m.		Shoeburyness	to Tilbury
9.18		Tilbury	to Fenchurch St.
10.45		Fenchurch St.	to Shoeburyness
3. 6 p.m.		Shoeburyness	to Tilbury
4.45		Tilbury	to Fenchurch St.
5.55		Fenchurch St.	to Shoeburyness
8.10		Shoeburyness	to Fenchurch St.
10.15		Fenchurch St.	to Shoeburyness

On Saturdays after

10.45 a.m.		Fenchurch St.	to Shoeburyness
1.50 p.m.		Shoeburyness	to Fenchurch St.
4.46		Fenchurch St.	to Tilbury
7.45		Tilbury	to Shoeburyness

No. 12 SHOEBURYNESS.

7.15 a.m.	(Carrs.)	Shoeburyness	to Westcliff	
7.40		Westcliff	to Fenchurch St.	
8.58	(Carrs.)	Fenchurch St.	to Plaistow	
12.28 p.m.	(Carrs.)	Plaistow	to Fenchurch St.	Sats.
1. 5		Fenchurch St.	to Shoeburyness	only
4.32	(Carrs.)	Plaistow	to Fenchurch St.	
5. 6		Fenchurch St.	to Shoeburyness	
7.50	(Carrs.)	Shoeburyness	to Southend	
8.30		Southend	to Fenchurch St.	Not Sats.
10.25		Fenchurch St.	to Plaistow	
11.20	(Light)	Plaistow	to Barking	
11.40		Barking	to Southend	
12.30 a.m.	(Light)	Southend	to Shoeburyness	

ENGINE WORKING.

Week Days, June, 1915, until further notice.

No. 13 SHOEBURYNESS.

8.19 . m.		Shoeburyness	to Fenchurch Street
9.30		Fenchurch St.	to Tilbury
2.35 p.m.		Tilbury	to Fenchurch St.
4. 7		Fenchurch St.	to Shoeburyness
6.16		Shoeburyness	to Barking
7.22	(Light)	Barking	to Shoeburyness

On Saturdays after.

9.39 a.m.		Fenchurch St.	to Tilbury
12.10 p.m.		Tilbury	to Fenchurch St.
2. 6		Fenchurch St.	to Shoeburyness

No. 14 SHOEBURYNESS.

8.27 a.m.		Shoeburyness	to Southend
8.58		Southend	to Fenchurch St.
10.17		Fenchurch St.	to Tilbury
3. 5 p.m.		Tilbury	to Fenchurch St.
4.27		Fenchurch St.	to Shoeburyness

On Saturdays after.

10.17 a.m.		Fenchurch St.	to Tilbury
1. 0 p.m.		Tilbury	to Fenchurch St.
2.26		Fenchurch St.	to Shoeburyness
5.20		Shoeburyness	to Fenchurch Street
7.20		Fenchurch St.	to Shoeburyness

No. 15 SHOEBURYNESS.

8.50 a.m.		Shoeburyness	to Fenchurch St.
10.28		Fenchurch St.	to Upminster
11.30	(Light)	Upminster	to Plaistow—Not Weds.
1.41 p.m.		Upminster	to Romford
1.55		Romford	to Upminster ⎱ Weds.
2.10		Upminster	to Barking ⎰ only
2.32	(Light)	Barking	to Plaistow
4.38		Plaistow	to Fenchurch St.
5.16		Fenchurch St.	to Shoeburyness

On Saturdays after.

11.30 a.m.	(Light)	Upminster	to Plaistow
11.40	(Light)	Plaistow	to Little Ilford S. Sidings
1.20 p.m.	(Carrs.)	Little Ilford S. Sidings	to Fenchurch St.
1.56		Fenchurch St.	to Southend
3.20	(Light)	Southend	to Shoeburyness

No. 16 SHOEBURYNESS.

9.20 a.m.		Shoeburyness	to Fenchurch Street
11. 0	(Carrs.)	Fenchurch St.	to Plaistow ⎱ Weds.
11.35	(Light)	Plaistow	to Tilbury ⎰ only
11.13		Fenchurch St.	to Tilbury—Not Weds.
12.53 p.m.		Tilbury	to Southend
2.12		Southend	to Tilbury ⎱ Not
4.10		Tilbury	to Fenchurch St. ⎰ Sats.

No. 17 SHOEBURYNESS.

9.45 a.m.		Shoeburyness	to Barking—Not Weds. & Sats
9.45		Shoeburyness	to Fenchurch St ⎱
11.45		Fenchurch St.	to Tilbury ⎮
1.40 p.m.		Tilbury	to Fenchurch St. ⎮ Weds.
3. 8		Fenchurch St.	to Shoeburyness ⎮ only
6. 5	(Light)	Shoeburyness	to Southend ⎮
6.35		Southend	to Fenchurch St. ⎱
8.25	(Carrs.)	Fenchurch St.	to Barking ⎮
9.41		Barking	to Southend ⎮
10.40	(Light)	Southend	to Shoeburyness ⎰
3.55		Barking	to Fenchurch St. ⎱
4.46		Fenchurch St.	to Tilbury ⎮ Not Weds.
6.11		Tilbury	to Southend ⎮ & Sats.
7.12	(Light)	Southend	to Shoeburyness ⎰
1.30	(Light)	Shoeburyness	to Tilbury ⎱
3. 5		Tilbury	to Fenchurch St. ⎮
4.27		Fenchurch St.	to Shoeburyness ⎬ Sats. only
8.10		Shoeburyness	to Fenchurch St. ⎮
10.15		Fenchurch St.	to Shoeburyness ⎰

No. 18 SHOEBURYNESS.

7.45 a.m.	(Light)	Shoeburyness	to Southend
8.20		Southend	to St. Pancras
12.28 p.m.		St. Pancras	to Southend
2.20	(Light)	Southend	to Shoeburyness
2.40	(Light)	Shoeburyness	to Southend
2.55		Southend	to St. Pancras
6.48		St. Pancras	to Southend
8.40	(Light)	Southend	to Shoeburyness

No. 1 KENTISH TOWN.

a.m.	(Light)	Kentish Town	to St. Pancras
8.45		St. Pancras	to Southend
10.35	(Light)	Southend	to Shoeburyness
11.35	(Light)	Shoeburyness	to Southend (11.30 Sats., 17th July to 11th Sept. inclusive).
12. 0 noon		Southend	to St. Pancras
3. 5 p.m.		St. Pancras	to Southend
4.50	(Light)	Southend	to Shoeburyness (4.55 Sats.)
7.20	(Light)	Shoeburyness	to Southend
7.54		Southend	to St. Pancras
—	(Light)	St. Pancras	to Kentish Town

No. 2 KENTISH TOWN.

a.m.	(Light)	Kentish Town	to St. Pancras
9.33		St. Pancras	to Southend
11.40	(Light)	Southend	to Shoeburyness

CARRIAGE WORKING,
WEEK DAYS, June, 1915, until further Notice.

No. 1 TRAIN.
Bogie Stock.

	1st.	Compo.	3rd.	B. Vans.	J. Brakes.	3rd B. Carrs
4.22 a.m. Barking to Fenchurch Street	1		3		2	PLV. 1
5. 5 Fenchurch Street to Shoeburyness						
7.40 Shoeburyness to Fenchurch Street	1		3		2	
9.39 Fenchurch Street to Tilbury						
12.10 p.m. Tilbury to Fenchurch Street (Sats.	1		3 3		2	
1.56 Fenchurch Street to Southend only						
2.35 Tilbury to Fenchurch Street Not	1		3		2	
3.25 Fenchurch Street to Southend Sats.						
6.20 Southend to Fenchurch Street	1		3		2	PLV. 1
8.25 (E) Fenchurch St. to Barking—Not Sats.	1		3 2a		2	PLV. 1
8.28 (E) Fenchurch St. to Barking—Sats. only	1		3 3		2	PLV. 1

Barking to detach 2 A Thirds from 8.25 p.m. Not Sats., and place next engine of 4.38 a.m. Down next day.

The six-wheeled Passenger Luggage Van to be next engine of 4.22 a.m. Up.

Tilbury to attach 2 A Thirds, Not Sats., 3 Thirds, Sats. only, and 1 six-wheeled Passenger Luggage Van daily to 6.20 p.m. Up.

Southend to detach Passenger Luggage Van from 5.5 a.m. Down daily and send to Shoeburyness. Shoeburyness to send this Passenger Luggage Van to Tilbury, except Fridays. The van received on Fridays to be attached next engine of 6.10 a.m. up Sats.

Southend to detach 3 A Thirds from 1.56 p.m. on Sats. and send to Shoeburyness for Nos. 7 & 15 trains on Sundays.

No. 2 TRAIN.
Bogie Stock.

	1st.	Compo.	3rd.	B. Vans.	J. Brakes.	3rd B. Carrs
4.38 a.m. (E) Barking to Dagenham	1	1	5 2		2	
4.58 Dagenham to Fenchurch Street						
5.45 Fenchurch Street to Shoeburyness						
10.17 Shoeburyness to Fenchurch Street	1	1	3		2	
12.15 p.m. Fenchurch Street to Shoeburyness						
2.25 Shoeburyness to Fenchurch Street						
4. 7 Fenchurch Street to Shoeburyness						
9.15 Shoeburyness to Fenchurch Street	1	1	5		2	
10.25 Fenchurch Street to Barking						

On Saturdays after.

	1st.	Compo.	3rd.	B. Vans.	J. Brakes.	3rd B. Carrs
5.45 a.m. Fenchurch Street to Shoeburyness						
10.17 Shoeburyness to Fenchurch Street						
12.15 p.m. Fenchurch Street to Shoeburyness	1	1	5		2	
5.20 Shoeburyness to Fenchurch Street						
6.53 Fenchurch Street to Tilbury						
9.14 Tilbury to Fenchurch Street						
10.25 Fenchurch Street to Barking						

2 A Thirds to be next engine of 4.38 a.m. Down.

Tilbury to detach 2 A Thirds from 5.45 a.m. Down.

No. 3 TRAIN.
B. Stock.

	1st.	Compo.	3rd.	B. Vans.	J. Brakes.	3rd B. Carrs
7.37 a.m. Barking to Fenchurch Street Mons.	2		8 3		3	
8.11 Fenchurch Street to Tilbury only						
7.37 Barking to Fenchurch Street Not	2		1 9 2		2 1	
8.11 Fenchurch Street to Tilbury Mons.						
5.52 p.m. Tilbury to Fenchurch Street Not	2		9		2	
7. 4 Fenchurch Street to Barking Sats.						

No. 4 TRAIN.
A Stock.

	1st.	Compo.	3rd.	B. Vans.	C. Brakes.	3rd B. Carr
†5.50 a.m. Plaistow to Tilbury	1	1	8	1	1	
7.24 Tilbury to Fenchurch Street						
8.29 Fenchurch St. to Tilbury						
4.45 p.m. Tilbury to Fenchurch St.	1	2	6	1	2	
5.46 Fenchurch St. to Tilbury						
9.14 Tilbury to Fenchurch Street	1	1	8	1	1	
10.25 Fenchurch Street to Plaistow						
†6.47 Tilbury to Southend		1	2— 4 on Frid.		1	

‡ On Mondays will consist of 14 A stoc coaches.

† To form 9.19 a.m. up following day. 1 Compo, 2 Thirds and 1 Carr. Brake to be next engine of 4.45 p.m. up.

ON SATURDAYS AFTER.

	1st.	Compo.	3rd.	B. Vans.	C. Brakes.	3rd B. Carr
8.29 a.m. Fenchurch Street to Tilbury						
10.55 (E) Tilbury to Little Ilford S. Sidings	1	2	6	1	2	
12.45 p.m. (E) Little Ilford S. Sdgs. to Fenchurch St						
1.15 Fenchurch Street to Tilbury						
†2.12 Tilbury to Southend		1	2		1	

† To form 9.19 a.m. np on Mondays. 1 Compo, 2 Thirds and 1 Carr. Brake to be next engine of 10.55 a.m. from Tilbury on Sats.

No. 5 TRAIN.
Close Buffer and B Stock.

	1st.	Compo.	3rd.	B. Vans.	C. Brakes.	3rd B. Carr
7.38 a.m. Plaistow to Fenchurch Street	2		11		3	
7.58 (E) Fenchurch Street to Plaistow						
2. 5 p.m. (E) Plaistow to Fenchurch St.						
2.30 Fenchurch St. to Shoeburyness Sats. only						
10.52 Shoeburyness to Tilbury						

No. 6 TRAIN.
B Stock.

	1st.	Compo.	3rd.	B. Vans.	C. Brakes.	3rd B. Carr
4.55 a.m. (E) Little Ilford S. Sidings to Barking	1		15			2
5.37 Barking to Fenchurch Street						
6.18 Fenchurch Street to Dagenham Dock						
7.10 Dagenham Dock to Fenchurch Street						
7.53 (E) Fenchurch St. to Little Ilford S. Sdgs						

No. 7 TRAIN.
B. Stock.

	1st.	Compo.	3rd.	B. Vans.	C. Brakes.	3rd B. Carr
7.25 a.m. (E) Little Ilford S. Sidings to East Ham	1		15			2
7.33 East Ham to Fenchurch Street						
8. 2 (E) Fenchurch Street to East Ham						

No. 8 TRAIN.
B Stock.
NOT SATURDAYS.

	1st.	Compo.	3rd.	B. Vans.	C. Brakes.	3rd B. Carr
6.27 a.m. Upminster to Fenchurch Street	3		11	1	2	PLV. 1
7.20 Fenchurch Street to Shoeburyness						
9.29 Shoeburyness to Fenchurch Street	2		8		2	
11.45 Fenchurch Street to Southend	2		6		2	
6.35 p.m. Southend to Fenchurch Street	2		8		2	
8.13 Fenchurch Street to Tilbury						
9.24 Tilbury to Pitsea	1		3		1	

For continuation of No. 8 Train, see page 2.

E. EMPTY TRAIN

CARRIAGE WORKING.

Week Days, June, 1915, until further Notice.

No. 8 TRAIN—*continued.*

NOT SATURDAYS

	1st	Compo.	3rd	B. Vans.	C. Brakes	3rd B.Cars.
9.53 a.m. Shoeburyness to Barking	1		8	1		
11.13 (E) Barking to Little Ilford S. Sidings ..						
6.43 p.m. (E) Little Ilford S. Sidings to Barking ..						
6.50 Barking to Pitsea	A		A	A		
10.10★ (E) Pitsea to Tilbury — Not Weds.	2 1	A6	3	1	1	
10.10★ (E) Pitsea to Tilbury—Weds. only ..	2	26	2	1	1	2

★ Coaches of 4.49 and 6.50 p.m. ex Barking, and 9.24 p.m. ex Tilbury

ON SATURDAYS.

	1st	Compo.	3rd	B. Vans.	C. Brakes	3rd B.Cars.
						PLV
6.27 a.m. Upminster to Fenchurch Street	3		11	1	2	1
7.20 Fenchurch Street to Shoeburyness ..						
9.29 Shoeburyness to Fenchurch Street ..	3		11	1	2	
11.45 Fenchurch Street to Southend	2		6		2	
6.35 p.m. Southend to Fenchurch Street	2		10		2	
8.13 Fenchurch Street to Tilbury						
†9.24 Tilbury to Pitsea	1		8		1	

† To form 6.30 a.m. up on Mondays.
Passenger Luggage Van to run on rear of 6.27 a.m. daily ; Shoeburyness to detach from 7.20 a.m. and attach to 11.18 a.m. up. Except Sats. Tilbury to detach 2 Thirds from 9.29 a.m. and attach 2 Thirds to 11.45 a.m. On Sats. Tilbury to detach 1 First, 5 Thirds and 1 Brake Van from 9.29 a.m. and attach 4 Thirds to 11.45 a.m.

No. 9 TRAIN. A Stock.

	1st	Compo.	3rd	B. Vans.	C. Brakes	3rd B.Cars.
5.30 a.m. Tilbury to Fenchurch Street	1	1	13		2	
6.52 Fenchurch Street to Tilbury {Not						
9.45 Tilbury to Fenchurch Street {Weds.	1		4		2	
11.13 Fenchurch Street to Tilbury						
5.30 Tilbury to Fenchurch Street	1	1	12		3	
6.52 Fenchurch Street to Tilbury } Weds.						
7.58 Tilbury to Shoeburyness } only.	1	1	3		2	
9.45 Shoeburyness to Fenchurch St.						
11.13 Fenchurch Street to Tilbury						
1.40 p.m. Tilbury to Fenchurch Street	1	1	4		2	
2.40 Fenchurch Street to Tilbury						
5. 5 Tilbury to Fenchurch Street {Not	1	1	9		2	
6. 7 Fenchurch Street to Barking {Sats. ..						
7. 7 Barking to Fenchurch Street						
7.41 Fenchurch Street to Tilbury						
1. 0 Tilbury to Fenchurch Street	1	1	10		2	
2.15 Fenchurch Street to Tilbury } Sats. ..						
3.13 Tilbury to Pitsea } only ..	1		5		1	
4. 5 (E) Pitsea to Tilbury (see No. 39)	1	1	9		2	
†10.30 Tilbury to Shoeburyness	1	1	4		2	

† To form 2.18 p.m. Shoeburyness to Barking on Sundays.
On Weds. 5.30 a.m. to be made up as follows :—C.B., 1 third, 1 first, 1 compo., 2 thirds, 1 C.B., 9 thirds and 1 C.B.

No. 10 TRAIN. A Stock.

	1st	Compo.	3rd	B. Vans.	C. Brakes	3rd B.Cars.
6.26 a.m. Tilbury to Fenchurch Street	1	1	9	1	2	
7.32 Fenchurch Street to Southend						PLV
9.36 (E) Southend to Shoeburyness	1	1	4	1	1	1
11.18 Shoeburyness to Fenchurch Street ..	1	1	4	1	1	1
1.35 p.m. Fenchurch Street to Tilbury—Sats. only	1	1	9	1	2	1
1.48 Fenchurch Street to Southend }	1	1	4	1	1	1
4.35 Southend to Fenchurch Street {Not						
6.38 Fenchurch Street to Tilbury {Sats.	1 1B	1	4 7B	1	1 1B	
†7 45 Tilbury to Pitsea	1B		8B		1B	

†To form 6.0 a.m. up following day.
Tilbury to detach 5 Thirds and 1 Carr. Brake from 7.32 a.m. down, and attach 5 Thirds and 1 Carr. Brake to 11.18 a.m. on Sats., and 1 First, 7 Thirds and 1 Carr. Brake B Stock, to 4.35 p.m. Not Sats.
P.L.V. to run on rear of 11.18 a.m Tilbury to detach this P.L.V. from 1.35 p.m. on Sats. and 1.48 p.m. not Sats.

No. 11 TRAIN. B Stock.

	1st	Compo.	3rd	B. Vans.	C. Brakes	3rd B.Cars.
5.45 a.m. (E) Tilbury to Grays	2		10	1	2	
6. 0 Grays to Tilbury						
6.12 (E) Tilbury to Grays						
6.25 Grays to Tilbury						
9.45 Tilbury to Fenchurch Street } Weds.	1		4		2	
11.0 (E) Fenchurch St. to Plaistow } only						
5.10 p.m. Tilbury to Purfleet Rifle Range } Not	3		11	1	2	
5.39 Purfleet Rifle Range to Tilbury } Sats.						PLV
6.20 Tilbury to Fenchurch Street ..	3		11	1	2	1
7.33 Fenchurch Street to Upminster ..						

The coaches of 11.0 a.m. from Fenchurch Street on Wednesdays to be sent from Plaistow to Tilbury by 2.40 p.m. ex Fenchurch Street.
6.20 p.m. to be marshalled as follows ; Except Fridays, C.B. train, 5 Thirds, 1 First, 1 Brake Van and 1 P.L.V. On Fridays, 1 Brake Van 1 First, 5 Thirds. C.B. train and 1 P.L.V.

No. 12 TRAIN. A Stock.

	1st	Compo.	3rd	B. Vans.	C. Brakes	3rd B.Cars.
8. 5 a.m. Tilbury to Fenchurch Street	1	1	5	1	1	
9.18 (E) Fenchurch Street to Plaistow ..						PLV
4.19 p.m. (E) Plaistow to Fenchurch Street ..	1	1	5	1	1	1
4.46 Fenchurch Street to Tilbury						(SO)
8. 5 Tilbury to Grays } Not						
9.45 Grays to Tilbury } Sats.						
10.50 Tilbury to Fenchurch Street	1	1	8 (6 on Sats)	1	1	
12. 0 mdt. Fenchurch Street to Tilbury ..						

No. 13 TRAIN. A Stock.

	1st	Compo.	3rd	B. Vans.	C. Brakes	3rd B.Cars.
9.18 a.m. Tilbury to Fenchurch Street	1	1	5		2	
10.28 Fenchurch Street to Upminster ..						
11.25 Upminster to Shoeburyness						
1.56 p.m. (E) Shoeburyness to Southend ..						
2.12 Southend to Fenchurch Street ..						
4.16 Fenchurch Street to Shoeburyness ..						
9. 5 Shoeburyness to Fenchurch Street ..	1	1	7		2	
10.45 Fenchurch Street to Tilbury						

Tilbury to attach 2 thirds to 4.16 p.m.

No. 14 TRAIN. B Stock.

NOT SATURDAYS.

	1st	Compo.	3rd	B. Vans.	C. Brakes	3rd B.Cars.
6.10 a.m. (E) Tilbury to Pitsea	1		8		1	
6.58 Pitsea to Tilbury						
9. 5 Tilbury to Barking						
2.35 p.m. Barking to Upminster—See No. 3 local						
7.27 Upminster to Tilbury						

ON SATURDAYS.

	1st	Compo.	3rd	B. Vans.	C. Brakes	3rd B.Cars.
6.10 a.m. (E) Tilbury to Pitsea	1		8		1	
6.58 Pitsea to Tilbury						
9. 5 Tilbury to Barking	2		6		2	
10.26 (E) Barking to Plaistow—see No. 18 train	3		11		4	
12.48 p.m. (E) Plaistow to Fenchurch Street ..	2		6		2	
1.11 Fenchurch Street to Upminster ..						
1.59 Upminster to Pitsea						
2.50 (E) Pitsea to Tilbury						

Plaistow to detach 1 First, 5 Thirds and 2 Carr. Brakes from 10.26 a.m. ex Barking to form 3 27 p.m. to Shoeburyness—See No. 18 train.

E EMPTY TRAIN.

CARRIAGE WORKING,

Week Days, June, 1915, until further Notice.

No. 15 TRAIN.
B Stock.

	1st.	Compo.	3rd.	B. Vans.	C. Brakes.	3rd B. Carr.
6.50 a.m. Pitsea to Plaistow		1	2		1	Milk Van 1
11.32 Plaistow to Pitsea—Sats. only						
11.45 (E) Plaistow to Barking } Not Sats.						
12.18 p.m. Barking to Pitsea						

No. 16 TRAIN.
B Stock.

	1st.	Compo.	3rd.	B. Vans.	C. Brakes.	3rd B. Carr.
8.7 a.m. Pitsea to Romford	1	1	3		2	
9.0 Romford to Upminster						
†9.14 Upminster to Barking						

† To form 6.40 a.m. down following day.

No. 17 TRAIN.
B Stock.

	1st.	Compo.	3rd.	B. Vans.	C. Brakes.	3rd B. Carr.
6.30 a.m. Pitsea to Upminster	1		3		1	
8.21 Upminster to Tilbury						

No. 18 TRAIN.
B Stock.
NOT SATURDAYS.

	1st.	Compo.	3rd.	B. Vans.	C. Brakes.	3rd B. Carr.
7.5 a.m. Tilbury to Barking	1		3		1	
7.50 (E) Barking to Ilford Southern Sidings						
6.11 p.m. (E) Ilford Southern Sidings to Barking						
6.15 Barking to Pitsea						

ON SATURDAYS.

	1st.	Compo.	3rd.	B. Vans.	C. Brakes.	3rd B. Carr.
★7.5 a.m. Tilbury to Barking	1		9		2	

★ Tilbury to place 4 thirds on rear of this train.—Barking to detach for 2.7 p.m. up; remainder of coaches to be attached to 10.26 a.m. empty train Barking to Plaistow. See No. 14 train.

	1st.	Compo.	3rd.	B. Vans.	C. Brakes.	3rd B. Carr.
†3.27 p.m. Plaistow to Shoeburyness	1		5		2	

† To form 8.10 a.m. up on Sundays.

No. 19 TRAIN.
Corridor Stock.

	1st.	Compo.	3rd.	B. Vans.	C. Brakes.	3rd B. Carr.
4.45 a.m. (E) Shoeburyness to Southend—Mons. only.		1	1		2	
5.5 Southend to Ealing		1	1		2	
10.42 p.m. Ealing to Southend						
12.30 night (E) Southend to Shoeburyness—Sats. only						

No. 20 TRAIN.
Corridor Stock.

	1st.	Compo.	3rd.	B. Vans.	C. Brakes.	3rd B. Carr.
7.20 a.m. Southend to Ealing		1	5		2	
9.32 Ealing to Shoeburyness						
6.16 p.m. Shoeburyness to Ealing						
8.36 Ealing to Southend—Not Sats.						

On Sats. the coaches of 6.16 p.m. will stow at Ealing for 10.26 a.m. on Sunday.

No. 21 TRAIN.
A Stock.

	1st.	Compo.	3rd.	B. Vans.	C. Brakes.	3rd B. Carr.
7.9 a.m. Upminster to Romford	1		3		2	
7.40 Romford to Upminster						
7.55 Upminster to Hammersmith						
1.42 p.m. Hammersmith to Upminster						
5.8 Upminster to Emerson Park						
5.24 Emerson Park to Upminster } Sats. only.						
5.34 Upminster to Romford						
5.51 Romford to Upminster						
4.50 Hammersmith to Upminster						
6.10 Upminster to Tilbury						
7.32 Tilbury to Romford						
8.18 Romford to Grays						
9.30 Grays to Upminster						
10.2 Upminster to Barking						
10.19 (E) Barking to Little Ilford S. Sidings						
12.25 ngt (E) Little Ilford S. Sidings to Barking						
12.30 Barking to Upminster						

(Not Sats.)

No. 22 TRAIN.
Bogie Stock.

	1st.	Compo.	3rd.	B. Vans.	C. Brakes.	3rd B. Carr.
6.10 a.m. Shoeburyness to Fenchurch Street	2	1	4		2	
7.42 (E) Fenchurch Street to Plaistow						
12.6 p.m. Plaistow to Shoeburyness—Sats. only						
4.38 (E) Plaistow to Stepney						
4.51 Stepney to Fenchurch Street } Not Sats.						
5.6 Fenchurch St. to Shoeburyness						
8.10 Shoeburyness to Fenchurch Street						
9.44 (E) Fenchurch Street to Barking						
10.40 Barking to Shoeburyness						

Passenger luggage van to run next engine of 6.10 a.m. up on Saturdays. Plaistow to detach from 7.42 a.m. down and attach to 4.19 p.m. up empty train.

No. 23 TRAIN.
Bogie Stock.
NOT SATURDAYS.

	1st.	Compo.	3rd.	B. Vans.	C. Brakes.	3rd B. Carr.
6.54 a.m. Shoeburyness to Fenchurch Street	1	1	4— 5 on Mons		2	
8.20 Fenchurch Street to Shoeburyness	1	1	2		2	
11.10 Shoeburyness to Fenchurch Street						
1.0 p.m. Fenchurch Street to Shoeburyness	1	1	5		2	
7.50 (E) Shoeburyness to Southend						
8.30 Southend to Fenchurch Street						
10.15 Fenchurch Street to Shoeburyness						

ON SATURDAYS.

	1st.	Compo.	3rd.	B. Vans.	C. Brakes.	3rd B. Carr.
6.54 a.m. Shoeburyness to Fenchurch Street	1	1	4		2	Milk Van 1
8.20 Fenchurch Street to Shoeburyness						
4.48 p.m. Shoeburyness to Plaistow	1	1	4		2	
6.55 (E) Plaistow to Fenchurch Street	1	1	4		2	
7.20 Fenchurch Street to Shoeburyness						

Plaistow to detach Milk Van from 4.48 p.m. on Sats. to work to Barking at 8.18 p.m. and be attached to 9.8 p.m. to Shoeburyness.—See No. 38 train.

No. 24 TRAIN.
Bogie Stock.

	1st.	Compo.	3rd.	B. Vans.	C. Brakes.	3rd B. Carr.
7.15 a.m. (E) Shoeburyness to Westcliff	1	2	8		2	
7.40 Westcliff to Fenchurch Street						
8.38 (E) Fenchurch St. to Little Ilford S. Sdgs.						
1.20 p.m. (E) L. Ilford S. Sdgs. to Fenc'h St. } Sats. only						
1.48 Fenchurch Street to Shoeburyness						
5.5 (E) L. Ilford S. Sdgs. to Fenchurch St. } Not Sats						
5.38 Fenchurch Street to Shoeburyness						

E Empty Train.

CARRIAGE WORKING,
Week Days, June, 1915, until further notice.

No. 25 TRAIN.

Bogie Stock

	1st	Compo.	3rd	B. Van.	C. Brakes.	3rd B.Carrs
7.30 a.m. Shoeburyness to Fenchurch Street	1	2	7— 8 on Mons.		2	
8.58 (E) Fenchurch Street to Plaistow						
12.28 p.m. (E) Plaistow to Fenchurch St. } Sats.	2		4		2	
1. 0 Fenchurch St. to Shoeburyness } only.						
6.55 (E) Plaistow to Fenchurch Street	1	2	7— 8 on Mons.		2	
7.20 Fenchurch St. to Shoeburyness (Fast) } Not Sats.	1	1	6— 7 on Mons.		1	
7.20 Fenchurch St. to Shoeburyness (Slow) }		1	1		1	
10.15 Shoeburyness to Fenchurch Street	1		3		2	
12.10 a.m. Fenchurch Street to Shoeburyness ..						

Brake to be on front of each portion on
6.55 p.m. Up—Not Sats.

No. 26 TRAIN.

Bogie Stock.

	1st	Compo.	3rd	B. Van.	C. Brakes.	3rd B.Carrs
8. 4 a.m. Southend to Fenchurch Street	2	1	8		2	
9.12 (E) Fenchurch Street to Little Ilford S. Sdgs.						
12.50 p.m. (E) Little Ilford S. Sidings to Fenchurch Street } Sats. only.						
1.25 Fenchurch Street to Southend						
5.45 (E) Little Ilford S. Sidings to Fenchurch Street } Not Sats.						
6.17 Fenchurch St. to Shoeburyness }						
10. 0 (E) Shoeburyness to Southend						

No. 27 TRAIN.

Bogie Stock.

	1st	Compo.	3rd	B. Van.	C. Brakes.	3rd B.Carrs
7.56 a.m. Shoeburyness to Fenchurch Street ..		2	6— 7 on Mons.		2	
9.26 Fenchurch Street to Shoeburyness ..		1	3		2	
12.40 p.m. Shoeburyness to Fenchurch St. }						
2. 6 Fenchurch St. to Shoeburyness } Not		2	7		2	
4.10 Shoeburyness to Fenchurch St. } Sats.						
5.55 Fenchurch St. to Shoeburyness }		1	1	7		2
12.40 Shoeburyness to Fenchurch Street }						
2. 6 Fenchurch Street to Shoeburyness } Sats	1		5		2	
4.20 Shoeburyness to Fenchurch Street } only.						
6.38 Fenchurch Street to Shoeburyness }	1	1A	1	5	2A	2

On Sats. Tilbury to attach 1 first and 2
thirds, A stock, to 4.20 p.m. up and detach 1
third from 6.38 p.m.

No. 28 TRAIN.

Bogie Stock.

NOT SATURDAYS.

	1st	Compo.	3rd	B. Van.	C. Brakes.	3rd B.Carrs
8.18 a.m. Shoeburyness to Fenchurch St... ..	2	1	7		2	
9.34 (E) Fenchurch St. to Plaistow :. ..						
6. 0 p.m. (E) Plaistow to Fenchurch St. ..						
6.26 Fenchurch St. to Shoeburyness ..						

ON SATURDAYS.

	1st	Compo.	3rd	B. Van.	C. Brakes.	3rd B.Carrs
8.18 a.m. Shoeburyness to Fenchurch St. ..	2	1	7		2	
9.34 (E) Fenchurch St. to Plaistow ..						
12.40 p.m. (E) Plaistow to Fenchurch St. ..	2	1	5		2	
1. 5 Fenchurch Street to Shoeburyness ..						
4.35 Shoeburyness to Fenchurch Street ..	1	2	6		3	
6.26 Fenchurch St. to Shoeburyness (Fast)	1		4		2	
6.26 Fenchurch St. to Shoeburyness (Slow)		2	2		1	

Brake to be on front of each portion on
4.35 p.m. Up on Sats.

No. 29 TRAIN.

Bogie Stock.

NOT SATURDAYS.

	1st	Compo.	3rd	B. Vans	C. Brakes.	3rd B. Car.
8.27 a.m. Shoeburyness to Fenchurch Street ..	2		6— 7 on Mons.		2	
9.45 (E) Fenchurch Street to Plaistow ..	1	1	5		2	
4.52 p.m. (E) Plaistow to Fenchurch Street ..						
5.16 Fenchurch St. to Shoeburyness ..						

Plaistow to detach 1 first and 1 third (2 on
Mondays) from 9.45 a.m. ex Fenchurch Street,
Not Sats. and send to Tilbury by 12.25 p.m. ex
Fenchurch Street, for No. 33 train.

ON SATURDAYS.

	1st	Compo.	3rd	B. Vans	C. Brakes.	3rd B. Car.
8.27 a.m. Shoeburyness to Fenchurch Street ..	2		6		2	
9.45 (E) Fenchurch Street to Plaistow ..						
4.52 p.m. (E) Plaistow to Fenchurch Street ..	2		7		2	
5.16 Fenchurch St. to Shoeburyness ..						

No. 30 TRAIN

Bogie Stock.

NOT SATURDAYS

	1st	Compo.	3rd	B. Vans	C. Brakes.	3rd B. Car.
8.58 a.m. Southend to Fenchurch Street	2	2— 3 on Mons.	5		2	
9.58 (E) Fenchurch Street to Plaistow .:						
4.32 p.m. (E) Plaistow to Fenchurch St.	2		5		2	
4.57 Fenchurch St. to Southend ..						

Plaistow to detach 2 compos. (3 on Mons.)
from 9.58 a.m. ex Fenchurch Street, Not Sats.;
place 1 compo. in 4.52 p.m. up and send 1
(2 Mons.) to Tilbury by 12.25 p.m. ex Fenchurch
Street, for No. 33 train.

ON SATURDAYS.

	1st	Compo.	3rd	B. Vans	C. Brakes.	3rd B. Car.
8.58 a.m. Southend to Fenchurch Street	2		6		2	
9.58 (E) Fenchurch Street to Plaistow ..						
12.10 p.m. (E) Plaistow to Fenchurch Street ..	1	2	6		2	
12.55 Fenchurch Street to Southend ..						

Southend to obtain from Shoeburyness the
stock required to make up 8.58 a.m. and on
Sats. detach 1 Third from 12.55 p.m. ex
Fenchurch Street and send to Shoeburyness.

NOTE.—Nos. 25, 29, 29 & 30 trains on
Sats.—After re-forming these trains and making
up the 12.10, 12.28, 12.40 and 4.52 p.m. empty
trains to Fenchurch Street as shown herein.
Plaistow will have 4 bogie thirds spare; these
coaches to be sent to Barking by 8.18 p.m. train
for Nos. 1 and 3 trains on Sundays.

No. 31 TRAIN.

Bogie Stock

NOT SATURDAYS.

	1st	Compo.	3rd	B. Vans	C. Brakes.	3rd B. Car.
8.50 a.m. Shoeburyness to Fenchurch Street ..	2	1	4		2	
10.17 Fenchurch Street to Shoeburyness ..						
5.20 p.m. Shoeburyness to Fenchurch St. ..	2		5 6 on Weds.		2	
6.53 Fenchurch St. to Shoeburyness ..						

ON SATURDAYS.

	1st	Compo.	3rd	B. Vans	C. Brakes.	3rd B. Car.
8.50 a.m. Shoeburyness to Fenchurch Street ..	2	1	4		2	
10.17 Fenchurch Street to Shoeburyness ..						
2.25 p.m. Shoeburyness to Fenchurch Street ..						
4. 7 Fenchurch Street to Shoeburyness ..						
9.15 Shoeburyness to Fenchurch Street ..	1	2	3		2	
★11.25 Fenchurch Street to Barking ..						

★ To part form 10.48 a.m. up on Sundays ..

E Empty Train.

CARRIAGE WORKING,
Week Days, June, 1915, until further notice.

Column headers (both sides): 1st | Compo. | 3rd | B. Vans. | C. Brakes. | 3rd.B.Carr.

No. 32 TRAIN. Bogie Stock.

	1st	Compo.	3rd	B. Vans	C. Brakes	3rd.B.Carr.
9.20 a.m. Shoeburyness to Fenchurch Street	1	3	2		2	
10.45 Fenchurch Street to Shoeburyness						
1.50 p.m. Shoeburyness to Barking						
3.55 Barking to Fenchurch Street						
4.27 Fenchurch St. to Shoeburyness						
6.55 Shoeburyness to Fenchurch Street	1	3	3		2	
8.41 Fenchurch St. to Shoeburyness						
On Weds. 9.20 a.m. to consist of	1	3	1ᴀ	2 1	2 1	

(A stock to be next engine).
On Mondays 9.20 a.m. Up to run with 1 Third extra.
On Wednesdays, Southend to detach 3 A Stock Coaches from rear of 10.45 a.m. down to part form 1.50 p.m. up.—See No. 40 train.

No. 33 TRAIN. Bogie Stock.
NOT SATURDAYS.

	1st	Compo.	3rd	B. Vans	C. Brakes	3rd.B.Carr.
10. 5 a.m. (E) Shoeburyness to Southend	1ᴀ	1	3— 2 Mons.		2	
10.18 Southend to Fenchurch Street						
12.25 p.m. Fenchurch St. to Tilbury						
6.55 Tilbury to Fenchurch St.	1	2— 2 Mons.	4		2	
8. 0 Fenchurch St. to Shoeburyness						

ON SATURDAYS.

	1st	Compo.	3rd	B. Vans	C. Brakes	3rd.B.Carr.
10. 5 a.m. (E) Shoeburyness to Southend	2		6		2	
10.18 Southend to Tilbury						
1.50 p.m. Tilbury to Fenchurch St.						
3. 8 Fenchurch St. to Shoeburyness						
7.50 (E) Shoeburyness to Southend	2		5		2	
8.30 Southend to Fenchurch St.						
10.15 Fenchurch St. to Shoeburyness						

Tilbury will receive 1 First, 2 Compos and 2 Thirds on Mondays, and 1 First, 1 Compo and 1 Third, Mondays and Saturdays excepted, from Plaistow by 12.25 p.m. ex Fenchurch St. to part form 6.55 p.m. up.

No. 34 TRAIN. Bogie Stock.
NOT SATURDAYS.

	1st	Compo.	3rd	B. Vans	C. Brakes	3rd.B.Carr.
12.16 p.m. Shoeburyness to Fenchurch St.		3	1		2	
2.25 Fenchurch St. to Shoeburyness						
7. 5 (E) Shoeburyness to Southend						
7.20 Southend to Fenchurch St.						
9.25 Fenchurch St. to Shoeburyness		3 1	2		2	

Tilbury to attach 2 A Thirds to 7.20 p.m. and detach from 9.25 p.m.

ON SATURDAYS

	1st	Compo.	3rd	B. Vans	C. Brakes	3rd.B.Carr.
12.16 p.m. Shoeburyness to Fenchurch St.	1	2	5		2	
2.26 Fenchurch St. to Shoeburyness	1		7		2	
7. 5 (E) Shoeburyness to Southend						
7.20 Southend to Fenchurch St.						
9.25 Fenchurch St. to Tilbury—to form 11.54 a.m. Tilbury to Fenchurch Street on Sundays						

No. 35 TRAIN. A Stock.

	1st	Compo.	3rd	B. Vans	C. Brakes	3rd.B.Carr.
7.58 a.m. Tilbury to Shoeburyness						
9.45 Shoeburyness to Barking } Not Weds. and Sats.	1		3		1	
4.49 p.m. Barking to Pitsea						
7.58 a.m. Tilbury to Shoeburyness						
11.10 Shoeburyness to Barking	1		4		1	
6.15 p.m. Barking to Upminster						
6.50 Upminster to Romford						
7.10 Romford to Upminster						
7.26 Upminster to Romford						
7.39 Romford to Upminster						
8.53 Upminster to Romford						
9. 4 Romford to Upminster						
9.28 Upminster to Romford						
9.43 Romford to Upminster						
10. 2 Upminster to Barking						
10.19 (E) Barking to Little Ilford Southern Sidings						
12.25 ngt. (E) Little Ilford Southern Sidings to Barking						
12.30 Barking to Pitsea—To form 6.0 a.m. up on Mondays						

(Saturdays only.)

The coaches of 4.49 p.m. ex Barking to be attached to 10.10 p.m. empty train Pitsea to Tilbury.

No. 36 TRAIN.
Bogie & A Stock.

	1st	Compo.	3rd	B. Vans	C. Brakes	3rd.B.Carr.
7. 0 a.m. Southend to Fenchurch St.—Mons. only	1		3		2	
7. 0 Southend to Fenchurch St.—Not Mons.	1		3 2ᴀ		2	
9. 5 Fenchurch Street to Shoeburyness						
8. 6 p.m. Shoeburyness to Fenchurch St. } Not						
5.25 Fenchurch Street to Southend } Sats.						
3. 6 Shoeburyness to Tilbury	1		3 2ᴀ		2	
4.10 Tilbury to Fenchurch St. } Sats.	1	1ᴀ	3 4ᴀ		2 1ᴀ	
5.25 Fenchurch St. to Southend } only.	1		3		2	
5.25 Fenchurch St. to Tilbury		1ᴀ	4ᴀ		1ᴀ	

On Mondays Tilbury to attach 2 A Thirds to 7.0 a.m. up.

No. 37 TRAIN.
A Stock.

	1st	Compo.	3rd	B. Vans	C. Brakes	3rd.B.Carr.
5.50 a.m. Shoeburyness to Grays	1	1	5		2	
7.21 Grays to Tilbury						
1.50 p.m. Tilbury to Fenchurch St. } Not						
3, 8 Fenchurch St. to Shoeburyness } Sats.						
11.14 a.m. Tilbury to Fenchurch St.						
12.25 p.m. Fenchurch St. to Tilbury } Sats.						
2.35 Tilbury to Fenchurch St. } only.						
3.25 Fenchurch St. to Southend						
5.20 (E) Southend to Shoeburyness						

No. 38 TRAIN.
B Stock.
NOT SATURDAYS.

	1st	Compo.	3rd	B. Vans	C. Brakes	3rd.B.Carr.
4.48 p.m. Shoeburyness to Plaistow	1		5		2	Milk Van 1
8.18 Plaistow to Barking						
9. 8 Barking to Shoeburyness						

Milk Van to be next engine of 4.48.

SATURDAYS ONLY.

	1st	Compo.	3rd	B. Vans	C. Brakes	3rd.B.Carr.
9.53 a.m. Shoeburyness to Barking	1		6		2	Milk Van 1
9. 8 p.m. Barking to Shoeburyness	1		6		2	

No. 39 TRAIN.
A Stock.

	1st	Compo.	3rd	B. Vans	C. Brakes	3rd.B.Carr.
9.19 a.m. Southend to Upminster		1	2— 4 Sats		1	
2.58 p.m. Upminster to Pitsea } Sats.		1	4		1	
4. 5 (E) Pitsea to Tilbury (coupled to No. 9) } only.						
3.16 Upminster to Romford		1	2		1	
3.35 Romford to Upminster } Not Sats.						
†3.50 Upminster to Barking						

† To be attached to 7.37 a.m. Barking to Fenchurch St. following day.

No. 40 TRAIN.
A Stock.
WEDNESDAYS ONLY.

	1st	Compo.	3rd	B. Vans	C. Brakes	3rd.B.Carr.
1.30 p.m. Southend to Barking		2	2		1	
†4.49 Barking to Pitsea						

†Coaches of this train to be attached to 10.10 p.m. (E) Pitsea to Tilbury

On Tuesdays, Tilbury to send Southend 1 compo., and 1 third A stock, to part form 1.30 p.m. on Wednesdays.

CARRIAGE WORKING

Week Days, June, 1915, until further notice.

		1st.	Compo.	3rd.	B. Van.	C. Brake	3rd B. Carr

ROMFORD, UPMINSTER AND GRAYS, ETC. LOCAL SERVICE.

No. 1 TRAIN.

B Stock.

		1st.	Compo.	3rd.	B. Van.	C. Brake
6. 0 a.m.	Upminster to Romford	1	1	3—4 on Weds.		2
6.15	Romford to Upminster					
6.30	Upminster to Romford					
6.50	Romford to Upminster					
7. 6	Upminster to Barking					
7.27	Barking to Upminster					
8.15	(E) Upminster to Emerson Park					
8.26	Emerson Park to Upminster					
8.39	(E) Upminster to Emerson Park					
8.49	Emerson Park to Upminster					
9.17	Upminster to Romford					
9.34	Romford to Upminster					
9.48	Upminster to Romford					
10. 1	Romford to Grays					
10.58	Grays to Romford					
11.56	Romford to Grays					
12.44 p.m.	Grays to Romford					
1.22	Romford to Grays					
2. 5	Grays to Romford					
2.40	Romford to Grays					
3.52	Grays to Romford					
4.36	Romford to Grays					
5.41	Grays to Romford					
6.40	Romford to Tilbury					
11.46	Tilbury to Pitsea—To form 8.7 a.m. up following day					

ON SATURDAYS AFTER.

11.56 a.m.	Romford to Grays
12.32 p.m.	Grays to Romford
1.15	Romford to Upminster
1.35	Upminster to Emerson Park
1.46	(E) Emerson Park to Upminster
1.56	Upminster to Grays
2.25	Grays to Romford
3.26	Romford to Upminster
3.41	Upminster to Emerson Park
4. 3	Emerson Park to Upminster
4.15	Upminster to Barking
11.48	Barking to Upminster

No. 2 TRAIN.

B Stock.

		1st.	Compo.	3rd.	C. Brake
7.16 a.m.	(E) Upminster to Emerson Park	1	1	3	2
7.27	Emerson Park to Upminster				
7.51	(E) Upminster to Romford				
8. 6	Romford to Upminster				
8.18	Upminster to Barking				
12.49 p.m.	Barking to Upminster—coupled to No. 3				
3.49	Upminster to Emerson Park				
4. 0	Emerson Park to Upminster				
5. 1	Upminster to Emerson Park				
5.12	Emerson Park to Upminster				
5.20	Upminster to Romford				
5.45	Romford to Upminster				
6.23	Upminster to Emerson Park				
6.32	Emerson Park to Upminster				

No. 2 TRAIN.—continued.

6.50 p.m.	Upminster to Romford
7.10	Romford to Upminster
7.26	Upminster to Romford
7.39	Romford to Upminster
8.33	Upminster to Romford
9. 4	Romford to Upminster
9.28	Upminster to Romford
9.43	Romford to Upminster
10. 0	Upminster to Romford
10.46	Romford to Upminster
11. 0	Upminster to Emerson Park
11.11	Emerson Park to Upminster
11.55	Upminster to Emerson Park
12. 7 nght	(E) Emerson Park to Upminster
12.50	Upminster to Emerson Park .. { Thurs
1. 0	(E) Emerson Park to Upminster } only

ON SATURDAYS AFTER.

8.16 a.m.	Upminster to Barking
12.47 p.m.	Barking to Grays
1.35	Grays to Romford
2. 9	Romford to Upminster
2.21	Upminster to Romford
2.34	Romford to Grays
3.52	Grays to Romford
4.36	Romford to Grays
5.41	Grays to Romford
6.30	Romford to Tilbury
7.21	Tilbury to Romford
8 18	Romford to Grays
9.30	Grays to Romford
10.46	Romford to Upminster
11. 0	Upminster to Emerson Park
11.11	Emerson Park to Upminster
11.55	Upminster to Emerson Park
12. 7 ngt.	(E) Emerson Park to Upminster
12.50	Upminster to Emerson Park
1. 0	(E) Emerson Park to Upminster

No. 3 TRAIN.

B Stock.

		1st.	Compo.	3rd.	C. Brake
6.40 a.m.	Barking to Grays	1	1	3	2
8. 4	Grays to Upminster				
10.14	Upminster to Romford				
10.39	Romford to Upminster				
10.55	Upminster to Romford				
11. 8	Romford to Grays				
11.48	Grays to Barking				
12.49 p.m.	Barking to Upminster—coupled to No. 2				
1.41	Upminster to Romford				
1.55	Romford to Upminster				
2.10	Upminster to Barking				
2.35	Barking to Upminster	2	1	6	3

The coaches of 9.5 a.m. from Tilbury, Not Sats., to be sent from Barking to Upminster by 2.35 p.m. train. See No. 14 train.

ON SATURDAYS AFTER.

		1st.	Compo.	3rd.	C. Brake
11.48 a.m.	Grays to Barking				
2. 7 p.m.	(E) Barking to Fenchurch Street	1	1	7	2
2.40	Fenchurch Street to Tilbury				
11.48	Tilbury to Pitsea—To form 8.7 a.m. up on Mondays.	1	1	3	2

Nos. 1 & 2 Locals to work alternate days on trips shown.

E Empty Train.

B Stock Coaches are not under any circumstances to be placed in Trains running with Bogie Stock.

Appendix III. Stations

London, Tilbury & Southend Railway stations (including joint lines) by line, giving opening dates and the original name where one or more name has been used.

Gas Factory Junction to Barking

		Renamings
Bromley	1858	
West Ham	1901	
Plaistow	1858	
Upton Park	1877	
East Ham	1858	

Woodgrange Park to Tilbury

Woodgrange Park	1894	
Barking	1854	
Dagenham Dock	1908	
Rainham	1854	
Purfleet Rifle Range	1911	Closed 31.5.1948
Purfleet	1854	
Grays	1854	
Tilbury Docks	1885	Tilbury Town 10.1934
Tilbury	1854	Tilbury Riverside 1935

Tilbury to Shoeburyness

Low Street	1861	
East Tilbury Halt	1936	
Stanford-le-Hope	1854	Opened as Horndon 14.8.1854, renamed in 1854
Pitsea	1855	
Benfleet	1855	
Leigh	1855	
Chalkwell	1933	
Westcliff-on-Sea	1895	Westcliff 1969
Southend	1856	Southend-on-Sea 6.1876
		Southend-on-Sea Central 1.5.1949
		Southend Central 1969
Southend East	1932	Southend-on-Sea East 1.5.1949
		Southend East 1969
Southchurch on Sea	1910	Thorpe Bay 18.7.1910
Shoeburyness	1884	

Barking to Pitsea

Upney	1932	
Gale Street	1926	Becontree 18.7.1932
Dagenham Heathway	1932	Heathway 1.5.1949
Dagenham	1885	Dagenham East 1.5.1949
Elm Park	1935	
Hornchurch	1885	
Upminster Bridge	1934	
Upminster	1885	
East Horndon	1886	West Horndon 1.5.1949
Laindon	1888	
Basildon	25.11.1974	

Romford and Ockendon Branches

Romford	1893	
Emerson Park	1909	
Ockendon	1892	
Chafford Hundred	1995	

Thames Haven Branch

Thames Haven	1855	Closed

Whitechapel & Bow Joint Railway

Whitechapel	1902
Stepney Green	1902
Mile End	1902
Bow Road	1902

Tottenham & Forest Gate Joint Railway

Black Horse Road	1894	
Walthamstow	1894	Walthamstow Queens Road 6.5.1968
Leyton	1894	Leyton Midland Road 1.5.1949
Leytonstone	1894	Leytonstone High Road 1.5.1949
Wanstead Park	1894	

Notes

Of the stations between Barking and Upminster with platforms on through lines, Becontree, Dagenham East and Hornchurch are not served by main line trains and the British Railways platforms were closed on 12 June 1961.

Bromley to East Ham: with the exception of West Ham the through line platforms were taken out of use on 18 June 1962.

West Ham: through line platforms were disused in 1913, became unusable in 1940 as a result of air raid damage and were removed in 1956. A new island platform for LT&S trains was opened on 30 May 1999.

Appendix IV. Locomotive Headlamp Codes and Route Indication

From almost the earliest years of the Victorian steam railway it was important to be able to identify the class of train and this was done by using the bell code (once the block system and telegraph was in operation) and by engine headlamp codes, made possible by arranging for the oil lamp or disc to be attached to different positions at both ends of the locomotives. Prior to 1903 there was a large variation in individual company approach to this matter but in that year a considerable amount of rationalisation came into being. The entire question of what happened across the railways of Great Britain is quite beyond the scope of this work, but it does serve to introduce readers to LT&SR practice.

To compile this information I have used an amalgam of the information contained in the LT&SR 1890 private timetables, together with details given by Dow in *Midland Style* and Leech in his various works.

	Ordinary Goods	1 green disc with white rim on centre of buffer beam + 1 white disc with red cross over centre of destination board	1 green light on centre of buffer beam + 1 green light on smokebox
	Special Goods	1 green disc with white rim on centre of buffer beam + 1 white round disc on l.h.s. of buffer beam + 1 white disc with red cross over centre of destination board	1 green light on centre of buffer beam + 1 green light on smokebox + 1 white light on l.h.s. of buffer beam
Upminster Grays and Tilbury via Ockendon	Ordinary Pass.	1 square green disc with white cross on smokebox	1 white light on smokebox + 1 white light on centre of buffer beam
	Special Pass.	1 square green disc with white cross on smokebox + 1 round white disc with green rim on r.h.s. of buffer beam	1 white light on smokebox + 1 white light on centre of buffer beam + 1 white light on r.h.s. of buffer beam
	Ordinary Goods	1 square white disc with green cross on smokebox	1 white light on l.h.s. of buffer beam + 1 white light on r.h.s. of buffer beam
	Special Goods	1 square white disc with green cross on smoke-box + round white disc with green rim on r.h.s. of buffer beam	1 white light on l.h.s. of buffer beam + 1 white light on r.h.s. of buffer beam + 1 white light on centre of buffer beam

By day *all* engines working into Fenchurch Street to have white square marked 'L.T.S.R.' on smokebox at base of chimney.

ENGINE AND TRAIN HEAD LIGHTS AND DISCS.

TRAINS.	DISCS BY DAY.	LIGHTS BY NIGHT.
MAIN LINE.		
Ordinary Passenger Trains	One White Square on Smoke Box marked L T&S R	One White Light on Buffer Beam right hand.
Special Passenger Trains	One White Square on Smoke Box marked LT & S R and One White Disc on Buffer Beam right hand.	One White Light on Buffer Beam right hand, and One White Light on Smoke Box.
Ordinary Goods Trains	One White Square on Smoke Box marked LT & S R and One Green Disc, with white rim, on centre of Buffer Beam.	One Green Light on centre of Buffer Beam, and One White Light on Smoke Box.
Special Goods Trains	One White Square on Smoke Box marked LT & SR One Green Disc, with white rim, on centre of Buffer Beam, and One Round White Disc on Buffer Beam left hand.	One Green Light on centre of Buffer Beam, One White Light on Buffer Beam left hand and One White Light on Smoke Box.
Via UPMINSTER.		
Ordinary Passenger Trains...............	One White Square on Smoke Box marked L T S R and One White Disc, with Red Cross over centre of destination Board.	One White Light on Buffer Beam right hand and One Green Light on Buffer Beam left hand.
Special Passenge Trains	One White Square on Smoke Box marked LTSR One White Disc with Red Cross over Centre of Destination Board, and One White Disc on Buffer Beam right hand.	One White Light on Buffer Beam right hand, One Green Light on Buffer Beam left hand, and One White Light on Smoke Box.
NORTH LONDON.		
Ordinary Passenger Trains	One Red Disc on Buffer Beam right hand.	One White and One Green Light placed side by side on Off-side Buffer.
Special Passenger Trains	Two Red Discs, one on each Buffer.	Ditto ditto with an additional White Light on Smoke Box.
GREAT EASTERN.		
Liverpool St. and Barking ...... — Ordinary Passenger Trains.	One Green Disc with White Rim at each end of Buffer Beam, & One White Disc on Smoke Box.	One Green Light at each end of Buffer Beam, and one White Light on Smoke Box.
Liverpool St. and Barking ...... — Special Passenger Trains...	Ditto ditto	One White Light on Smoke Box, and an additional White Light on Buffer Beam left hand.
Stratford and Barking......... — Ordinary Goods Trains ..	One White Disc on Smoke Box, and One Green Disc with White Rim on Buffer Beam right hand	One White Light on Smoke Box, and One Green Light on Buffer Beam right hand.
Stratford and Barking......... — Special Goods Trains	NIL.	One White Light on Smoke Box, and an additional White Light on Buffer Beam, left hand
Fenchurch St. and Woolwich via Bromley ...... — Ordinary Passenger Trains.	One Green Disc, with a White Rim, at each end of the Buffer Beam.	One Green Light, at each end of the Buffer Beam.
Fenchurch St. and Woolwich via Bromley ...... — Special Passenger Trains...	Ditto ditto.	Ditto ditto.
London Docks and Victoria Docks via Bromley .... — Ordinary Goods Trains ..	One Green Disc, with a White Rim, on the Buffer Beam right hand, and One White Disc on the Smoke Box	One Green Light on Buffer Beam right hand, and One White Light on Smoke Box.
London Docks and Victoria Docks via Bromley .... — Special Goods Trains	Ditto ditto.	Ditto ditto.

42

The extract from the 1890 LTSR Working Timetable (WWT).

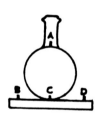

Other trains

(1)	Breakdown van train going to clear line	ABD green discs with white rims	ABD	green lights
(2)	Breakdown van train not going to clear line	A green disc with white rim	A	green light
(3)	Chalk Farm-Southend through train from North London Railway	ABD lamps C white square board lettered LT&SR	ABD	white lights
(4)	P&O boat specials from Tilbury to Liverpool Street	A white disc BD green discs with white rims C white square board lettered LT&SR		

Additional information taken from George Dow's *Midland Style* in respect of the 1904 and 1912 Working Timetables.

Index

(Chapters 5-11 are self-indexing and only references to subjects that are not the main chapter topic have been included below.)